D0884254

The
African Heritage
of American
English

Lorenzo Dow Turner, from the *Chicago Sun Times,*
May 19, 1962. Reproduced with permission.

The
African Heritage
of American
English

JOSEPH E. HOLLOWAY
and WINIFRED K. VASS

INDIANA UNIVERSITY PRESS
Bloomington & Indianapolis

R01640132l9
humca

HOUSTON PUBLIC LIBRARY

All illustrations except number 6 are reproduced courtesy of the Amistad Research Center, New Orleans.

© 1993 by Indiana University Press

All rights reserved
No part of this book may be reproduced or utilized in any form or by any means, electronic or mechanical, including photocopying and recording, or by any information storage and retrieval system, without permission in writing from the publisher. The Association of American University Presses' Resolution on Permissions constitutes the only exception to this prohibition.

The paper used in this publication meets the minimum requirements of American National Standard for Information Sciences—Permanence of Paper for Printed Library Materials, ANSI Z39.48-1984.

$\otimes$^{TM}

Manufactured in the United States of America
Library of Congress Cataloging-in-Publication Data
Holloway, Joseph E.
    The African Heritage of American English/Joseph E. Holloway and Winifred K. Vass.
        p. cm.
    Includes bibliographical references and index.
    ISBN 0-253-32838-1 (cloth)
        1. Afro-Americans—Language—Dictionaries. 2. English language—United States—Foreign elements—African—Dictionaries. 3. African languages—Influence on English—Dictionaries. 4. Black English—Dictionaries. 5. Americanisms—Dictionaries. I. Vass, Winifred Kellersberger. II. Title.
    PE3102.N4H65 1993
    427'.973'08996—dc20   92-18270

1 2 3 4 5 97 96 95 94 93

Contents

Acknowledgments vii

Lorenzo Dow Turner
A Biographical Dedication ix

Introduction
The African Connection xiii

Abbreviations xxxv

One
The Bantu Vocabulary Content of Gullah 1

Two
Black Names in the United States 78

Three
Africanisms of Bantu Origin in Black English 93

Four
Bantu Place Names in Nine Southern States 107

Five
Africanisms in Contemporary American English 137

Notes 161
Bibliography 179
Index 189

Maps

1. Western Africa (Westernmost Part) — xxi
2. Western Africa (Easternmost Part) — xxii
3. Culture Groups in Africa and North America — xxviii
4. Geographical Locations of Turner's Linguistic Sources of Gullah Vocabulary — 8
5. Location of Bantu Place Names in Nine Southern States — 109
6. Alabama — 111
7. Georgia — 112
8. Florida — 115
9. Mississippi — 117
10. North Carolina — 119
11. South Carolina — 120
12. Virginia — 122
13. Louisiana — 123
14. Texas — 124

Tables

1. Africans Imported into South Carolina, by Culture Cluster — xxvii
2. Distribution of African Words Found in Gullah, as Identified by Turner (1949) — 4–5
3. African Linguistic Sources of Gullah, after Turner (1949) — 5–6
4. Geographical Locations of Turner's Linguistic Sources of Gullah Vocabulary — 6–7
5. Days of the Week with Corresponding African Names — 81
6. African Names from South Carolina Gazette, 1732–1775 — 83–84
7. Names Listed on the Dutch Slave Ship Wittepaert — 84–85

Acknowledgments

We would like to extend a special acknowledgment to Dr. William S. Pollitzer of the Department of Cell Biology and Anatomy, School of Medicine, the University of North Carolina at Chapel Hill, for his numerical compilation in tables 2, 3, and 4 of Turner's amazing work of research on Gullah. He had the map accompanying table 4 made to show the general location on the African continent of each language group referred to. He is also responsible for the preparation of all the maps in chapter four.

Dr. Pollitzer read several chapters, and his comments were greatly appreciated. His suggestions and input significantly influenced this volume. Without his strong participation the manuscript would be quite different. Dr. Pollitzer approaches the search for the original African linguistic sources of Gullah from a biomedical viewpoint. His special area of research is on the physical anthropology of the black people of coastal South Carolina and their African ancestors, including blood types and the sickle cell trait.

Acknowledgment is made to Gina Harrison of the University of North Carolina at Chapel Hill for her excellent cartographic work on the language distribution map in chapter one and all the maps in chapter four. We also thank Mthobeli Guma for locating many of the place names researched.

Sincere thanks are expressed for the secretarial work which made the preparation of the manuscript possible, including the strong editorial assistance of Mrs. Winifred K. Vass and the welcome assistance of her husband, the Reverend Lachlam C. Vass, and his nimble fingers on his word processor. We also would like to thank Minghoi Cheng and Trinh Hoang, who helped in the preparation of the manuscript.

A special mention is made of Professor George Jackson, who did the statistical analysis of slave populations entering the United States, and Dr. Rosentene Purnell and Dr. Selase W. Williams, both of the California State University, Northridge, Department of Pan African Studies, who read the manuscript and gave useful criticisms.

We are grateful to the Center for Afro-American Studies of the University of California at Los Angeles for permission to use material from Vass, *The Bantu Speaking Heritage of the United States.*

And we would like to extend special thanks to the Gullah people on the island of St. Helena and to the Penn Center and its director, Emory Campbell, for preserving their culture. This book is our gift to the Gullah people toward the restoration and preservation of the Gullah language.

Lorenzo Dow Turner

A BIOGRAPHICAL DEDICATION

Since Turner's *Africanisms in the Gullah Dialect* (1949) serves as the main source of Gullah used in this book, it is only fitting that a biography of the author, Lorenzo Dow Turner, and his research be presented.

Lorenzo Dow Turner was born in Elizabeth City, North Carolina, on August 21, 1895. His family moved to Maryland near Washington, D.C., when he was six years old. His father founded the Roanoke Institute in Elizabeth City and took a post as a high school principal.

In 1910 Lorenzo Dow Turner enrolled at Howard University in Washington and worked his way through school as a Pullman porter until he became a professional baseball player. He played eight summers for the Commonwealth Giants in New York's old Negro league. He received a B.A. degree from Howard University in 1914, and a master's degree from Harvard University in 1917. With an M.A. in English, he returned to Howard to teach English. There he taught for three years while working on his doctorate at the University of Chicago. During the summers of study, he took one year of leave from Howard to finish work on his doctoral thesis, "Anti-Slavery Sentiment in American Literature Prior to 1865." (This 1926 thesis was reprinted in 1966 by Kennikat Press, Port Washington, N.Y.)

He turned down the chairmanship of the English Department at Fisk University in Nashville, Tennessee, to take a post at South Carolina State College in Orangeburg, where he focused on linguistics and English. While working in South Carolina, he noticed two women in his class who spoke Gullah. Little did he know that this brief encounter would change his life and the focus of his research for the rest of his life. He investigated further and found that they came from neighboring coastal islands isolated from the mainland, where strong African retention in language and culture was still present. Having worked with Melville J. Herskovits as a student, he was keenly aware of the importance of documenting these Africanisms as soon as possible. He spent his weekends on the island of St. Helena studying the Gullah dialect.[1] Excited about the possibilities of documenting direct African retentions in African-American speech, he received a Rockefeller Foundation grant to study and record the speech mannerisms in the South Carolina Sea Islands. A year later the grant was renewed, and he spent one winter studying African languages in New York and another at the Linguistic Institute at Brown University.

Turner mastered five African languages, Kongo, Igbo, Yoruba, Krio (Creole), and Mende (Mande), including a dozen African dialects. In addition to these African languages, he learned Portuguese, Arabic, German, French, and "a little Dutch." He had reading knowledge of Latin, Greek, and Italian. Turner wanted to know and learn the ancestral languages of African-American forebears who had come to America on slave ships. With this knowledge, he wanted to document a study of Africanisms in Gullah.

After a third year in the Sea Islands among the Gullah, he received two grants, one from the Rosenwald Fund and another from the American Council of Learned Societies (ACLS). While in the Sea Islands, he made a connection between Gullah, Louisiana Creole, and Creole spoken in West Africa and the West Indies as one and the same. In 1935 he left for Louisiana to study Creole, to see if it was related to the Sea Island Creole (Gullah).

The next year he took a sabbatical leave from Fisk and traveled to London to study additional African languages. At an exposition held in France he met Professor Henri Labouret, a French linguist, who helped him link African languages and Gullah. In his discussion with Labouret he discovered numerous Arabic words in Gullah.

In 1939 he went to Yale on a fellowship to learn Arabic. He found Arabic useful in deciphering some Arabic words found in Gullah. He also studied two Native American languages to see if Gullah had been influenced by Native Americans. He found no traces of Native American speech in coastal Sea Island Gullah.[2]

Later he turned his interest toward Brazil. He wanted to see if there was any relationship between Gullah in the United States and black dialects in Brazil. With partial funding from the American Philosophical Society and ACLS grants, he studied and recorded the speech of African-Brazilians and found that they spoke the same Gullah or Creole as the blacks in the Sea Islands.[3]

In 1944 he returned to Fisk to teach English and prepare his seminal study of African retention in African-American speech, *Africanisms in the Gullah Dialect,* published in 1949 by the University of Chicago Press. By the sheer weight of the material he gathered, he refuted the theory of Krapp, Gonzales, and Mencken that the special features of Gullah "represented the inability of the Negroes to learn the language of their masters and that their dialect represented carry-overs of the speech of Elizabethan England spoken by early whites."[4] Turner agreed with Herskovits's hypothesis that "structurally, the special traits in Gullah speech, like those in other New World dialects, could be ascribed to the retention of certain African grammatical forms, into the mold of which were cast English and French words pronounced by speakers whose phonemic patterns were wholly or partially African."[5]

In an article published by the American Dialect Society in 1948, Turner explicitly described what he felt were the important requisites for an objective approach to the study of Gullah:[6]

> One of the requisites is adequate knowledge of the conditions surrounding the importation of slaves to the United States. . . . Another of these requisites is some acquaintance with the speech of Negroes in some areas of the New World where they could have had no contact with the English language of the seventeenth and eighteenth centuries—such areas, for example, as Haiti, Brazil and other non-English regions of the New World. A study of the speech of the Negroes in these

areas reveals the same characteristics that one finds in the non-English portions of Gullah. A third requisite for an adequate study of Gullah, and a highly important one, is some familiarity with African culture, especially with the African languages spoken in those areas from which the slaves were brought to the United States. In this requirement the advocates of the theory that Gullah is merely the English of the seventeenth and eighteenth centuries were conspicuously lacking.

If an investigator met these requirements, Turner believed, he or she had gone a long way toward solving the first problem confronting the investigator of this dialect—the problem of acquiring an adequate background for the study.

In April 1946 Turner became a member of the Roosevelt University. In 1951 and 1952 he received a Fulbright Fellowship. While in Africa he collected more than 8,000 proverbs, 1,600 folk tales, and thousands of other pieces of folklore, including many in Krio and Nigerian languages. Turner was sixty-nine years old when he finished his *Anthology of Krio Folklore and Literature* for the United States Department of Health and Welfare and seventy when he wrote *Krio Texts with Grammatical Notes and English Translation for the Peace Corps.*

Introduction

THE AFRICAN CONNECTION

The purpose of this book is to make available comprehensive lists of linguistic Africanisms drawn from a wide range of domains, including personal names, place names, language usage, foods, folklore, aesthetics, and music. The book includes Africanisms in the Gullah dialect, Africanisms in American names, and words borrowed from African languages found in Standard and non-Standard American English. While we have relied heavily on word lists compiled by Turner (1949), Puckett (1975), Dalby (1972), Vass (1979), and others, this book does not simply duplicate their works. Instead, it seeks to correct the mistaken assumption that only West Africans had a linguistic influence on African-American culture by showing that both West and Central African languages contributed to the diversity of Africanisms found in American English.

Turner's *Africanisms in the Gullah Dialect* (1949) serves as the major source of Gullah material used in chapter one, by Winifred K. Vass, "The Bantu Vocabulary Content of Gullah." The aim is not to duplicate Turner's findings but to point out the Bantu content in his list of Africanisms found in Gullah—in other words, to provide a more comprehensive listing of Africanisms retained in Gullah from Bantu. This is significant: of 3,938 Gullah terms listed by Turner as originating in West Africa, Vass has identified 1,891 as Bantu words still in use today in Zaire, giving Gullah a core Bantu lexicon of 35.2 percent.

Vass's word-for-word translation of the Gullah to Bantu meaning identifies the Luba-Kasai area of Zaire as the source. Three-quarters of all Bantu speakers are in three groups in northwest and west central Angola: the Kikongo-speaking Bakongo, the Kimbundu, and the Umbundu-speaking Ovimbundu. Luba-Kasai, or Tshiluba, is one of the four vernacular languages given special status by the government of Zaire, the other three being Kikongo, Lingala, and Kiswahili. According to Guthrie in *Comparative Bantu* (1967), the linguistic homogeneity of the Bantu is identified by a common core language. Luba-Kasai is one of the core languages of Central Africa, having 47 percent of the more than 500 terms common to all the Bantu languages of sub-Saharan Africa.

In giving a word-for-word translation of Turner's list and comparing it to Bantu meaning, we do not intend to suggest that all of Turner's entries are of Bantu origin. Rather, we are pointing out that the majority of words Turner identified as other than Bantu are still in use in Zaire. When Turner published his seminal work in 1949, spoken Gullah was different from its source language at the time of slavery. Like culture, language (which is a part of culture) is always in a state of flux. Turner relied heavily on dictionary meanings because many of his informants could only recall English meanings in some cases. Nevertheless, Turner provided us with a list of African words retained in Gullah. Vass's Bantu meanings provide a link to understanding Gullah as it was probably spoken at midcentury based on current meanings and usage in Zaire.

Many words Turner listed have multiple African etymologies. For example, the word *aba* is found in both Twi and Tshiluba. In Twi, *aba* is a day name given to a female child born on Thursday. In Tshiluba it is a verb. Twi is a West African language completely unrelated to the Bantu languages. This shows that it is quite possible for the same word to exist in one language as one part of speech and in another as a different part of speech and to have very different meanings.

There is an unusually close relationship in Bantu languages between nouns and verbs. A basic verb root presents a wide range of possibilities for creating nouns out of it. One characteristic of Bantu languages is the grammatical process called agglutination by which nouns may be formed from verbs. There are several kinds of these derived nouns, such as nouns of agent, nouns of place or manner, abstract concepts, and even words denoting ineptitude or incongruity. For example, the performer of an act is expressed by changing the final *a* of the verb root to *i* and connecting it to the prefixes of class I nouns, referring to persons.

muibi,	a thief, is derived from *-iba,* to steal
mutudi,	a blacksmith, is derived from *-tula,* to forge
musungidi,	a savior, is derived from *-sungila,* to rescue

The place where an action is performed is expressed by suffixing *-ilu* or *-elu* and prefixing *tshi-* or *bi-* (class VII nouns, indicating size, space, or bigness) and changing the final *a* of the verb root to *u*.

tshibandilu,	a stairway, comes from *-banda,* to go up
tshishikidilu,	a destination, comes from *-shika,* to end
tshilambilu,	a kitchen, comes from *-lamba,* to cook

An abstract idea of the verb root may be expressed by using the singular prefix of class IV nouns, *lu-*, with the final vowel of the root generally changed to *u* or *o*.

luendu,	a journey, derives from *-enda,* to go
lulelu,	fertility, derives from *-lela,* to give birth
lulamatu,	loyalty, derives from *-lamata,* to adhere, stick to
lufu,	death, derives from *-fua,* to die

The idea of worthlessness is contrived by using the prefixes of class VII nouns, *tshi-*, *bi-*, and doubling the verb root.

tshiendenda,	vagrancy, comes from *-enda,* to walk
tshiakulakula,	chatter, gibberish, comes from *-akula,* to talk[1]

The vocabulary list in chapter two, "Black Names in America," is compiled from Puckett's *Black Names in America: Origins and Usage* (1975). Vass identified the Bantu lexicon in Puckett's list of African words and includes Tshiluba meanings. This list thus provides additional names of Bantu origin not listed in Turner's study.

Chapter three by Vass, "Africanisms of Bantu Origin in Black English," is a list of words used by African Americans. This list, taken from Vass's *Bantu Speaking Heritage of the United States* (1979), provides an important list of Bantu words used by African Americans.

Chapter four by Vass, "Bantu Place Names in Nine Southern States," documents Bantu place names throughout the South. Place names are extremely important in identifying possible early plantation sites and African population areas. Here Vass provides a detailed list of African place names that were contributed by Tshiluba, or Luba-Kasai.

Chapter five, "Africanisms in Contemporary American English," is compiled from several sources. This chapter is comprehensive in scope, listing linguistic Africanisms of both Bantu and Mande origin found in both Black and Standard American English. Thus it illustrates the African linguistic heritage of both black and white Americans. This chapter is further divided into Africanisms in foods, crops, animals and insects, cowboy culture, musical instruments, dance, celebrations, gestures, and social culture.

THE STUDY OF AFRICANISMS

The debate over the survival of linguistic Africanisms in North America has been controversial since Melville J. Herskovits's pioneering study, *The Myth of the Negro Past,* was published in 1941. The debate is deeply rooted in a controversy between Herskovits and E. Franklin Frazier. Frazier believed that the institution of slavery completely destroyed any surviving African culture and that African-American culture developed without any African antecedents. In short, Frazier emphasized African discontinuity, advocating a deculturalization hypothesis. To refute this deculturalization hypothesis, Herskovits argued that African cultural influences survived in the New World and were retained by the process of acculturation and adaptation. Herskovits believed that there was an African continuum and continuity in African-American language.

While Herskovits recognized the need to study, research, and document specific African cultural diversity in American culture (see his article "The Ancestry of the American Negro," 1938–39), he was not successful because of a lack of ethnographic data. Herskovits's methodology of establishing an African cultural baseline from which to assess New World Africanisms was correct, however, even though he searched for Africanisms in different places, mainly West Africa.

Herskovits's *Myth of the Negro Past* was pioneering in that it allowed detailed analysis of African survivals and retentions based on the West African cultural zones he outlined. However, the apparatus of only a West African baseline for Africanisms is no longer applicable for examining New World Africanisms. Following Herskovits, Whitten and Szwed (1970), Bastide (1971), Mintz (1974), Mintz and Price (1976), Levine (1977), and Moreno Fraginals (1984), either implicitly or explicitly suggested a West African baseline for New World Africanisms. But Wood (1974),

Vass (1979), Stuckey (1987), and Holloway (1990) have revised Herskovits's baseline to include a Bantu origin for many facets of American culture.

This book, unlike Herskovits's study and others', cites specific examples of linguistic Africanisms of Bantu origin. It uses two cultural baselines to assess linguistic Africanisms in North America, i.e., a West African baseline for assessing New World Africanisms among whites and a Central African baseline for assessing Africanisms among African Americans.

There are several dictionaries and related works on African-American culture, history, and language, but none provides a comprehensive documentation of linguistic Africanisms except Turner's *Africanisms in the Gullah Dialect.* His study provided the first comprehensive dictionary documenting Africanisms in the speech of African Americans. It lists approximately 5,000 words that originated in West and Central Africa.

The next important dictionary to appear after Turner's was Gold's *Jazz Lexicon* (1960), which traces the history and origins of jazz to the old Congo Square in New Orleans, one of the North American Bantu culture centers. The word *jazz* comes from *jaja,* which means "to make or cause to dance."* Jazz was closely associated with the language used by black musicians. "Jive talk" was coded language used by enslaved Africans to communicate a double entendre meant to conceal meanings from whites. *A Jazz Lexicon* is an important dictionary of jazz words along with usage and meanings in the context of language used in the jazz era. Gold's list captures important linguistic Africanisms. He gives a number of words of African origin, including *baad* (bad), *boo, boogie-woogie, bug, cool cat, cootie, cop, chick, daddy, dig, dirt* (dirty), *fuzz* (fuss), *gully, gutbucket, jam, jamboree, jitterbug, jive, jook, ofay,* and *uno* (you know). All of these African-derived words formed an important part of black slang in the 1930s, '40s, and '50s.

The next significant study was Puckett's collection, *Black Names in America* (1975), which is the most important available source of black personal names, providing information on words of possible African origin and meaning with possible ethnic group and gender identification. This volume is the largest collection of black names in America from 1619 to 1940. Puckett lists approximately 500,000 African-American names, 340,000 used by blacks and 160,000 used by whites. His study shows that in the early years both enslaved African Americans and free African Americans identified strongly with their African culture and heritage as demonstrated in the retention of African personal names and naming practices. Puckett's collection suggests that the greatest percentage of Africanisms in black names were in popular use in the eighteenth century. By the middle of the nineteenth century fewer names of African origin were used by blacks. As a direct result of pressures from white Americans, African Americans gave up their Africanity and began to conform to the traditions and practices of Western Europe.

Dalby's "African Element in Black English" (1972) provides a dictionary of linguistic Africanisms from Wolof found in American English and black slang.

---

*The Bantu root for "dance" is *ja. Jaja,* which doubles the verb root, is the causative form of the verb, "to make or cause to dance." Jazz was music that made people dance.

Dalby identified early African linguistic retentions or Wolof-Mande origins and traced them back to Africa. He traced many Americanisms to Africanisms: *A.O.K.* (okay), *bogus, boogie woogie, bug* (insect), *cat, dig* (to understand), *fuzz* (police), *hep cat, hippi, honkie* (pink white man), *jazz, jam, jamboree, jive, mumbo-jumbo, phoney, rap.*

Major's *Dictionary of Afro-American Slang* (1978) provides a list of slang words credited to and used by African Americans, including word definitions, dates of usage, and geographical areas of usage. Black slang is deeply based in African linguistic retention. Many Africanisms used in the 1960s were first heard on plantations in the American South during the slavery era and reemerged in the 1960s as an important part of black dialect before moving into white speech.

Dillard's *All-American English* (1975) focuses primarily on the impact on the American English system of pidgins and creoles, such as Gullah or Geechee, Louisiana French Creole, and New Jersey American Trade Pidgin. Pidgin is formed when two cultures first come into contact; creole is established when the pidgin becomes the mother language of the next generation. Dillard shows how some Africanisms became Americanisms. One example is the expression "to kick the bucket." Originally the terms used by blacks were kickerapoo[2] and kickatavoo,[3] which meant "killed" or "dead." According to Dillard, these words came from two African sources: Krio (the English-based creole of Sierra Leone) *kekrebu* or *kekerebu,* meaning "dead" or "to wither" (as fruit or leaves), and Gã (a West African language) *kekre,* "dry, stiff," and *bu,* "to befall, end."

Dillard's *Black Names* (1976) examines Africanisms in African-American naming practices: personal names, jazz, blues, church names, vehicle names, shops, vendors, and things for sale. Names used by black Americans tell much about the people because names retain important vestiges of Africanisms. Dillard points out that Africanisms in black naming practices are not unique to blacks but that Africanisms such as *big eye, bad mouth,* and *O.K.* are also used by whites.

Dillard's *Lexicon of Black English* (1977) is an important work for understanding ebonics, or black English. It is not really a lexicon of Black English but rather a dictionary of non-standard English as used over time by African Americans. Dillard does not concentrate on Africanisms in black American speech but seeks to understand the myriad of language changes among blacks living in the ghettos and in the northern United States. He argues that language used among blacks derives from a complex set of culture transparencies and is maintained by an equally complex set of societal and communication networks, but he nonetheless concludes that black vernacular survives from Africa in new structural linguistic forms.

Smitherman's *Talkin and Testifyin: The Language of Black America* (1977) provides a list of African-American slang and African-derived words found in American English. Smitherman examines words of direct African origin, such as *yam* (sweet potato) from Wolof *nyam* (to eat). She gives special attention to American words surviving in Standard English, such as *banana, banjo, cola* (as in Coca-Cola), *elephant, goober, gorilla, gumbo, juke* (jukebox), *oasis, okra, sorcery, tater, tote* (to carry), and *turnip.* She also examines African loan translations from Africa found almost exclusively in black slang, such as *bad mouth, bogus, cool, dig, fat mouth, hip, mean, okay,* and *skin.* Smitherman concludes that African-American language is deeply based in an African linguistic structure reflecting an African heritage, meaning, nuance, tone, and gesture.

Vass's *Bantu Speaking Heritage of the United States* (1979) presents a compelling account of African retention within American folk tales, folklore, folk songs, place names, and other facets of American English. Vass opened a new dimension in the study of linguistic Africanisms. She analyzed and determined the African content in various aspects of American language and culture by using a methodological approach similar to Turner's: she elucidated the contributions of Tshiluba, a Bantu language of Zaire. Her in-depth focus on Central Africa rather than West Africa distinguishes her study from previous scholarship. She pioneered the thesis of a Bantu origin for black American culture.

Vass explores Bantu content within American language and culture. Her book makes a significant contribution by demonstrating a methodological approach that is useful for historical research. It shows how language can be employed as a tool to conduct historical research. Through language and linguistic survivals, Vass provides a comprehensive historical reconstruction of the world of the slaves who were brought to North America from the Congo (Zaire). The significance of her work is the revelation of Bantu contributions to American culture. She provides a dictionary list of words of Bantu origin used by African Americans.

Nunes's *Dictionary of Afro-Latin American Civilization* (1980) is useful as a historical and descriptive dictionary of terms, phrases, and selected biographies of African-Latin political leaders. It includes more than 4,500 entries from English, French, Portuguese, and Spanish sources, along with a brief bibliography of dictionaries, glossaries, books, monographs, articles, and periodicals.

Dalgish, in *A Dictionary of Africanisms: Contributions of Sub-Saharan Africa to the English Language* (1972), attempts to list African-derived words and phrases used in English. He cites numerous usages and references in Western and African publications. The major problem and failure of his study is its definition of *Africanism.* African words cited in European and African publications cannot serve as the basis for Africanisms. By definition an Africanism is any cultural (material or nonmaterial) or linguistic property of African origin surviving in the New World or in the African diaspora.

Cassidy and LePage's *Dictionary of Jamaican English* (1980) is a comprehensive listing of words in everyday Jamaican English. While the dictionary cross-lists a few Africanisms in North America, it does so within the context of Jamaican English. In other words, the book is not a dictionary of Africanisms. Still there are numerous examples of cross-referenced words common to Jamaican English and American Sea Island Creole (Gullah). There exists a strong relationship between Jamaican English and Gullah in that both form the basis for Sea Island Creole with regional variations. For instance, the word *buckra* originates from both Igbo and Efik and means "white man" in both dialects. The term is still current in both Jamaican English and Gullah literature. Some nicknames are still current, such as *bobo* from Twi and *baba,* Yoruba for "father" but used in black American English as a nickname for either male or female. The demonstrative pronoun *da* is still current in black English and Jamaican English. The word *daadi* (daddy) from Fante *dadd* is used almost universally by both blacks and whites as an affectionate term for father. In the areas of musical instruments and food culture there are some similarities. *Jenkoving* (horn blowing), *mojo, tom tom,* and *banjo* are identical in both dialects. The *calemba* (funeral dance performed in eighteenth-century New Orleans) is still performed in Jamaica. *John Canoe* festivals were strong in the eighteenth century in both the United States and Jamaica. A food called *fungee* or *fufu* (corn-turn) found its equivalency in the Sea Island "turn meal and flour."

Holm and Shilling, in *The Dictionary of Bahamian English* (1982), provide a comprehensive list of words in Bahamian English, which forms an important link between Caribbean English and Gullah, the dialect spoken by African Americans in coastal communities from northern Florida to North Carolina. This dictionary is relevant because of the numerous North American cross-references in linguistic Africanisms with African idioms found in both Barbados and South Carolina, such as *big eye* (greedy), *hoe cake, hoppin John, bad mouth,* and *buckra* (poor white). The dictionary presents new perspectives for the study of Black English in the United States because of the similarities found in Bahamian English and Gullah.

Miller and Smith's *Dictionary of Afro-American Slavery* (1988) focuses on blacks in the United States, starting with their first arrival in Jamestown, Virginia, in 1619 and continuing through the Civil War, the Reconstruction era, and beyond. Included are entries on such topics as abolition, the slave trade, and the theater during the Harlem Renaissance. Appendices provide a listing of plans, musical entertainments, and publications by and about African Americans. There is also an extensive glossary of Harlem slang in which a large number of Africanisms are found.

Finally, Keller's *Harlem Renaissance: A Historical Dictionary for the Era* (1989), a work of nearly 800 entries, contains a wide range of information about the personalities, places, and events that relate to African-American aesthetics and politics.

THE AFRICAN HERITAGE OF BLACK AMERICANS

At least 70 percent of the ancestors of Americans of African descent came from the Mande (West African) and Bantu (Central African) ethnic groups. These two cultures contributed substantially to the diversity of the ethnic stock in North America.

The West Africans

Africans from the Senegambia region of West Africa included the Bambara, Wolof, Mandingo, Fula, and Serer. Over 30 percent of Africans arriving in South Carolina during the transatlantic trade were Mande speakers. The Mande civilization was the greatest and most advanced of the Sudanic empires. It was also the earliest and most complex civilization to emerge in the western Sudan.

The Mande civilization began with ancient Ghana and developed between A.D. 200 and 1200 in the region between the bend of the Niger River and the middle reaches of the Senegal River. Ancient Ghana was not the sole state in the region, but it was the first of many kingdoms to emerge as a powerful and wealthy state. Others were Mali, Songhai, Tekrur, and, to the east, the Hausa states and Kanem and Bornu in the Chad basin. The Soninke (Mandingo), Serer, Wolof, Susu, and Foulah (Fula) lived in the Senegambia region. The founders of ancient Ghana were the Soninke, a Mande-speaking people who, along with the Malinke, shared a common history and culture. Among the most important clans were the Sisse, Draine, Sylla, and Kante. Each clan represented a specific division of labor. The Sisse were the ruling class from which the principal political officials and governors of the provinces were chosen. The Kante clan provided the artisans and craftsmen who engaged in metal working, pottery, and carpentry.[4] Most of the New World artisans were selected from Kante guilds. Linguistically the Mande include the Soninke, Malinke, Bambare, Dyula, Koranko, Khasonke, Susu, Mande (Mandingo), Gbandi, and Ebunde, including the Wolof, Serer, Temne, Kissi, Limba, Gola, and western Fulani.

The Wolof (Mande) arrived exclusively in South Carolina between 1650 and 1700. This large influx of Wolofs can be explained by the disintegration of the Sudanic empires, the beginning of the transatlantic slave trade, and the breakup of the Wolof empire in the 1670s instigated by the Mauretanian Marabouts. The fall of this empire created a state of continual warfare as rival political factions attempted to fill the power vacuum. One result of this instability was the holding of prisoners of war. This was the only time the Wolof had a great influence on the American slave markets. Never again would they be transported in any appreciable numbers to the North American continent.[5]

The Wolof, along with the Mandingo and Bambara, were fairly prominent in the trade but were relatively few in comparison to neighboring ethnic groups such as the Foulah. They were thinly dispersed on the north bank states of Niami, Salnia, Baddibu, and Niani. A large community of Wolofs lived on the island of Goree, a major center from which enslaved Africans were transported to America to cultivate rice in the South. These Wolofs formed a class of small traders and artisans. During the colonial period planters had little trouble finding Wolof speakers to translate for newly arrived Africans from the region.

In North America, Wolofs were primarily employed as house servants. Many of the Senegambians were already familiar with domestic service. They had lived in highly developed cities, and most of the skilled artisans were members of several endogamous castes, which included the smiths, leather workers, butchers, and griots. Many of these skilled artisans continued their trades in South Carolina, and many griots' stories found their way to the Sea Islands in the form of Brer Rabbit stories.

The Brer Rabbit, Brer Wolf, Brer Fox, and Sis' Nanny goat stories were among the Wolof folk tales brought to America by the *Hausa, Fula* (Fulani), and *Mandinka*. Mande tales of Tricksters and Hares were also introduced. The Hare (Rabbit) story is also found in parts of Nigeria, Angola, and East Africa. Tortoise stories are found among the Yoruba, Igbo, and Edo-Bini peoples of Nigeria. Other examples of

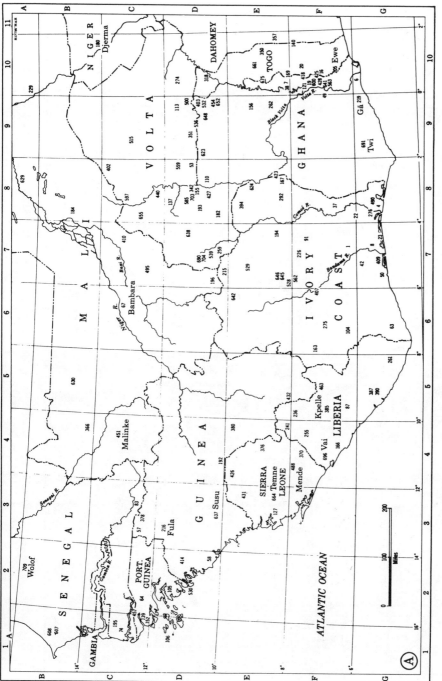

MAP 1. Western Africa (Westernmost Part). From "The Languages of Africa," by Joseph H. Greenberg, publication no. 25, January 1963, of the Indiana University Research Center in Anthropology, Folklore, and Linguistics; map inset A. Used by permission.

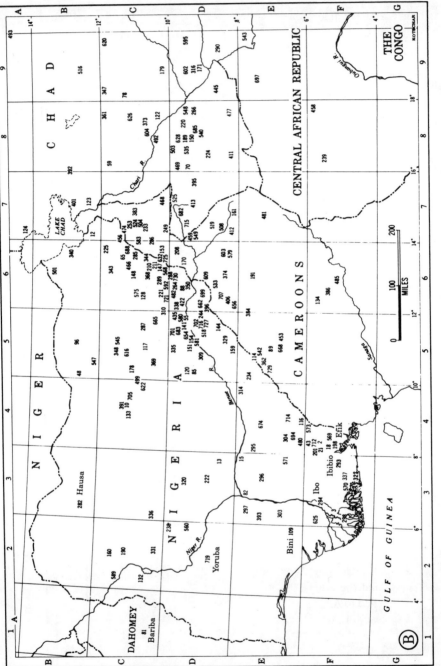

MAP 2. Western Africa (Easternmost Part). From "The Languages of Africa," by Joseph H. Greenberg, publication no. 25, January 1963, of the Indiana University Research Center in Anthropology, Folklore, and Linguistics; map inset B. Used by permission.

folklore from West Africa are tales such as the "Hare Tied in the Bean Farm" and the "Three Tasks of the Hare" (where he goes to ask God for more Wisdom). These tales are widespread among the Mandinka and Wolof of West Africa and common in black folklore in the United States.[6]

The Hare and Hyena (corresponding to Brer Rabbit and Brer Wolf) tales are told all over the West African Sudanic (Sahel) zone among the Fula, Wolof, and Mandinka and eastward to the Hausa of Nigeria. In North America the slaves who fled to the Creek Indians introduced West African tales in their region; the tales later gained acceptance as Trickster and Hare tales among various Indian groups. Tales from the Mandinka heartland spread south to such countries as Liberia, Sierra Leone, Ivory Coast, and wherever the Mandinka Jula traders migrated. The Africans who came from those areas to the New World via the transatlantic slave trade brought the folk tales as part of their oral tradition. These tales later resurfaced as the Uncle Remus stories retold in the Georgia and Carolina Sea Islands. Most of the folk tales told by Uncle Remus are Hausa in origin and were transported to North America by the Mandinkas (Mandingos).

The Mande were the first enslaved Africans to arrive in South Carolina, bringing with them a unique cultural heritage. In the 1700s Wolof was by far the dominant African culture on both sides of the Atlantic, in the upper Guinea coast and the coast of South Carolina. The Wolofs' skills became an integral part of the practices of North American plantations, where numerous African carryovers of Wolof origin found their way into European-American culture. As a result, Wolofs were the first Africans to have elements of their language and culture retained within the developing American culture. Mande and Wolof were the two most widespread languages of the Senegambia. Bilingualism was important for the trade and commerce in the region.

West Africans traded between Sierra Leone and Liberia, transmitting their culture with trade and commerce. There is an interesting case in which one of these traders crossed the Atlantic to consolidate relations with her American trading partners. Fenda Lawrence, a Gambian slave trader, visited the American South in 1772 as a tourist. The government of Georgia issued her a certificate stating that "a free black woman and heretofore a considerable trader in the River Gambia on the Coast of Africa, hath voluntarily come to be and remain for some time in this province, with the permission to pass and repass unmolested within the said province on her lawful and necessary occasion."[7] Apparently she moved throughout the South without any problems and returned to Gambia to continue her trade in slaves.

Another Gambian, Job Ben Solomon, spent a brief time enslaved in Maryland until he attracted the attention of James Oglethorpe and was eventually freed in 1734 and returned to Africa as a celebrity among his fellow Foulah and neighboring Wolofs and Mandingos.[8] Abd al-Rahman Ibrahima (known as "Prince" on the plantation), a West African prince from the kingdom of Tambo, was kidnapped from Africa and sold into slavery in New Orleans in 1788. He was Fulbe (Fulani) and spoke fluent Arabic, Wolof, and Mande, the lingua franca of the plantation before the 1730s.[9]

Much of Mande culture was transmitted to white Americans by way of the plantation "Big House." African cooking in the Big House creolized into southern cooking. The relationship between house servant and master was bidirectional and reciprocal in nature, with each adopting something of value from the other's culture. The masters acquired such knowledge as the herbal cure for snakebites and innovations in animal husbandry practice and rice cultivation. From the mammies, white American children learned and passed on African folk beliefs, tales, and stories as told by Uncle Remus. From the Mande, American English borrowed numerous words now a part of everyday English. African culture and linguistic retentions moved into American culture via the Mande and the Bantu; the Mande displayed the greatest influence on white American culture, the Bantu on black American culture.

The Central Africans

The Bantu formed the largest homogeneous group among Central Africans enslaved in South Carolina. The Central Africans came from Kongo, Cabinda, Loango, Luanda, Luba, Mbanza, and Ndongo. Angola and the Congo played key roles in the American slave market. While roughly 60 percent of the Africans came from West Africa over the whole period between 1700 and 1808, about 40 percent came directly from the Angolan and Congo ports of Loango, Malemba, Cabinda, Pinda, Ambriz, Kitungo, and St. Paul-de-Luanda.

Africans were taken from the deep interior of Central Africa to the coastal areas. In Angola the largest and most organized were the Mbundu, or Ovimbundu. Their king was the N'gola of Ndongo, and from this title the kingdom was called N'Angola by the Portuguese. Enslaved Africans in South Carolina thus became known as N'gola, or Gulla(h). A drawing of Loango from the period (fig. 5) suggests that Angola at the height of the slave trade was a well-organized country equal in size and organization to any in Europe at the time.

What accounts for Bantu unity is a common origin. The Bantu dispersal into the Kasai region of Central Africa was completed by A.D. 500. By 1150 the Bantu were located west along the Kongo River (Zaire) toward the Atlantic Ocean; it was there that the Portuguese Diego Cao "found" the mouth of the Kongo in 1487. By 1550 the Yaka had pushed the Bantu westward to their present location. In the process there were several internal migrations, which account for the formation of the various related ethnic divisions—the Mbamba, Mpemba, Mbata, Nsundi, and Mpangu. Between 1300 and 1500 the kingdom of the Kongo was at the height of its power. The reign of the Christian kings (*manikongo*) took place under the influence of the Portuguese as they searched for the legendary kingdom of Prester John.

The Lunda people formed themselves into a vital center of the Central African slave trade. Their empire lasted from 1665 to 1860, paralleling the most intensive era of the slave trade. During the reign of Mwata Yamvo (1660–75), the Lunda of Bushimayi extended their confederation westward to include the Bangala kingdom, stretching to territories formerly belonging to the manikongo of the Kongo King-dom. The period between 1650 and 1885 was marked by corruption and moral decay. This period involved the greatest migration of Africans to Brazil and South Carolina, from 1780 to 1807.

While many of the Senegambians were enslaved as craftsmen and artisans, the field slaves were mainly Central Africans who, unlike the Senegambians, brought a homogeneous, identifiable culture. The Bantus often possessed good metallurgical and woodworking skills. They had a particular skill in iron working, making the wrought-iron balconies in New Orleans and Charleston. But as field workers the Bantus were kept away from the developing mainstream of white American culture. This isolation worked to the Bantus' advantage in that it allowed their culture to escape acculturation, maintain uniformity, and flourish. The Bantus had the largest constituency in South Carolina and possibly in other areas of southeastern United States as well.* Given the homogeneity of the Bantu culture and the strong similari-ties among Bantu languages, this group no doubt influenced West African groups of larger size.

After 1730 Bantus were imported in large numbers in South Carolina. Once they reached America they were able to retain much of their cultural identity. Enforced isolation allowed them to retain their religion, philosophy, culture, folklore, folk-ways, folk beliefs, folk tales, storytelling, naming practices, home economics, arts, kinship, and music. Their Africanisms, shared and adopted by various African ethnic groups of the field-slave community, gradually developed into African-American cooking (soul food), music (jazz, blues, spirituals, gospels), dance, lan-guage, religion, philosophy, customs, and arts.

Vass has documented a substantial number of Bantu speech survivals in folk tales and songs. She used Luba, a core language in the Bantu nucleus identified by Guthrie, as the basis for her analysis of Gullah. Luba has 47 percent of all general terms common to the Bantu languages. Its extension to the south, Luba-Katanga, has 50 percent. Luba is surpassed only by the closely related Bemba, with the highest, 54 percent.[10] Its language area covers some 800,000 square kilometers, a major block of Central Africa.[11]

Curtin has shown that 58.8 percent of the enslaved Africans imported in ships known to the British Foreign Office between 1817 and 1843 came from Kongo North and Angola, the Bantu sources. His analysis, covering 100,000 enslaved Africans imported during those key years in the southern slave purchase, revealed that trade was concentrated in a few ports; "although this whole coastline stretches more than 1,000 miles, about three-quarters of all the Africans exported came from a distance of about only 300 miles." All the ports listed exported Bantu-speaking Africans who came to North America as slaves.[12] Wood's research shows that "roughly seven out of every ten Africans imported into Charleston during this period came from the area then called 'Angola' near the Congo River."[13]

---

*We are aware of the ambiguity of the term *Bantu*: Afrikaners refer to white South Africans as "Africans" and black Africans as "Bantus." For us, the term *Bantu* serves to describe the cultural homogeneity of Central Africans brought to the New World.

In Bantu survivals in the United States, the Luba appear to have dominated the other Bantu groups. At least 260 place names of Bantu origin are found throughout nine southern states. The predominance of Bantu linguistic survivals in American folk tales and songs suggests a Bantu diaspora in the American South.[14] Herskovits noted that the Bantu culture had survived in the Sea Islands and that blacks there had retained the strongest African heritage, second only to Brazil, because of their isolation from the mainland.[15] Bastide identified three main centers of Bantu culture in the United States: the Sea Islands, the coastal region of Virginia, and the area centered on New Orleans. He found a double level of African culture in Louisiana, Dahomean in religion (voodoo cult) and Bantu in regard to folklore and aesthetic culture.[16] Bantu contributions to South Carolina and Louisiana include not only wrought-iron balconies but also wood carvings, basketry, weaving, clay-baked figurines, and pottery. Cosmograms, grave designs and decorations, funeral practices, and the wake are Bantu in origin. Bantu musical contributions include drums, diddley bow, mouth bow, quills, washtub bass, jug, gongs, bells, rattles, ideophones, and the *lokoimbi,* a five-stringed harp.

THE AFRICAN SLAVE TRADE INTO SOUTH CAROLINA

The transatlantic slave trade was of course the main avenue for the transmission of African culture to the New World. This trade, as Holloway has pointed out, "established a permanent link between Africa and North America as Africans sold into slavery transplanted their cultures to the New World. The largest forced migration in history, the slave trade brought an estimated half-million Africans to what is now the United States over some two hundred years. This total is thought to represent about 7 percent of the entire transatlantic slave trade. . . . If one considers those who perished in the stockades and on the cargo ships in estimating the volume of traffic to the New World, the total may well be over forty million."[17]

An estimate of fifteen million was commonly accepted by scholars as the total volume of transatlantic traffic until Curtin's *Atlantic Slave Trade* revised this figure down to 9,566,000.[18] Rawley, in *The Transatlantic Slave Trade,* revised Curtin's figures up to 11,345,000, suggesting that the total volume was even greater than the previous estimates by 1,779,000.[19] Not all scholars agree with either Curtin's global estimates or Rawley's revisions. In a history of the transatlantic slave trade published by UNESCO in 1979, J. F. Abe Ajayi and J. E. Inikori believed that Curtin's global estimate was at least 10 percent too low. They suggested that it would be more realistic to raise Curtin's figures by 40 percent, making the total export from Africa "by the way of that trade 15.4 million."[20]

The total volume of the slave trade may never be known. But any tally of the mass human exportation must include not only the Africans who arrived alive but also those who died. For every African who arrived alive, many others died in interethnic warfare generally instigated by "pombieros," powerful mulatto chiefs, motivated by their white fathers and implemented by the black connections of their

TABLE 1
Africans Imported into South Carolina, by Culture Cluster

Country	Culture Cluster	Number	Percent
Ghana	Akan	9,851	10.8
Senegal	Mande	22,874	25.0
Liberia	Mano River	6,099	6.7
Nigeria	Niger Delta	1,301	1.4
Zaire	Bakongo	9,807	10.7
Angola	Ovimbundu	24,346	26.6
Mozambique	Yao	473	0.5
Africa	Unknown	16,840	18.4
Total		91,591	

mothers for the purpose of acquiring slaves through raids. More Africans perished inside the stockades called "factories" while awaiting shipment to the New World. In addition, one-fourth of the cargoes was lost to sickness and death. If one considers all these factors in estimating the volume of the traffic to the New World, the total may exceed even Holloway's estimate. It may be over sixty million.

The transatlantic slave trade was in full-scale operation by the late 1600s. Documents from 1700 to 1730 are vague in identifying African ethnicity, but we do have data on total recorded importations. In just twenty years after the original settlement, the African population in the Carolinas was equal to that of Europeans. By 1715 Africans outnumbered Europeans 10,500 to 6,250. Between 1706 and 1724, 5,081 Africans arrived in colonial South Carolina; between 1721 and 1726, 3,632 were imported.[21] Even though relatively few Africans were imported during the early years of the Colonial period, they outnumbered the white population. By 1720 Africans had outnumbered Europeans for more than a decade. In 1724 the white population in Colonial South Carolina was estimated at 14,000, the black population at 32,000. A Swiss newcomer, Samuel Dyssli, observed in 1737 that Carolina "looks more like a negro country than like a country settled by white people."[22]

The slave trade into South Carolina between 1700 and 1808 totaled 91,591 Africans (table 1). By clusters we can identify the African culture and language groups.[23]

The accompanying cultural map shows the relation of Africans arriving in South Carolina from each cluster to the corresponding culture in the United States. Of the culture clusters that entered (Akan, Bantu, Mande, Mano River, Niger Cross River, Niger Delta, and Sudanic), the Bantu are divided into Bakongo, Ovimbundu, and Luba Lunda.

There were three slave trade periods: 1700–40, 1750–75, and 1776–1807. As Creel pointed out, the Donnan and Treasury Report data, based on documents from the early period, show that 60 percent of the Africans entering South Carolina were from Angola in Central Africa.[24] During the middle period, the figure dropped to

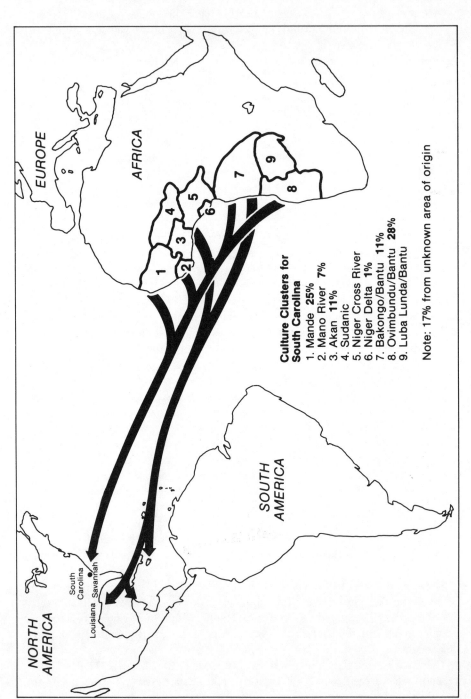

Culture Clusters for South Carolina
1. Mande **25%**
2. Mano River **7%**
3. Akan **11%**
4. Sudanic
5. Niger Cross River
6. Niger Delta **1%**
7. Bakongo/Bantu **11%**
8. Ovimbundu/Bantu **28%**
9. Luba Lunda/Bantu

Note: 17% from unknown area of origin

MAP 3.   Culture Groups in Africa and North America

15 percent because of the Stono Rebellion. In the final period, Bantu forced immigration rose to 53 percent. Toward the mid-1700s, then, more Angolans than any other African group were being imported into South Carolina. Wood found documents showing that between 1735 and 1740, 70 percent of all incoming Africans were Bantu from the Angolan region near the Congo River. Of 11,562 Africans imported in that five-year period, 8,045 were from Angola. The next largest group listed (2,719) was from "elsewhere in Africa." From Gambia only 705 Africans (6 percent of the total) were brought into South Carolina, probably to be trained as house servants.[25]

After 1739 fewer Angolans were brought into the colony, for by then the southern planters were prejudiced against them. In the southern planters' minds, Angolan dominance contributed to the unrest of 1739, in which Angolans revolted, killing whites while en route to Florida. Documents describing the Stono uprising mention that "amongst the Negroe Slaves there are a people brought from the kingdom of Angola in Africa." In 1739–40 only 692 Angolans were imported into Charlestown, the Carolina port (now Charleston), and during the rest of the century Angolan importation dropped to 40 percent of the Africans imported into South Carolina. But even with this 30 percent drop, the Bantus still remained the largest cohesive group on the American plantations.[26]

1.   A Mandingo.

2.   Voodoo dance.

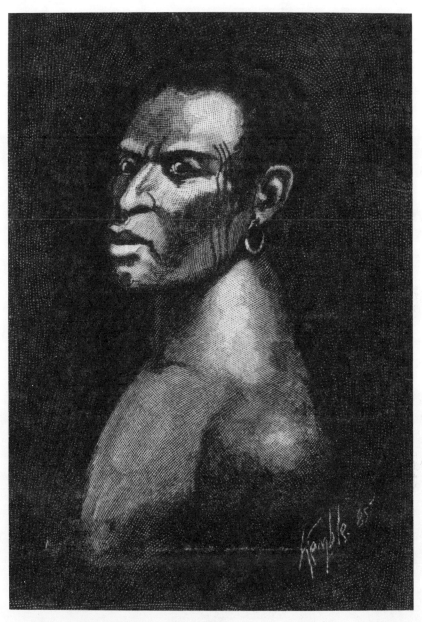

3.   A Yoruba man with ethnic markings.

4. Calalou.

5. Mulatto woman.

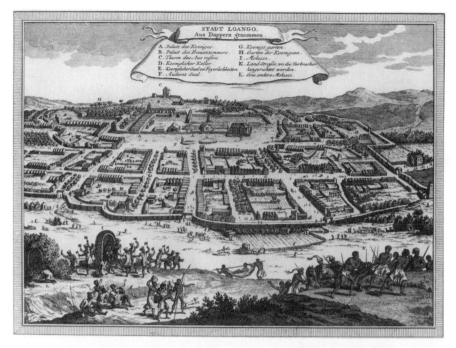

6. Loango. Drawing from *Allgemeine Historie der Reisen zu Wasser und Lande oder Sammlung aller Reisebeschreibungen,* vol. 4 (Leipzig, 1749); translation of *Histoire générale des voyages* (Paris, 1747). Courtesy of Peter H. Wood.

7. The bamboula.

8. The love song.

9. Africa House, Natchitoches, Louisiana. Architectural style particular to the Congo.

Abbreviations

adj.	adjective
adv.	adverb
cf.	compare
conj.	conjunction
dem.	demonstrative
esp.	especially
excl.	exclamation
i.	intransitive
imp.	imperative
int.	interrogative
inv.	invariable
lit.	literally
loc.	locative
neg.	negative
n.	noun
num.	number, numerical
part.	participle
pl.	plural
poss.	possessive
prep.	preposition
pres.	present
pron.	pronoun
purp.	purportive mood
sing.	singular
t.	transitive
temp.	temporal clause
v.	verb

The
African Heritage
of American
English

One

THE BANTU VOCABULARY CONTENT
OF GULLAH

The Bantu vocabulary content of Gullah—that is, the Central African origin for many words used in African-American culture—becomes apparent in a simple word-for-word comparison of the vocabulary collected by Turner (1949) among the Gullah speakers of the southeastern United States with equivalent words currently in use by Luba-Kasai (Tshiluba) speakers in present-day Zaire (formerly Congo) in Central Africa. Of the 3,938 Gullah terms that Turner lists, 1,891 are recognized by Vass in current Luba use today, giving Gullah a core Bantu lexicon of 35.2 percent (see tables 2 and 3; for geographical locations, see table 4 and map 4).

This vocabulary comparison of Gullah and Luba, with grammatical classifications and meanings, will be of interest to all who seek "roots" by means of the superb tool of linguistics. Two points should be noted:

1. The orthography of spoken Tshiluba is in constant flux. In this dictionary it is brought up to date as much as possible, but variations in the spelling of certain words will be found because of dialectical differences.

2. Turner called attention to the fact that Bantu languages have words that are spelled exactly alike but have differing meanings. The differentiation is made by syllables that are variously pronounced, with high or low, long or short, rising or falling glides. Whenever readers see a puzzling duplication of words spelled alike, they should keep this aspect of Bantu languages in mind.

Three Tshiluba dictionaries were used in compiling this vocabulary list: Nzongola (1967), Morrison (1939), and DeClerq (1960). Turner had access to Morrison's *Dictionary of the Tshiluba Language;* reference is made to it in *Africanisms in the Gullah Dialect,* 303.

The system used by DeClerq and Willems to mark tonemes has been used only when necessary to indicate the differing tonal patterns of identically spelled words. All unmarked tones are high; low tones are indicated by a grave accent (`) a period following a syllable indicates the prolongation of the vowel sound; a circumflex (ˆ) indicates a tonal glide.

> *bàtà. (first tone low and short, second low and long)
> -bà.ta (first tone low and long, second high and short)
> -ba.ta (first tone high and long, second high and short)
> -bàta (first tone low and short, second high and short)

This duplication of the rising and falling inflections of the human voice is the secret of the "talking drums" and communication whistles heard in spoken Tshiluba.

Certain Bantu syntax forms are found in Gullah and Tshiluba:

1. **Use of the preposition "for"** ("fuh" = "bua" to express purpose or use)

   Sumpm *fuh* nyam   tshintu *tshia* kudia   something *for* to eat[1]
   Eh bim want *fuh* axe me sometin. Wakasua *bua* kungebesha bualu. He wanted *for* to ask me sometin.[2]
   Den e beggin *fuh* walk. Hashishe, wakutuadisha *bua* kuenda. Then he started in *for* to walk[3]

2. **Of**

   A heap *of* ting   Bintu *bia* bungi.   Things *of* muchness, many things.[4]

3. **Locatives** (prepositional forms that follow and are attached to verb)

you going *at*	udi uya*ku*	you are going-*to*[5]
you stay *at*	udi ushala*ku*	you are staying-*at*
Put that right down *here*.	Utshiteka*pu*	Put it right-*here*.
Dem look *pontopper* me.	pambidi *panyi*	*On top of me*[6]

4. **Distinctive verb forms**

   Hotten up the coffee. *Temesha* cafe. Cause the coffee to be hot. *Causative* form of verb "tema" to burn, be hot.[7]
   Joe gone on *dig dig*.   Wakuya bua ku*dimadima*. He has gone to work for a long time in his field (hoe-hoe)[8] *Repetitive* form of the word to hoe, showing repeated action. "Say-say," *kuambamba*, to say over.

5. **Tenses**

we dun duh nyam	*tukadi badie*	we are already having eaten	Present Perfect
ef I ben know	*bu meme mmanye*	if I had known	Past Perfect
I be tired	*ntu ngikala mupungile*	I am always tired	Present Habitual[9]
Soon, meaning "early," too soon to start	*tukadi pa kuya*	we are about to go	Imminent, Tense[10]

---

*For meanings of these words, consult chapter one.

6. Pronominal infixes and suffixes

Uh yeddy '*um* but ent sh*um*. Nkadi *bu*mvue kadi tshiaku*ba*mona. I heard-them but did not see-them. (Pronominal direct object infix)

You wantuh sh*um*, suh? Udi musue ku*ba*mona? Do you want to see-them, sir? (Note ellision of direct object pronoun with the verb in Gullah and Tshiluba.)

Massuh quizzit '*um*. Mukelenge waka*mu*ebesha. The master questioned him.

7. No differentiation in gender of pronouns

E hab a chile.	*Yeye* wakalela muana	He (or she) has a child.
Him a bad ooman.	*Yeye* mmukaji mubi	She (or he) is a bad woman.
Him's a gal.	*Yeye* udi muana wa bakaji.	She (or he) is a girl child.[11]

8. Onomatopoeic expressions in Gullah found exactly in Tshiluba

Shubbles go *shu-shu* een de sand.

W'en shubble hit de nail, e gone *kong! kong!*[12]

Bim!	Violently.
Pak! Pak! Pak!	Knocking
Ban! Ban! Ban!	Pounding[13]

9. Tshiluba idioms carried over into Gullah

Expressions of time

Cock crowing	*hadi hasama tshitala*	when the rooster crows[14]
Day-clean	*kutoka kulu*	clean high (in the sky)
High sun	*diba kulu*	high sun (forenoon)[15]
De sun duh lean	*diba diakuhuka*	the sun has stepped aside (afternoon)[16]
Deep dus'	*kajimb'a buenyi*	guest-disappearance hour, the hour the guest becomes part of the family

10. Other terms

Knee-high men	*mitumbula*	little knee-high men of Zaire folklore[17]
He yent crack e teet	*kena muleje menu*	he hasn't shown his teeth (said a word)[18]
Tek yo foot in yo han'	*ambula dikasa*	pick up your foot (literally)[19]
Snake bite de chile e lef han feet	*nyoka musume muana ku dikasa dia bakaji*	The snake bit the child on the woman's (left) foot[20]
All-two	*bonso babidi*	all-two[21]
Greebunce gottum	*dikenga diakamukuata*	trouble has caught him[22]
Possit your word	*punga diyi diebe*	contract your word[23]
Enty?	*nasha?*	Isn't it? (after a statement)[24]

TABLE 2
Distribution of African Words Found in Gullah, as Identified by Turner (1949)

Language	Meanings*	Percent
Bantu†		
Bobangi	30	
(Djema)	4	
(Fang)	239	
Kongo	805	
Kikongo	21	
Kimbundu	203	
(Manyika)	210	
(Songye)	2	
Tshiluba	148	
Umbundu	229	
Total	1,891	35.2
Benue-Congo		
Efik	22	
Ibibio	2	
Total	24	0.4
Niger-Congo		
Nupe	3	
Gbari	2	
Total	5	0.1
Chad (Afro-Asiatic)		
Hausa	272	5.1
Kwa (Sudanese)		
Bini	76	
Ewe	420	
Gã	29	
Igbo	44	
Fante	16	
Twi	295	
Yoruba	788	
Total	1,668	31.1
Mandinka‡		
Mandingo	87	
Bambara	345	
Kpelle	4	
Mende	528	
Malinke	9	
Susu	6	
Vai	275	
Total	1,254	23.4
West Atlantic		
Fula	75	
Temne	38	

TABLE 2 *(continued)*

Language	Meanings*	Percent
Wolof	<u>138</u>	
Total	251	4.7
Grand Total of All African Language Meanings Given by Turner for 3,382 Gullah Words	5,365	100.0

*Compilation of numerical count by William S. Pollitzer.
†Guthrie, *Comparative Bantu,* 11–15.
‡Turner mistakenly listed Mandinka as Bantu. Apparently he was confused by the striking similarity of Mandinka, a Niger-Congo language of Senegal and Eastern Nigeria (1A2 on Greenberg's "Summary of Classification" map), and Manyika, a Bantu language of the Shona group in Mozambique and Zimbabwe (T13 in Guthrie's *Classification of Bantu Language* and S13 in his *Comparative Bantu,* vol. 1, 87). This explains the presence of this body of definitively Bantu words in the category that Turner lumped together as "Mandinka." Those in parentheses corrected by Winifred K. Vass, Joseph Holloway, and William Pollitzer.

TABLE 3
African Linguistic Sources of Gullah, after Turner (1949)

	Personal Names (3,595)		Words, Conversation (251)		Words, Stories (92)		Total (3,938)	
Language	No.	%	No.	%	No.	%	No.	%
Kongo	706	14.5	99	24.8			805	15.0
Yoruba	775	15.9	13	3.2			788	14.7
Mende	433	8.9	31	7.8	64	68.8	528	9.8
Ewe	405	8.3	15	3.8			420	7.8
Bambara	323	6.6	21	5.2	1	1.1	345	6.4
Twi	281	5.8	14	3.5			295	5.5
Vai	218	4.5	30	7.5	27	29.0	275	5.1
Hausa	251	5.2	21	5.2			272	5.1
Fon	229	4.7	10	2.5			239	4.4
Umbundu	211	4.3	18	4.5			229	4.3
Mandinka	207	4.2	2	0.5	1	1.1	210	3.9
Kimbundu	188	3.9	15	3.8			203	3.8
Tshiluba	130	2.7	18	4.5			148	2.8
Wolof	114	2.3	24	6.0			138	2.6
Mandingo	79	1.6	8	2.0			87	1.6
Bini	74	1.5	2	0.5			76	1.4
Fula	50	1.0	25*	6.2			75	1.4
Igbo	40	0.8	4	1.0			44	0.8

TABLE 3 *(continued)*

Language	Personal Names (3,595)		Words, Conversation (251)		Words, Stories (92)		Total (3,938)	
	No.	%	No.	%	No.	%	No.	%
Temne	35	0.7	3	0.8			38	0.7
Bobangi	28	0.6	2	0.5			30	0.6
Gã	24	0.5	5	1.2			29	0.5
Efik	18	0.4	4	1.0			22	0.4
Kikongo	18	0.4	3	0.8			21	0.4
Fante	15	0.3	1	0.2			16	0.3
Malinke	8	0.2	1	0.2			9	0.2
Susu	6	0.1	0	0.0			6	0.1
Kpelle	1		3	0.8			4	0.1
Djerma	0		4	1.0			4	0.1
Nupe	1	0.1	2	0.5			3	
Songhay	1		1				2	0.2
Ibibio	1		1	0.5			2	
Gbari	2		0				2	
Totals	4,872	100.0	400	100.0	93	100.0	5,365	100.0

Compiled by William S. Pollitzer and used by permission.
*Includes numerals 1–19.

TABLE 4
Geographical Locations of Turner's Linguistic Sources of Gullah Vocabulary

Bantu	Guthrie's Classification	Geographic Location
Bobangi	C 32	Central African Republic, Zaire
(Djema)	A 84	Gabon, Congo-Brazzaville
(Fang)	A 75	Gabon, Congo-Brazzaville
KONGO	H 16	Zaire, Angola
Kikongo*	H 10	Zaire, Angola
KIMBUNDU	H 21	Zaire, Angola
(Manyika)	S 13a	Zimbabwe, Mozambique
(Songye)	L 20	Zaire
TSHILUBA†	L 31	Zaire (Zambia)
UMBUNDU	R 11	Angola

Benue-Congo	Greenberg's Classification	Geographic Location
Efik (198)	I.A.5, B-F 4	Nigeria
Ibibio (293)	I.A.5, B-F 3	Nigeria

TABLE 4 *(continued)*

Chad (Afro-Asiatic)

Hausa (282)	III. E, B-B 3	Nigeria

Kwa (Sudanese)

Bini (109)	I.A. 4, B-E 2	Nigeria
Ewe (205)	I.A.4, A-F 10	Togo
Ga (219)	I.A.4, A-G 9	Ghana
Igbo (294)	I.A.4, B-F 3	Nigeria
Twi (691)	I.A.4, A-G 9	Ghana
Yoruba (7119)	I.A.4, B-D 2	Nigeria

Mandinka

Bambara (67)	I.A.2, A-C 6	Mali
Kpelle (385)	I.A.2, A-F 5	Liberia
Mende (488)	I.A.2, A-F 4	Sierra Leone
Malinke (451)	I.A.2, A-C 4	Mali
Susu (637)	I.A.2, A-D 3	Guinea
Vai (696)	I.A.2, A-F 4	Liberia

West Atlantic

Fula (216)	I.A.1, A-D 3	Guinea
Temne (664)	I.A.1, A-E 3	Sierra Leone
Wolof (709)	I.A.1, A-B 2	Senegal

Compiled by William S. Pollitzer and used by permission.

Capital letters indicate a language spoken by more than one million people according to Gregersen (1977). Numbers in parentheses refer to maps in Guthrie (1967). All languages are listed by Turner (1949) except those in parentheses. Vass (1979) finds indications in Gullah of Djema, Fang, Manyika, Songye.

*Kikongo is considered by some a form of Kongo.

†Tshiluba is also called Luba-Kasai. Luba is geographically divided into Luba-Kasai and Luba-Katanga, with smaller subdivisions such as Luba-Lulua. Kasai and Lulua are names of rivers.

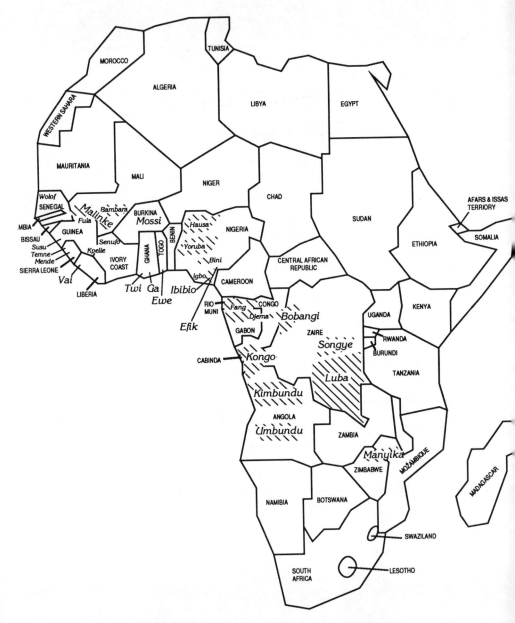

MAP 4. Geographical Locations of Turner's Linguistic Sources of Gullah Vocabulary

Vocabulary List

Column one lists Gullah words collected by Turner (1949); colum̄
Turner's English meanings for these words. Column three lists equivalent words
identified by Vass as currently in use by Luba-Kasai speakers in Zaire; column four
gives their English meanings.

A

aba	name given a girl born on Thursday	-aba v.i.	click, crack
		-aba v.i.	feel grief, pain
		-aba v.t.	divide, distribute
abashe	the work of a laborer	abashe purp.	let him build, cónstruct
adi	feasting, a meal	adiye purp.	let him eat
agogo	bell	ngongo n. sing.	bell
agoli		ngole n. sing.	zebra
akasa	corn meal or corn beverage	nkasa n. sing.	palm-leaf ball, corn shuck ball bounced on palm of hand
		nkasa n. sing.	toe
akele	name given one who is small but obstinate	nkela n. sing.	sneer
akiti	monkey	nkima n. sing.	monkey
akwenu	rich	kwenu loc. poss.	*"chez vous"*
Alaba	Arabian, Arabic	Alaba n. sing.	Arab, Arabian
alabalashe	goddess who foretells future	-alapala adj.	backwards (belief that *back* is turned to the unknown future
alala	slowly flowing stream	alale purp.	let him sleep
alama	a sign	alame purp.	let him keep, guard
alamisha	Thursday	-alamisha v.t.	cause to lie down on the ground
alaye	living	alaye purp.	let him say goodbye, promise
anani	name given fourth son	anayi num. adj.	four
anga	stone containing iron	-anga v.i.	be furious, angry
		-anga v.i.	shine, glow, as the moon
		-anga v.t.	seek, go in search of
anima	animal	nyama n. sing.	animal
anu	only	anu adv.	only

anyi	we, us, our	anyi poss. adj.	my
		-anyi conj.	or
anyika	"She is very beautiful"	-anyisha v.t.	praise, compliment, extol
apa	agreement	apa adv.	here
apara	raillery, jest	-pala v.i.	be crazy, drunk, foolish
arakana	the body pains him	-alakana v.t.	desire greatly, long for
asa	shield	-asa v.t.	shoot (an arrow, a gun); make, begin to do, initiate, undertake
ashale	personal name	ashale purp.	let him remain, stay
ashipe	accidental murder	ashipe purp.	let him kill
asoso	fruit of plant	nsoso n.s.	pockmark, blister
atanu	rejected	atanu num. adj.	five
awoni	visitor (personal name)	mwenyi n. sing.	visitor, guest
awu	dress, garment	awu dem. adj.	that
awulu	much, many	muvule adj.	much, many, abundant
awusa	walnut, pepper	musa n. sing.	nut, kernel
aya	sacred tree	-aya v.i.	be sour, acid
aye		aye purp.	let him go
ayedele	joy, pleasure	ayendele purp.	let him court, woo

B

ba	to meet	ba prep.	(people) of
baba	father	baba n. sing.	woman, mother
babadu	eaten by termites	babadi n. pl.	eaters, those who are eating
babaluaiye	god of smallpox	mbalanga n. sing.	smallpox
babalorisha		babalotshisha	they are causing them to dream
babata	feel one's way	-babata v.i.	walk blindly, feeling one's way
babatunde	name given male child born soon after death of grandfather	-tunda v.i.	wander about, go someplace else, migrate (idea of transmigration, soul of grandfather is in child)
babayi	male persons	bambayi n. pl.	husbands
babu	conversation	babu n. pl.	friends

badi	native cloth	badi verb to be	they are
		mbadi n. sing.	room, place, space, position, situation
bafa	to argue with	bafue n. pl.	the dead
bafata	high tide, be full	-pa.ta v.i.	go far away, travel abroad
		-pàta v.i.	be strong, vigorous, robust
		-pàta v.i.	be constipated
baka	to keep	-baka v.t.	marry, wed
bakalenge	to grow	bakelenge n. pl.	chiefs, leaders, head men
bala		-bala v.t.	read, count
balana	accidentally	tshimbalantan- ta adv.	suddenly, unexpectedly
balaye	personal name	balaye purp.	let them promise, say goodbye
bale	landlord	bale adj.	tall (people)
		-bale adj.	few, short, small, scarce
balema	sore, ulcer	balema n. pl.	crippled, handicapped people
bamba	to tie well	-bamba v.i.	hide, keep hidden
		-bàmba v.t.	fix, join together; sew, patch
		badi bamba	they say (-amba, say)
bambo	crocodile totem	mbamba n. pl.	scales of a snake or crocodile, scabs
bambula	transfer by witchcraft the property of one person to another	-bambula v.t.	reveal, remove the covering
		-bambula v.t.	forge, fashion metal by beating
bana	to spend together	bana n. pl.	children
banda	climb	-bànda v.t.	climb up, mount, ascend
		-banda v.t.	accuse falsely, calumniate
		-banda v.t.	braid the hair
bandakana	to be piled one on top of the other	bandakana v.t. & v.i.	stacking up, piling up on top of one another
bando	fee given a doctor	mbandu (wa tshilamba)	double arm's length of cloth
banduka	be disfigured (personal name)	-banduka v.i.	get up from a cramped position, stretch, stop field work

banga	begin, be betrothed to	-banga v.t.	begin, commence, start; be betrothed to a woman
		banga adv.	actually, truly, really
bangabanga	long ago	bangabanga adv.	long ago, in olden times
bangi	herbalist	bangi adj.	many (people)
		mubangi n. sing.	a starter, commencer
banyika	send a person out into very hot sun	-anyika v.t.	dry by the fire or in the sun; cook, roast, toast (badi banyika)
bangula	lift up, open, notch a gun	-bangula v.t.	open up that which was closed; unfasten, unlatch something shut, attached; cock a gun
banja	a kola nut of only two sections	mbanji n. sing.	rib
		banji v.t.	let them first do
banza	to think	-banza v.t.	establish a home after the definitive conclusion of a marriage
base	name of a place in the Mandinka country	-basa v.t.	build, construct
basala	personal name	-sàla v.t.	tatoo (badi basala)
		-sa.la (tshisuku)	stir, beat the bush, rouse
		sala v.t.	defy, provoke to war
basi	amulet	mbashi n. sing.	species of antelope
		mbashimbashi n. sing.	fear, timidity, shyness of a wild animal
bata	drum used by sango worshippers	bàtà.	picture word for calm, quiet
		-ba.tà v.t.	beat the earth underfoot
		-ba.ta v.t.	feel about for
		-bàta v.t.	examine, scrutinize
		mbàta n. sing.	a debt for credit
		mbata n. sing.	fist
		mbata n. sing.	fern, bracken
batika	to stick on	-batuka v.i.	be worried, lose calm
batumba	equality	-tumba v.i.	be renowned, acclaimed, famous
baula	coffin	-baula v.t.	listen, prick up ears, be alert

baya	personal name	-baya v.t.	hold steady, uphold, sustain, strengthen, complete
		badi baya	they are going (-ya, go)
		baya n. sing.	husband
bayani	object venerated	mbayanyi n. sing.	my husband
bayi	to leave	mbayi n. sing.	they have gone
be	to hide	be, postpositive adv.	exceedingly, very, quite, extremely
bedi		mbedi adv.	first, beforehand
bela	to perch	-bela v.t.	warn, instruct, exhort, teach
		-bèla v.i.	be sick, suffering
		-bèla v.t.	crack, crush, break (nuts); shell, hull (peas)
		mbèlù n. sing.	doorway, entrance
beli	weak, sickly	mubè.di n. sing.	sick person
		mube.di n. sing.	teacher, exhorter
bena	born on Tuesday	bena n. pl.	people of
benda	to be crooked	-benda v.t.	curve, bend
bende	a rat	bende inv. n.	someone else, another
		mbende n. sing.	lever, crowbar
bendesa	make crooked	bendesha v.t.	make crooked, bend
beng		mbenga n. sing.	wild olive seeds used in gambling
benyi		benyi n. pl.	guests, visitors
bento		bintu n. pl.	things, objects
benyin		-benya v.t.	flatten out, clear away brush
		-benya nyima v.t.	turn back on someone
bese	amulet	-besa v.t.	draw palm wine
		mbese n. sing.	side, flank
		munene mbese n. sing.	big, strong man
		kuasa mbesa	grow fat
bete	personal name	-bè.ta v.t.	tell jokes, pleasantries, have fun (bete, past part.)
		-bè.ta v.t.	beat grain, flatten

		mbeta n. sing.	type of reed, thick straw used in fence-making
betela	equality, accord	-betula (luendu)	march proudly, stride along
beya	to come	-beya v.t.	shave, cut the hair
bezuyi	the hare	-beza v.t.	strangle, suffocate; crush, tread on someone's toes
		bezuyi n. pl.	stranglers, treaders
beyi	goat	mbuji n. sing.	goat
bi	evil-doing	-bi adj.	bad, wicked, evil
biba	a meeting	-biba v.t.	choose, select at random
bibi	begotten	bibì adv.	terribly, strongly, greatly
		bibi n. pl.	thieves
bidi	an abundance	bidi	they are (v. to be, "things" as subject)
		pambidi adv.	on the body (pa mubidi)
		mbidi n. sing.	small type of Kanyoka house
bidibidi	small bird	bidibidi (picture word)	shuffling of feet
		mbidibidi n. sing.	child growing well
		lubidibidi n. sing.	pale, undetermined color; pink, yellow
biji	uncooked meat	mubiji adj.	raw, green, uncooked
bikira		-bikila v.t.	call
bikula	drink voraciously	-bikula v.t.	exaggerate; drink voraciously
		-bikula v.t.	abdicate, renounce the chieftainship
		bikulu n. pl.	grandchildren
bila	to boil, roar; call	-bila v.i.	boil, bubble, roar (as falls)
		-bìla v.t.	call, make come, yell for
bilu	to push against another	bilu n. pl.	blades, stalks of grass
		bilù n. pl.	naps, sleep
		munkatshi mua bilu	middle of the night
bim	term imitative of sound of beating	bim (picture word)	sound of beating
bimba	personal name	-imba v.t.	sing (badi bimba)
		maja bimba	singing dance

bimbi	personal name	bimbi n. pl.	singers, players of instruments
		mbimbi n. sing.	waterfalls
binda	to braid, to bolt	-binda v.i.	walk with chest sticking out; hurt, pain the chest
binga	to be acquitted	-binga v.i.	be acquitted, be right, win a cause
		-binga v.t.	coax, wheedle, cajole
bintu	daughter of Mohammed	bintu n. pl.	things, objects
bisa	to question	-ebisha v.t.	ask a question
bitonga	open wide, large	bitonga n. pl.	gourds cut crosswise
		bitonga n. pl.	edible fruit of rubber plant
		mesu bitongatonga	deep-set eyes, wide-open, large
bitsi	a swoon, a faint	bitshiyu n. pl.	obstinacy, insubordination, willfulness, stubbornness
biya	to burn	biya pres. part.	they (things) are going (bidi biya)
biyola	personal name	biyola v.i.	belch, "burp"
bo	name of a town in Sierra Leone	bo (picture word)	hardness, force, vigor, strength
boba	be soft, mild	-boba v.i.	ripen, mature, get soft; cook till done
		-bo.ba v.t.	hit, strike (a ball)
bobi	quiet, bashful	mbabi n. sing.	guile, finesse, shrewdness, quickness, alertness
bobo	personal name	bobo pron.	they, them
bobobo	make a hollow sound	kukola bobobo v.i.	grow stronger and stronger
bobola	make a hollow sound	-bobola v.t.	make a yodeling sound
		bobola miadi	cry out while hitting hand over mouth, funeral wail
boi	from English "boy"	mboi n. sing.	a personal servant
		mboyi n. sing.	type of snake
boku	diviner, priest	mbuku n. pl.	divinations, sorceries, witchcrafts
boma	black python	moma n. sing.	large black snake
		Boma n.	town at mouth of Congo River

bombo	small pox	mbombo n.	personal name for child for whom a special charm has been made, because of death of previous children
		mbombo n. pl.	thousands
		-bomba v.t.	calm, quiet, caress, flatter
		-bòmba v.i.	remain unfinished, incomplete
		-bomba v.i.	walk quietly, seek to slip out furtively
		-bomba v.t.	steep, soak, immerse
bong	cloth, goods, property	mbongo n. sing.	goods, wealth, possessions
		bongo n. sing.	brain
bondo	ceremonial rites of sande (female organization)	mbondo n. sing.	large frog
		mbondo n. pl.	deep, round baskets
bosa	to crush, break	-bosa v.t.	crush, shell, hull
bote		-bòta v.i.	be beaten down, pulverized, trodden underfoot
		-bòta v.t.	test, taste
		-bòta v.i.	be clean, cared for, in good condition
		botà. adj.	clean, spick-and-span
		mbote	lower Congo word of greeting
bowe	to tattoo	bowa n. sing.	mushroom
		bo.wa n. sing.	fear, terror
		mbowà n. sing.	buffalo
boya	clear away	-boya v.t.	clean up, pick up trash
bozo	great cheapness	-boza v.t.	crush, flatten, bruise; pound by trampling, treading on
bu	waste, loss	bu prep.	like, as
		bu conj.	if
buala	no	bwala neg.	no, not at all
buba	personal name	bubau n. sing.	fish, poison plant
		-buba v.t.	beat in order to soften, grind
		dibuba n. sing.	cloud
		dibuba n.s.	blister made by fire or hot water
bubu	gloom	mbubù n. sing.	imbecile

		mbubu n. sing.	ravine
		dibù.bù n. sing.	tsetse fly
budi	sheep	mbudi n. sing.	antelope
		mbuji n. sing.	goat
		budi v. to be	it is (abstract class)
budisa	cause to break	-budisha v.t.	deprive of, cause to lack
bugikai	something frightful	bungi kai int.	how much, how many?
buje	plant used in tattooing	buji n. sing.	act of dancing
buka	to heal, cure	-bùka v.t.	consult a diviner, consult the spirits
		-bù.kà v.i.	take flight, fly away
		-bù.ka v.t.	pluck, pick off leaves for cooking
bukra		bakulu n. pl.	elders, rulers
buku	to increase, bless	buku n. sing.	state of being mother-in-law or father-in-law
		buku n. sing.	alliance in African family
		bukue	sense
		bukuà n. sing.	race, type, family, gender
bula	size, importance	bula n. sing.	palm cabbage
		bula v.i.	be without, lack
		-bula v.t.	open with fingers, shell (peas)
		-bula v.i.	be straight (njila mubule, a straight path)
bulanda	Western Sudanic language	bulanda n. sing.	poverty, need, want, destitution
bule	impose fine	bule n. sing.	length
		bule adj.	long (bualu bule)
bulu	edible animal	mubulu n. sing.	ball, clod, bunch, bundle
bulunga	to be spherical	bulunga v.i.	be round, spherical
bumbu	take, lift, personal name	-bumba v.t.	carry and put in another place, deposit, stack
		-bumba v.t.	knead, mix as clay for pots
bumbu	to take	mbumbu n. sing.	weevil

bumbulu	a foolish person	-bumbula v.t.	knock things about, turn over, cause to crash down, chase away
		-bumbula biuma	dissipate funds
bundi	oil palm	bundi (relative)	that which I am (doing)
		mbunda n. sing.	drunkard
bundu	disgrace	bundu n. sing.	shame, modesty, disgrace
bunga	personal name	bunga adj.	bunga bualu, another matter
		-bunga v.i.	mildew, get moldy
bugikai		bungi kai? int.	how many?
bungo		mbùngù n. sing.	tube, pipe, gun barrel; oil lamp, vase
		mbungu n. sing.	loom; art of handweaving
bunji		bunjiya n. sing.	rage, fury, madness
buno		bunu n. sing.	act of drinking
buzu		buzazu n. sing.	nervousness, disquietude, acidity
		buzo n. sing.	acidity
bwila		bwila n. sing.	night (bwila butshia, night fades away)
		-bwila v.t.	gnaw away, erode (as banks by a stream of water)

D

dabidi	never, by no means	kashidi adv.	forever, eternally (lit. never ends)
dafa	fat	difu n. sing.	stomach, belly, womb
daha		ndapu n. sing.	indiscretion, divulgation, babbling, prating
daku	personal name	ndaku imp.	go there, "get gone"
dala		ndala v.i.	I am sleeping (ndi ndala)
dama	value, treasure	ndama v.t.	I am guarding, keeping (ndi ndama)
damana		ndamuna v.t.	I am pulling apart (ndi ndamuna)

damba	alligator, crocodile	dibamba n. sing.	fish scale
dambo	personal name	ndambu n. sing.	small portion, morsel, bit
dami		ndami n. sing.	chief's ring ("keep-me")
danda	exterior, surface	ndanda n. sing.	cotton
		-landa v.t.	buy (ndi ndanda, I am buying)
		-landa v.i.	be poor, indigent
		-landa v.i.	crawl, as a bug, snake
		-landa v.t.	think, reflect, meditate
		-lànda v.t.	lay low, level, flatten
dango		ndanga n. sing.	afterbirth
dayi		ndayi n. sing.	female ancestral name of Baluba; charm for obtaining husband's fidelity; buanga bua Ndayi
degu		ndengu n. sing.	shred, scrap, fragment
deji	a nurse	ndeji n. sing.	nursemaid for children
deka	finally, after that	ndekelu adv.	finally, at the end
deli		ndelà n. sing.	prolific man, father of many children
delu		ndelu n. sing.	descendants, progenitors, generation
demba	name given the third son	-lemba v.t.	touch (ndi ndemba, I am touching)
		-lèmba v.i.	hang, dangle, sway, swing; be agile, swift in the hunt (ndi ndemba, pres. tense)
dente		ndende n. sing.	trigger, tumbler of gunlock; spring of a trap
di	to take and use	-di v.i.	verb to be: ndi, I am
		diyi n. sing.	word, voice
		ndi, ndu	picture word for dispersion: lubilu bonso ndi!
diabu	any bad spirit of the white people's mythology	diaba n. sing.	space, interval between two objects
diakala		diakalu n. sing.	act of speaking, talking
dibala	a game	dibala n. sing.	counting, reading

		dibala n. sing.	a group (kuenda dibala, walk in a group)
		dibàla n. sing.	baldness
		dibàlà n. sing.	palaver house, tribunal; guest house
dibi	darkness, obscurity		
didi	to eat	didi v.i.	to be, it is (fourth class, sing.)
		didia n. sing.	act of eating
		ndidi n. sing.	manner of eating
		mudidi n. sing.	a weeper, one who cries
		mudidi n. sing.	large drum
didididi	feed	dididisha v.t.	cause to eat, feed oneself
difi	to protect	difi n. sing.	a lying word
digi	to plait the hair	ndinga n. sing.	red earth used to smear on the body after birth of a child
dikanu	mouth	mukana n. sing.	loc. n.; in the mouth
dikuba	bundle	dikuba n. sing.	large bundle, package
dikunda	the back, shoulders, ribs	dikunda n. sing.	type of tree
		dikunde n. sing.	detachment, displacement, removal of an object from one place to another
dile	a boa constrictor	dile adj.	long (fourth class, sing.)
		dila n. sing.	intestine, entrail, gut
		-dìla v.t.	cry, weep, wail
		dì.la v.t.	eat with, applied form of -dia: eat
dileli	peace, contentment	dilela n. sing.	birth, delivery
dilolo	a lake in Angola	dilolo n. sing.	evening
dilewe		dilewo n. sing.	faintness, stupor
dilonga	plate, dish, bowl	dilonga n. sing.	dish, plate, bowl
dima	earth used in making pot	dima n. sing.	clay for pottery-making
	hoe, cultivate	-dima v.t.	work, hoe, cultivate
dimba	tell an untruth	-dimba v.t.	tell a lie, falsehood; trick, deceive, fabricate
		ndimbi n. sing.	a liar
dimbu	gum, resin, pitch	budimbu n. sing.	gum, resin, pitch

dimi	personal name	dimi n. sing.	seed, unborn offspring; udi ne dimi: she is pregnant
dimina	pain	dimina n. sing.	audacity
		diminu n. sing.	throat
		dimi.nu n. sing.	grain, seedling, good plant which will keep propagating
dimindi	to hurt (someone)	ndimina n. sing.	reason for cultivating food
		ndiminu n. sing.	manner of cultivating food
diminka	personal name	dimweka n. sing.	apparition, revelation
dimo	to grasp	dimona n. sing.	act of seeing
		-dimona v.t.	see oneself
		dimono n. sing.	fingerprint
dina	to obstruct a passage	dina n. sing.	name
		dì.na n. sing.	hole, pit
		-dina v.i.	sink; drown; swoop, plunge down
dingo	personal name	-dìnga v.i.	swell up, take on large proportions, as ripening fruit
		-dinga v.t.	fool, seduce, lie to, entice
dingila	personal name	-dingila v.t.	lie about, accuse falsely, misinterpret another's actions
dingu	personal name	dingungu n. sing.	reeds, rushes used in mat-making
		ndingilu n. sing.	manner of lying
dinketi	personal name	dinkenke n. sing.	light, glow, sunlight
dinu	tooth, tusk, fang	dinu n. sing.	tooth
diokolo	a tadpole	diokola n. sing.	suffering
ditemu	hoe	ditemu n. sing.	hoe
dito	to pass very close to	ditu n. sing.	forest, woods
		ditshiyo n. sing.	ear
diwale	a kind of mushroom	diwala n. sing.	kind of tree with yellow wood (chrysophyllum)

diya	forgetfulness	diya n. sing.	departure, act of leaving, going away
		diya n. sing.	civet cat
diyadi	this	diadi dem. adj.	that (fourth class, sing.)
diyala	place for throwing rubbish	diala n. sing.	dunghill, place for throwing refuse, trash
diyukisa	to dip into water	diowesha n. sing.	washing in water
doba	light-colored horse	ndobo n. sing.	fishhook
dodi	to assist	ndiodi dem.	that's it
dodo	fried ripe plantain	ndondo n. sing.	pact, blood covenant; depth, deep pit
dolu		ndolo n. sing.	generosity, bounty
dombe		ndombi n. sing.	winnings, profits from gambling, earnings
		ndombo n. sing.	charm for making childbirth easier
		ndombwe n. sing.	kutua ndombwe: beat water with hands to make musical, rhythmic noise
dongo	student, disciple	ndongo n. sing.	species of bird
		-longa v.t.	learn (ndi ndonga: I am learning, am a student)
dopo	child, personal name	ndopolopo n. sing.	babbling, revealing secrets
doto	to listen	ndoto n. sing.	a dream
duba	the branch of a tree	nduba n. sing.	web-footed waterbird
dudu	a fool	ndudi n. sing.	marksmanship, good aim
dufu	darkness	ndufu	it is death
duku	napkin, towel	nduku n. sing.	friend, companion
dulu	to smoke	ndululu n. sing.	dispute, difference of opinion, vehemence, bitterness
dumaya	sorcery	lumanyi n. sing.	pupil of the eye (ndumanyi)
dumuna	to root up	lumuenu n. sing.	mirror (ndumuenu, with enclitic n)
dunga	a drum	ndunga n. sing.	type of tree (Xylopia aethiopica)
dungu		ndungu n. sing.	pepper

E

e		eè adv.	yes
eba	the oil-palm	-eba v.t.	hunt, chase, cause to flee
ebi	hunger; journey	ebi dem. adj.	these
ebo	European white man	ebu dem. adj.	this
		ebe poss. adj.	your
edi	charm, enchant	edi dem. adj.	this, (fifth class, sing.)
egede	incantation, magical formulas	ngele n. sing.	bells, strips of metal hitting together, tinkling
		ngela n. sing.	agent, official doer of some action
eka	fingernail, paw	eku dem. loc.	here, hence, hither
ekala	ashes, charcoal	dikala n. sing.	charcoal, coal of fire
ekaya	the tobacco leaf	dika.ya n. sing.	shoulder
		dikaya n. sing.	species of fox
ekofi	a blow with the fist	dikofi n. sing.	fist
		nkofi n. sing.	eyelash
ekuti	large brown pigeon	nkutshi n. sing.	dove, pigeon
eli	far off	-le adj.	long (kule: far away; kale: long ago)
elimi	tongue, language	ndimi n. sing.	tongue
elo	yes	eyo adv.	yes
elundu	nest of the white ant	tshilundu n. sing.	white anthill
ema	something strange	-kema v.i.	wonder at, be amazed
emba		-emba v.t.	blow the breath
emu	interior, in the middle	emu loc. adj.	herein, in the middle of
ena	two, second	-ena	neg. of v. to be (kena; he is not)
enu fole		udi ne difu	she is pregnant
epapi	wing of a bird	dipapu n. sing.	bird's wing
esalu	witchdoctor's bundle of charms (often includes feathers)	disala n. sing.	feather
		nsala n. sing.	summit, tip, top
		nsalo n. pl.	tattoo marks
esamba	a variety of the oil-palm	disambwa n. sing.	edge of path, crossroads

esanzu		nsanzu n. pl.	firewood
		nsanzu n. sing.	ruse, finesse, malice
		nsanzu n. pl.	sorts, degrees, situations
ese	father	diese n. sing.	fortune, good luck
eseke	bird, land	diseke n. sing.	vine bridge
		diseku n. sing.	wild goose
esenu		busenu n. sing.	slipperiness, sleekness, smoothness
eshimu		dishima n. sing.	act of lying
		nshima n. sing.	manioc bread, cassava mush
eshu		ditshiu n. sing.	ear
esinde	a blade of grass	dishinda n. sing.	grass
esiya	name given sixth child	isambombo num.	six
esole	a garden cleared in a wood or forest	-sò.la v.t.	clear forest to make a field
		-sola v.i.	be in heat
esuenga		-suanga v.t.	shuck (corn)
esundi	animal	disundu n. sing.	fist; knot
etamba	a fragrant-leaved tree	ditamba n. sing.	branch of a tree
etamina	a small basket	ntamina (mu luendu) v.i.	be away, absent for a long time (on a journey)
etele	a whale	ditele n. sing.	species of mushroom (common saying: Udi wasa matele, anyi? "Have you sprouted mushrooms for ears?")
etenji	small china or pearl button	ntenji n. sing.	translucence, transparency, clarity, pearl-like quality (ntenji wa disu-iris; of the eye) (ntenji wa ngondo-halo: round the moon)
etshi	this	etshi dem. adj.	this (thing)
etu	we, ours	etu poss. adj.	our, ours
etumbi	bed of burned roots and earth	ntumbi n. sing.	tinder for fire, touchwood
ewele	thorny, creeping plant	diwele n. sing.	species of tree
eweta	hunt with dogs	-ta v.t.	hunt with dogs

ewina	thirst	-ina v.t.	soak, submerge; plunge an object into water; dye by soaking
eya	palm tree	-eya v.i.	breathe
		-eya v.i.	be at peace, rest, relax
eyala	refuse, ash heap	diala n. sing.	refuse pile, garbage pit, dunghill

F

fa	to snore	pa v.t.	give
fabi	to surpass	pabi adj.	bad (surface, area)
fafa		-papa v.i.	become frightened, be afraid
		-papa v.i.	become hardened, indifferent
fakala		pakula (temp.)	when (he) speaks
		pakola (temp.)	when (he) grows strong, well
fakamba		pakamba (temp.)	when (he) said
fale	solid; to push; to change	pale adv.	far away, distant
fama	a king	-pama v.t.	settle, reside in a place, establish a domiclile, residence
fana	to knead	-pana v.t.	sell, betray
fande	to dispense with supper	-panda v.t.	cleave, split, cut open
fanga		-panga v.i.	be ignorant, fail, not know; lack, be without
		-pànga v.t.	make, fabricate; think, resolve
fangana		-pangana v.t.	confess, admit a fault
faniya	personal name	-panya v.t.	torment, vex, importune
fasai	to explain	-pasa v.i.	be full, filled up
fatama	personal name	-patama v.i.	be held fast, caught, squeezed
fatu	personal name	patu adv.	outdoors, outside
fatuma	personal name	patuma temp.	when (he) sends
fayema		-payama v.i.	be wrapped, packed up
fefe		pepi adv.	near, close by
		-pepa v.i.	be intense (cold, hunger)
		-pepa v.t.	agitate, blow about

fefe	air, wind	lupepele n. sing.	the wind, air
fela		-pè.la v.t.	to give to
		-pela v.t.	grind, crush, pulverize
		-pela v.t.	polish, scrape, scrub clean
		-pèla v.i.	be poor, needy
fele	personal name	pele adj.	poor, needy, destitute
feniya	to take snuff	-penya v.t.	lightning flash; grimace, show the teeth
fetel	a gun	-petela v.i.	hand to, pass on, to reach out hand to
feya	personal name	-peya v.t.	scrape, scour, peel, shave off
fiba	suckle	-fiba v.t.	suckle
fidi	personal name	-pidia v.t.	refuse
		mupidi n. sing.	a refuser
		mufidi n. sing.	an escort, one who conducts (from -fila)
fila	personal name	-fila v.t.	conduct, escort, accompany
		-pila v.i.	be guilty, convicted of
fimba	search, examine	-fimba v.t.	make pots, mold clay
fina	strife, magic spell	-fina v.t.	press, squeeze, compress
finama	hear, personal name	pinama	when (he) bends over
finda	kill, dispatch, forest, to be cloudy	-finda v.i.	get dark, cloudy, overcast
findi	flower, bud	mpindieu adv.	now
fino	black	mfinu n. sing.	immature, underdeveloped corn, peanuts, etc., not to be used for planting
fishi	itch	-pì.sha v.t.	burn up, consume
		-pì.sha v.t.	condemn, convict of wrong
fita	ascend	-pita v.t.	pass, surpass, overtake
		-fita v.t.	rub on, anoint with, smear on
fiya	whirling, buzzing	-piya v.t.	injure
		-pia v.t.	seize, grip
		-pia v.i.	be burned up, be consumed
fiyakalu	strike	-fiekela v.t.	squeeze, throttle, press
fiye	boil	-pie adj.	ripe, mature

fofo	father	-fofo adj.	blind
fu	defect	fue neg.	categorical no!
fufu	yam, cassava	mfufu n. sing.	blind man
		-pupa v.t.	blow
fuka	religious formalities	-fùka v.t.	create, shape, form, invent
		-fùka v.t.	neglect, pay no attention to
		-fuka v.i.	rot, become inedible
fukula	uncover	-fukula v.t.	heap up in mounds, like a mole (gardening term)
fula	working in metals	-fula v.i.	go the limit, go to the bitter end
		-fùla v.t.	forge, make iron objects
		-fula v.t.	lift, lengthen, raise
fumina	quiet, vexed	pumina temp.	when (he) tries, dares, makes an attempt
fumu	chief, nobleman, sovereign	mfumu n. sing.	chief, king, ruler
funa	threaten	-funa v.t.	defy, threaten, be fierce, flaunt one's powers
funga	to be sufficiently cooked	-funga v.t.	tie up
		-mfungu n. sing.	menace, threat
futisa	extort	-futshisha v.t.	cause to pay, force to pay, extort money
fwa	to die, a corpse	-fwa v.i.	die
		-fwa v.i.	abandon oneself, let go entirely
fwalansa	French	fwalansa adj.	French

G

gala	mat	ngala n. sing.	dam made for fishing in a stream
		ngala n. pl.	claws, nails
galu	moon, month; egg	ngalu n. sing.	red banana (tshibote tshia ngalu)
gama	eye, face	ngema n. sing.	palm-wine gatherer
gana	proverbs, folklore	ngana n. pl.	fables, proverbs, folklore
ganda	city in Kongo	nganda n. sing.	interior court of chief's enclosure
ganyi	pain, anger	nganyi int.	who?

ganu	metal implement	ngandu n. sing.	crocodile
gasa	rivalry, ditch	ngasa v.t.	I am building, constructing
gebu	under the sky	ngabu n. sing.	shield
gela	good marksman, personal name	ngela n. sing.	good marksman
gele	sky, heavens, lightning	ngele n. sing.	bells, small strips of metal tinkling together
gelede	Lagos masquerade	ngeledi n. sing.	one who throws to someone, does a favor for another
		keledi n. sing.	gives a gift to, offers food to ancestral spirits
gelema	end, termination, personal name	kelemena v.i.	be equal, of the same value
geli	elephant, personal name	ngelu n. sing.	kuela ngelu: sulk, hide oneself
gene	insect, circle	ngeni n. pl.	intelligence, wisdom
		ngendu n. pl.	journeys
		kena n. sing.	patron, namesake
		kena neg.	he is not
gidi	violently, with a loud noise	kidi	picture word for trembling, shaking
goba	bent, crooked, hollow	nkobo n. sing.	crook, staff with bent handle
goigoi	sluggishly (personal name)	ngonyangonya adv.	slowly, carefully, deliberately, sluggishly
gole	gun, cannon, pipe	ngole n. sing.	zebra
goma	drum	ngoma n. sing.	round, skin-covered drum
gombo	charm, witch-doctor	ngòmbà n. sing.	drummer
		ngombà n. sing.	cave, tomb
gone		ngongo n. sing.	species of rat
gongolo	cart, gig, king	-kongolo v.t.	return marriage dowry
		dikongolo n. sing.	millipede, gallery worm
gonji	a rope	mwonji	rope
gonu, konu	enemy	lukuna n. sing.	hatred, hostility
guba		nguba n. sing.	peanut, ground nut
gudi		ngudi	where is
		nkudi	where it is at

gula	to fall, drop off; name of ethnic group in Liberia	-kù.la v.t.	dislocate, pluck off; remove the handle; kula muoyo: to die
		-kù.la v.t.	redeem from slavery, deliver
		-kula v.t.	grind, masticate, chew, crush
		-kùla v.i.	endure, live a long time, grow old
gula		ngulube n. sing.	pig
gumba	shirt, gown, personal name	-kumba v.t.	set aside, dismiss, discharge
		nkumba n. sing.	toilet
gumbo		tshingombo n. sing.	okra
gunga	a bell	ngonga n. sing.	bell
guwu	hippopotamus	nguvu n. sing.	hippopotamus

H*

hadi	yes	padi	when it is
haima	evaluate, estimate	-pima v.t.	measure, weigh, examine
hala	hyena	-pa.la v.i.	be crazy, be deranged
		-pala v.t.	clear away for construction
		-pala v.t.	refuse to give to, be stingy, selfish
hale	superiority	-pa.le adj.	crazy, deranged
		pale adv.	far away
haluwa		palua	when (he) comes
hama	rainy season	-pama v.i.	settle, inhabit, establish a permanent residence
hani	prohibiting	panyi pron.	meme panyi, as for me
		panyi apa loc.	here at my home
		panyi? int.	where?
hanji	door-sill	panshi adv.	on the ground
hanu	misfortune	panu adv.	here below, here on earth

*Some words beginning with "p" are listed here under "H." In Tshiluba, "h," a voiceless glottal fricative, is interchangeably related to "p," a unique voiceless fricative, marking dialectical differences in pronunciation. Other words beginning with "p," a voiceless stop, often combined with "m," are listed under "P."

hate	Good! Well done!	-pata v.i.	become strong, robust
		-pate past part.	strengthened, made strong
		-pàta v.i.	be stopped up, obstructed, constipated
		mupate n. sing.	a constipated person
		-pa.ta v.i.	go far away, travel abroad
hawanga		pawanga	when (he, you) becomes, become furious, outraged
hayi	ascend, music	paya pres. part	when (he) becomes, goes
		-paya v.t.	place small objects in a container, wrap up in a package, bundle
heke	mix mud	peku loc.	on the hearth, fire
helenga	dusk	Pelenga	Bushongo proper name
hema	queen mother	-pema v.i.	roar, bellow
		pema n. sing.	white earth, whitewash
hembe	crown, kingdom	Pembe	Bushongo proper name
		lupemba n. sing.	white earth, whitewash
henga	deformed	-penga v.t.	push through, force one's way in
hima	monkey	nkima n. sing.	monkey
hinda	place, thing, circumstance, act	-pinda v.i.	accumulate, acquire goods, pile up
hiye	deceive, fail, prosperous	-pia v.i.	be ripe, mature
		-pie adj.	ripe, mature
hoho	many-voiced	-po.pa v.t.	nail, hammer, pound
		-po.pa tshianza v.t.	wave hand to restore calm
hombo	goat	-pomba v.i.	be weak, thin, skinny
hona	practitioner of witchcraft	-pona v.i.	fall, drop down, descend
hondo	personal name	-ponda v.t.	crush, pulverize, shred, grind into flour
honga	to practice witchcraft	muhongo	witchcraft
hota	stranger, visit	-pota v.i.	be foolish, stupid, ignorant
hujukulu	waste	kujukula v.t.	to manifest, divulge, reveal, explain something secret

hula	ravage	-pula v.t.	put down, set down
		-paula v.t.	loot, plunder, ravage
huma		-puma v.i.	groan, growl, grunt
		puma	when (it) dries
huta	steal, theft	-puta v.t.	draw, drag, trail, stretch; snuff, inhale, suck up
hutu	bag	tshiputu n. sing.	hat, cap
		tshibute n. sing.	leather bag
		mputu n. sing.	child born just after twins
huwa	elder brother	-puwa v.i.	be silent, be quiet

I

iba	lizard	iba mulolo	in the afternoon, evening
		-iba v.t.	steal
ibogidi	edible fruit	mbokoto n. sing.	gossip, tattle, chit-chat, chatter
ibola	act of respect	-ibula v.t.	burn the skin, scorch, peel off
idi	eagle	idi v. to be	they are
ife	cup	difi n. sing.	a lying word
ifu	intestines	difu n. sing.	stomach, intestines
igunuko	personal name	kunoko adv.	here, to this place
		iya kunoko	come here
ikija		-ikija v.t.	rest, be at ease, repose
ika	word, speech	-ika v.i.	grow long, mature (food crops)
		-ika v.i.	descend upon, rest upon, hover over (such as a blessing)
ila	circumcision line, mark, tattooing	-ila v.t.	try, learn
		-ila v.t.	become dark, blacken
		ila butuku	night is coming
ilaiya	courage, boldness	yilaiyi imp.	go round about, detour
		dilaya n. sing.	promise, vow, farewell
imbuwa	dog	mbwa n. sing.	dog
imi		dimi n. sing.	germ of life, seed, udi ne dimi: she is pregnant
ina	immerse, dye	-ina v.t.	immerse, dye

mother		ina n. sing.	mother (in'anyi, my mother; in'ebe, your mother)
inama	stoop	-inama v.i.	stoop, bend, bow down
invulu	rain	mvula n. sing.	rain
ipampa	traders agreement	mpampa n. sing.	master, conqueror, ruler
ipanda	you alone	mpanda n. sing.	savior, guardian; a protecting charm
ipete	intention	mpeta n. sing.	a rich man
isala	a dialect of Gurunsi	-isula v.t.	bear children frequently
isa	Jesus	disua n. sing.	bird's nest
		disuà n. sing.	love, desire, longing
ise	denial, five	disue n. sing.	slip knot, snare
isha		-disha v.t.	feed, nourish
		-yisha v.t.	teach, instruct
ishagidi		-dishangana v.t.	feed each other
		-yishangana v.t.	teach each other
ishai		dishayi imp.	feed
		yishayi imp.	teach
ishi		dishi n. sing.	clot of blood
		dishi n. sing.	caterpillar
		di.shi n. sing.	salt lick, salt works
iso	eye	disu, diso n. sing.	eye
ita		-ita v.t.	row, paddle, pull an oar
		-ita v.i.	to do evil
		-ita v.t.	to call by gesturing
itadi	money	ditadi n. sing.	rock, slate
itondi	what is your name?	ditonda n. sing.	recognition, acknowledgment
iwale		diwala n. sing.	species of tree
iwalula	remember	uvuluka imp.	remember
iya	mother	-iya v.i.	come
		diya n. sing.	departure, going away
		diyà n. sing.	civet cat
iyaba	elderly woman	diyeba n. sing.	granary, storehouse
iyaji	member of royal family	nyanji n. pl.	sentiments, desires
iyakala	personal name	ngikala v. to be	that I be, that I may be
iyama		nyama n. sing.	animal

iyami-iyami	My mother! My mother!	inanyi-inanyi	excl. my mother! my mother!
iyaha		iyaha imp.	come here!
iyoyo		diyoyo n. sing.	noise, sound
izaba	shoulder	dizaba n. sing.	game, play
izola	European week	nzolo n. sing.	chicken

J

ja	break	-ja v.t.	dance
jabalaiyo	personal name	-jabalala v.i.	sit on the ground
jabata		-jabata v.i.	be in deep grief, very troubled, afflicted
jala		jala adv.	absolutely, clearly, frankly, openly
jalawa	personal name	-jalama v.i.	stand erect, be stable
jama	be steadfast	-jama v.i.	be stuck in the sand, mud; be steadfast
jambila		ndambilu n. sing.	manner of speaking
janga		-janga v.i.	be naked, immodestly clad
je		nje	kudia njenjeje: sound of grating the teeth
jeke		njeku n. sing.	a paralytic
jiana		-jiana v.t.	murmur, complain against
jiba	wink, close the eye	-jiba v.i.	wink, blink, close the eye
jiku		-ji.ka v.t.	bury, inter
		-jika v.t.	block, head off, intercept
		-jika v.t.	be finished, completed
jikujiku		njiku-njiku n. sing.	I bury and bury (name of child born after series of deaths of older siblings)
jima	whole, perfect	-jima adj.	whole, entire
		-jima v.t.	put out, extinguish (fire, lamp)
		njima n. sing.	long black snake
jimba		-jimba v.t.	cause to disappear, kill in secret
		njimba n. sing.	raw rubber for applying to drumskins

jimbu		njimbu n. sing.	anteater
		dijimbu n. sing.	secret, an enigma, puzzle
jimi	pregnancy	dimi n. pl.	udi ne dimi: she is pregnant (had seed)
jinga	bedfellow, companion	-jinga v.t.	love, want, desire, long for
		-jinga v.t.	roll, roll up
jinisa	to burn	-shidisha v.t.	cause to burn, scorch food
jiwa		njiu, njiwu n. sing.	danger, peril, accident
		njiya n. sing.	bitterness, resentment
jogal		juka kulu imp.	rise up! stand up! get up!
jojo		-joja v.t.	stare at, look at fixedly
jolo		njolo n. sing.	cracks, crevasses
jowo		njowo, njo	Here I am!
jula	to lift	-jula v.t.	raise, lift up
		-jiula v.t.	bruise, wound

K

ka		ka dem.	here it is, there it is
		ka adv.	therefore, consequently, so
		ka! ka!	exclamation of surprise
		ka neg.	kambualu: it's nothing!
kaba	cassava	kaba n. sing.	small place, spot
		kabà n. sing.	snare for birds, bird trap
		-kàba v.i.	shine, scintillate, sparkle
		-kàba v.i.	be worried, nervous, preoccupied
		kaba	picture word showing disquietude: Kadima mesu kaba-kaba
kabala	sandal	ka.bàlà n. sing.	crime, evil deed
		kabala n. sing.	small space, short distance
		kabala n. sing.	wooden sandal
		kaba.la n. sing.	quail, partridge
kabi	thick, deep	kabi n. sing.	bad luck, crisis, tragedy
kabila	personal name	-kabila v.t.	urge on, stimulate, cheer on

kabindi		kabindi n. sing.	peanut
		kabindi n. sing.	big, vile man, savage
kabo		kabo	picture word indicating quantity, no measurement possible Kufuisha bantu kabo-kabo
kabokolo		kapokolo n. sing.	small depression; scooped-out, carved-out hole
kadi		kadi conj.	but
		kadi v. to be	it is (dim. class)
kado		kadiu n. sing.	disdain, displeasure, lack of appreciation
kafi	rectum	kafi n. sing.	sexual parts of the body
		nkafi n. sing.	oar, paddle
		kafu neg. imp.	let him not die
kai		kai? int.	what? who? which? where? why?
kaiba		kayiba n. sing.	striped cloth
		Kayiba	female personal name
kaili		kayidi neg. imp. of -yila	let him not learn
		kayidi neg. imp. of -ya	let him not go round about, circumvent
kainyi		kanyi poss.	my (dim. class)
		nkanyi n. pl.	wisdom, intelligence, wit, sharpness, acumen
kaji		-kaji adj.	female
		ngaji n. sing.	eleais: palm nut
kakatulu		kakatula	he did not put down; pull out; forge
kakela	cackle	kakela n. sing.	small egg
		kakele adv.	generously, beyond measure
kala	cut, scratch, strike	kala n. sing.	side, alongside, edge
	small wire	kala n. sing.	small wire ring, earring
		-kàla v.t.	cut off, chop off, sever
		-kala v.t.	scratch (as a fowl)
		-kàla v.t.	cry out, blow (horn, whistle)
kalaba	crawl	-kalaba v.i.	crawl, creep
Kalala	personal name	Kalala n. sing.	tribal deputy, officer; male proper name

kale	until the end of time	kale adv.	long ago, formerly
kalima	nephew	Kadima	male proper name
kalo	moon	nkala n. sing.	crab, lobster
kalumba		kalumbu n. sing.	partridge
kalundi	large hyena	kalunda n. sing.	isolation, separation from others, restriction
		kabundi n. sing.	ground squirrel, chipmunk
		kalunga n. sing.	honorary title for chief
kalunga	sea, ocean, abode of the dead	kalunga milabi	place of the good dead
		kalunga misona	place of the wicked dead
kama	to encircle	kama n. sing.	a mute
		nkama n. pl.	hundreds
		nkama n. pl.	claw prints, animal tracks
		-kàma v.i.	abate, dry up, diminish
		-kàma v.t.	arrest, restrain, repress, curb, bridle
		-kàma v.t.	desire, seek, love
		-kàma v.t.	squeeze, press between the fingers
kamaina		kumanyina v.i.	to be amazed
kamba	grave, personal name	nkamba n. sing.	prison
		nkambua n. sing.	ancestor
kambalala		kambambala n. sing.	fieldmouse
kamo	to reckon	kamue n. sing.	mosquito
		kamue adj.	one (dim. class)
kampuku	small rat	kampuku n. sing.	small rat
kamubika	a little slave	kamupika n. sing.	small slave, servant
kamushasha		kamushisha n. sing.	small tip of hoe affixed to the handle
kana	plan	kana n. sing.	small child, baby
		-kàna v.t.	menace, threaten; refuse to give; be determined
kanda		-kànda v.t.	separate
		-kànda v.t.	refuse to give permission or authorization; forbid, prohibit

	tie, forbid	-kànda v.t.	close up an opening by tying
		nkanda n. sing.	rat trap
kandalala		kuandalala v.i.	to be ignorant, pigheaded, stupid
kandi	palm nut	kandi poss.	his, hers, its
		nkande n. pl.	shackles, fetters, hobbles
kandimba	small hare	kandimba n. sing.	gunshot, shell for gun
kandingu		kandingundi-ngu	small annoyance, hindrance, interference, bother
kane	stinginess; competition	-akane adj.	good, beautiful, nice
kani	implore	kanyi poss.	my, mine
		kanyi kanyi adj.	very, very small
kanina	personal name	-kanina v.t.	threaten, menace
kaniya	personal name	-kanya lubilu v.i.	rise quickly, get up in a great hurry
		-kanya v.t.	scratch, scrape, erase
kanjama	personal name	kanjiabala n. sing.	sadness, sorrow, grief
kanjiya	a quarrelsome person	kanjiya n. sing.	pettiness, resentment
kanjolo	at once	kanjolo n. sing.	small crack; chink, cleft
kankan	hastily	-kanka v.i.	tremble, shake, quiver
kanu	Temne-speaking area of Sierra Leone	nkanu n. pl.	rings, chains, bracelets
kanza	snap, bite	nkanza n. pl.	knife with four points
		nkanzu n. pl.	suits, dresses, clothing
Kasai		Kasai	main tributary of Zaire River that drains the south-central Kasai provinces
kasanji		kasanji n. sing.	small musical instrument
kase	Wolof family name	-kasa v.i.	be better, get well, recover, convalesce
		-kase adj.	better, well, recovered
kasi	importance	nkashi n. pl.	hand clapping
kasike		kuajiki!	all finished!
kasite		kashidi adv.	forever, eternally
kasiya	suddenly	kashiyi bibishi	month of January
kaso	strike	nkasu n. pl.	hoes

		nkesu n. pl.	fragility, quality of breakableness
kasula		kasulu n. sing.	small brook, stream, creek
kata	venereal disease	kata n. sing.	venereal disease
		kata n. sing.	large measure of glass beads, former currency
		nkata n. sing.	wheel, coil, circular pad
katama	umbrella	kata.mu n. sing.	confusion, embarrassment
		katamu n. sing.	footstool
katende	personal name	katèndè n. sing.	species of dwarf palm
		katendè n. sing.	small yellow bird
katshinze-ngela		-nzengela v.i.	be weary, exhausted
katsina	town in northern Nigeria	katshina pres. part.	fears, is afraid of
katutu	bird	katutu n. sing.	species of mushroom
kaule		-kaula v.t.	remove the charm placed at edge of field to prevent thievery
kaya	to trouble	-kàya v.t.	observe certain ceremonies in order to protect property, prevent thievery
		-ka.ya v.t.	worry, trouble, cause distress to
		nkaya n. sing.	paddle, oar, scull
kayakaya	hornbill	nkaya nkaya	all alone, solitary
kaye	number, reckon	kaye past. part.	gone (dim. class)
kayi	a cutlass	kayi neg. imp.	let him not go
kayisa	greet, parch, distribute	-kayisha v.t.	cause to observe ceremonies for protection of property
ke		ke indicative particle	this is, here is
		ke neg. particle	is not
		nke	picture word for solidly, strongly
keba	take care of	-keba v.t.	seek, hunt for, search for
		nkeba n. sing.	seeker, hunter, searcher

kejo		-keja v.t.	hunt for, seek for
keke		-ke.ka v.i.	shine, glow
		-kè.ka v.t.	scorn, disdain, depreciate, lower, despise
		-kèka v.t.	cut into slices, cut greens into short lengths
kela	cut to pieces	-kèla v.t.	sever, cut with one stroke
		-kela v.t.	train, instruct by drilling
		-kela v.t.	clean up, straighten up
kela		nkela n. sing.	sneer
		nkèlà n. pl.	knives, points for incisions
kele	drum	kele n. sing.	small knife
kelele		kankelenkele n. sing.	small bird
kelu	faint	kelu	picture word for following closely, right on the heels of: kulonda kelu-kelu
kema	personal name	-kema v.t.	admire, wonder at, be amazed
kemba	decorate, deceimal	-kemba v.t.	look at carefully, observe
kena	white spots in the skin caused by destruction of colored pigmentation	kena neg. v. to be	he, she is not
	mother's brother	kena n. sing.	patron, namesake
		nkena n. sing.	bright, striking colors, brilliant purple, red, blue
		-kena v.i.	be bright red, glow with color
keniya	grin	-kenya v.i.	shine, flash (as lightning); throb with pain, stab with pain
kenga	filter	-kenga v.t.	need, lack, be in want for
kenji	a fire	kenji neg. imp.	let him not do, make
kenza	filter	-kenza v.t.	purify, render clean, cleanse
kese	baboon	-kese adj.	small, few
		nkese n. sing.	hedgehog, porcupine
		-kesa v.i.	rejoice, be happy

keta	mischief	-keta v.i.	do, execute perfectly, exactly
		-keta v.i.	gnaw with hunger, stomach growl with hunger
		nkete n. sing.	stomach wrinkle
		mukete n. sing.	arrow with metal tip
		Mukete	ethnic group in Kasai area of Zaire
kianyi		tshianyi poss.	my, mine
		tshianya n. sing.	part, portion
		nkayanyi pron.	I, myself
kiata	to form a line	kiata n. sing.	small mat, rug (diminutive)
kiayiba		kuayike v.t.	to leave unburied the body of one condemned to death, cast out
kiba		kiba pres. part.	stealing
kibamba	commission, payment	tshibamba n. sing.	hardiness, assurance, audacity
kibi	pluck	kibi neg. imp.	let him not steal
		ngibi n. sing.	thief
		tshibi adv.	at least, only
		tshibi n. sing.	door
kidi	gum copal	kidi	picture word for trembling: kukanka kidikidi
kididi	warmth, tepidity	tshididi n. sing.	division, partition of a house
		tshididi	picture word: red as blood, black as night
		nkidikidi n. sing.	long, thin caterpillar
kiebe		kebe poss. adj.	your, yours
kiese	joy, personal name	diese n. sing.	joy, good fortune, happiness
kijila	fasting	kujila v.t.	fast, abstain from food
		tshijila n. sing.	a taboo, anything forbidden
kika	refusal	-kika v.i.	ape, mimic, "get a rise out of someone"
kikula	carry away	-pikula v.t.	set free, deliver from bondage

		tshikulu n. sing.	site of an old village
		tshikulu n. sing.	elder, notable
kikulakaji	old person	mukulakaji n. sing.	an old person
kilama	personal name	tshilama n. sing.	vine
		-lama v.t.	guard, watch over
kilamba	to be still	tshilamba n. sing.	bridge
		tshilamba n. sing.	cloth
		-lamba v.t.	cook, prepare food, stretch out, grow long, climb up (as a creeping vine)
		-lamba v.i.	touch, handle
kile	pledge	-kile adj.	long (diminutive)
		nkila n. sing.	dam in a stream
kilembe		tshilembe n. sing.	hunter, fisherman
kilombo		tshilomba n. sing.	parasol, umbrella tree
		tshilombe n. sing.	species of fish
		kalumbu n. sing.	quail
kilundu	spirit	tshilundù n. sing.	termite hill, anthill
		tshilundu n. sing.	sore throat
kima	monkey, personal name	nkima n. sing.	monkey
		nkima n. sing.	name given child born in a crouching position
kimana		kimana pres. part.	standing
		tshimana n. sing.	wall
kimaniya	lazy	kumanya v.t.	to know
		tshimanye n. sing.	one who knows, a good judge
kimba	secret society	ngimba n. sing.	a singer
		tshimbe adj.	foolish, stupid, silly

kimbi	hawk, buzzard	nkumbikumbi n. sing.	hawk
kimbiji	animal	kambiji n. sing.	cat
kimbimbi		tshimpin-dim-pindi adj.	small, short
kina		-kina v.t.	denounce, renounce, disown
kinga		nkinga n. sing.	bicycle
kini		nkindi n. sing.	riddle, folk tale, hidden meaning
kinkuba	personal name	nkuba n. sing.	lightning, lightning-spider
kinsanga	personal name	kansanga n. sing.	somebody-or-other
		nsanga n. sing.	mediator, intermediary
		nsanga n. sing.	survivor of twins
kinunu	nature of a bird	nyunyu n. sing.	bird
kisa	fade	-kisa v.t.	be cruel to, mean to, hate
		tshisa n. sing.	ethnic group, clan, extended family
		tshisa n. sing.	heart pang, pity, regret
kisala		tshisala n. sing.	leafy branch
feather		disala n. sing.	feather
kise	fatherhood	tshise n. sing.	compassion, pity, nostalgia
kishi		kishi n. sing.	small insect
kitanda	Portuguese language, culture	tshitanda n. sing.	open shed
kituta	Angola folklore	tshitù.ta n. sing.	short throwing-knife
		tshitu.ta n. sing.	stalk of thick grass used in house construction
		tshitutu n. sing.	bud
kiwawula	door, much	tshiawula n. sing.	sleep-talking, revelation of the meaning of a dream communicating response of the diviner
kiwula	toad	tshiula n. sing.	toad, frog
kiya	take a walk	tshiya n. sing.	journey
kiyadi		tshiadi n. sing.	chest, bosom

kiyelo	door, gate	kumbelu loc. n.	at the door, on the threshold
kiyunga	to whine	kunyunga v.t.	to shake, sift
kizomba	dancing party	kusomba v.i.	to sit, sit down
kizu	bush	nkisu n. pl.	hatreds, animosities, bad attitudes
ko	deficiency, sterility	ko adv.	strongly, solidly
		nko adv.	very, completely
		nkoo adv.	truly, verily
koba	leaves	-koba v.i.	win a game, gain a point, make a goal
		nkoba n. pl.	skins, hides
kobena		kabena neg v. to be	they are not
kobola		-kobola v.i.	cry out, raise shout of alarm by slapping hand rapidly over mouth
kodi		nkodi n. sing.	vine, creeper
kofi	Akan day name	nkofi n. sing.	eyelash
koja		kodya-kodya	picture word: pellmell, in disorder
koji		nkoji n. sing.	convulsion, spasm, fit
		nkoji n. sing.	white frog
		nkoyi n. sing.	blunt arrow made of wood
koko		koko adv.	vainly, uselessly, in vain
		-koka v.t.	draw, drag, pull along
		-koka v.i.	get weak, feeble, grow old
		-koke adj.	old, weak, feeble
		nkoka n. sing.	ditch, rut, gulley
		mukoko n. sing.	sheep
kokola		-kokola v.t.	knock on, strike, hit (drum, door)
kola	become hard	-kola v.i.	be strong, grow strong; grow up, be mature
		kola v.t.	care for a woman in childbirth
		nkola n. sing.	a drunkard
kole		-kole adj.	strong, well, vigorous; stable, firm
		nkole n. sing.	a powerful man; strong, eminent
		Nkole n. sing.	God

kolisa	intensify	-kolesha v.t.	strengthen, intensify, tighten, support, refresh
kolo	redheaded lizard	nkò.lò n. sing.	grasshopper
		nkòlo n. sing.	site of abandoned village, band of unworked land between two fields
kolombolo		kulombola v.t.	to lead
koma		-koma v.t.	smooth out, straighten out, iron
		nkoma n. sing.	fruit used to improve taste of palm wine
komba	personal name	-komba v.t.	sweep, brush
kombo	personal name	nkombo n. pl.	staves, strong staffs for travel
		nkombò n. sing.	beer dregs
		nkòmbo n. pl.	brooms, brush for sweeping
komena		-komena v.t.	keep locked, closed, shut up
kona		-kona v.t.	scrape, peel, clean
kone		-kone adj.	sharpened, filed
kongo		nkongo n. sing.	age group, generation
konko		dikonko n. sing.	question
		-konka v.t.	ask a question
		nkònko n. sing.	sternum
		nkonko n. sing.	finger ring
kono		kuonona v.t.	to snore
kosa	drum	-kosa v.t.	cut off, sever, chop off
kose		nkose n. sing.	house rat, small rodent
koshi		nkoshi n. sing.	nape of the neck
kota		-kota v.i.	curl up, shrivel up
		-kota v.t.	cut, chop, split wood
kote		nkote n. sing.	pangolin
kowa		kowa n. sing.	species of fish
koya		-koya n. sing.	be tender, soft, easy to eat
koyo		nkoyo n. sing.	terminal point of banana bunch
kuama		-kuama v.t.	yield, bear fruit

kuba	care for, await	-kuba v.t.	care for, watch over, oversee
kucina		kutshina v.i.	to be afraid
kuda	Wednesday	nkuda n. sing.	turtle, tortoise
kudima	hoeing	kudima v.t.	to dig, hoe, cultivate
kudiya	food	kudia v.t.	to eat
kuelu	style of hair dressing	nkuele n. sing.	sister-in-law
kufi	shortness	nkufa n. pl.	ticks, animal lice
kufiya	death	kufinya v.t.	to press, compress, stuff
		kufinya v.i.	to sniff the nose
kuha		kupa v.t.	to give
		kuupa v.t.	to winnow, fan, sift
		kuupa buatu	to row a boat, paddle
		kuupa munda	to have diarrhea
kukuta	chew	kukuta v.t.	to wrap up, make into a bundle
		kukuta v.t.	to be thick, dense, bushy
		kuukuta v.i.	to be full, satisfied, have enough to eat
kula	grow	kù.la v.t.	dislocate, pluck off, remove the handle
		-kula muoyo	die
		-kù.la v.t.	deliver, redeem from bondage, slavery
		-kula v.t.	grind, masticate, chew
		-kùla v.i.	endure, last a long time, become old
		kuula v.t.	to buy, purchase
		kuula v.i.	to be or become full
kuli	fish trap	kule adv.	far off, far away
kulu	antiquity	kulu adv.	up high
		nkulu n. sing.	center, middle
		mukulu n. sing.	elder, older brother
kuma	chastise	-kùma v.t.	beat, strike, chastise
	cover a house (with thatch)	-kuma v.t.	thatch the roof of a house
		kuuma v.i.	to be or become dry, dried out
kumba	roar, graze	nkumba n. sing.	a childless woman
		nkumba n. sing.	toilet
		kuumba v.t.	to do soon, shortly
		kuumba v.t.	to gather, lay by, save

kumbi	drum	nkumbi n. sing.	insect; large drum beaten on both sides
		nkumbikumbi n. sing.	hawk
kumona	to see	kumona v.t.	to see, perceive
kuna	to plant	-kùna v.t.	plant in the ground
		-kuna v.i.	to be intimate with, know
		kunua v.t.	to drink
kunci		kunshi adv.	down below
kuni	planter	kunyi? int.	where? where at?
		nkunyi n. pl.	firewood
kunini	distinguished, eminent	kunene adj.	big, important
kuno		nkuno n. pl.	plants, seedlings
kunu	here	kunu adv.	here, to this place
kunza	funeral feast	-kunza v.i.	be red, get red
kusa	rub	-kusa v.t.	shake the head, refuse
		kusua v.t.	to want, like, love, desire
kusha		kuuja v.t.	to fill, inflate, cause to expand
kushi		kushiyi neg.	don't leave
		nkutshi n. sing.	pigeon
kushila		kushila v.i.	to be consumed, burned up
		kushì.la v.t.	to leave for another
kusu		nkùsù n. sing.	head louse
		nkusu n. sing.	parrot
kuta		-kuta v.t.	wrap up, tie into bundle
		-kuta v.i.	be thick, dense, bushy
		nkutu n. sing.	forked pole for supporting ridge pole
kuta	water turtle	nkuda n. sing.	turtle, tortoise
kutama	assemble	kutama v.i.	to get fat, become important, famous
kutu	ear	nkutu n. sing.	spoon
		nkùtù n. sing.	covering, wrapping
kutukudiya	personal name	kutukudia n. sing.	"always eating"
kuwa	strike with a blunt instrument	-kùwa v.i.	get cold; be stunted, dwarfed
kwa	back	kua prep.	of, at
kwakuwa	personal name	kwakwa prep.	over there, yonder

kwasa	scratch	kwasa v.t.	to build, construct
		nkwasa n. sing.	chair
kwata	catch	-kwata v.t.	catch, take hold of
kwefi	dayname	kwepi? int.	where? to where?
kwenda	to go, advance	kwenda v.i.	to go, march, walk along
kwenga	tight	kwenga v.i.	to be shiny, sparkling
		kwenga v.t.	to filter, distill water in order to get salt
kwenu	yours	kwenu prep.	at your place, at your home

L

la		laa	excl. of contempt, taunting: kuela laa
lakana		-elakana v.i.	hesitate, be uncertain
lakumuna	move the tongue	-laka mukana v.t.	lick the inside of the mouth
lala	sleep, dream	-lala tulu v.i.	lie down, go to sleep
		-lala v.i.	have value, cost
lalula	pick up	-lalula v.t.	lead astray, misguide
		-lalula v.t.	extend, stretch
lama	salute, join	-lama v.t.	keep guard, watch over
lambi	a cook	ndambi n. sing.	a cook
lamika	stick, fasten	-lamika v.t.	fasten, fix, tie together
lamini	personal name	ndaminu n. sing.	motive for keeping
lamuna	detach	-lamuna v.t.	detach, separate
landa	pursue, escort	-landa v.t.	buy, purchase
		-landa v.i.	be poor, indigent
		-landa v.i.	creep up, crawl up
		-landa v.t.	lay waste, level
landu	disobedience	ngandu n. sing.	crocodile
lauwila		-awila v.t.	tell a dream, recount a dream
		luaula n. sing.	species of bird
lawo		ndawo n. sing.	medicinal plant
laya	mouth word	-laya v.t.	promise, announce, be committed to

le	able, powerful	-le adj.	long, tall, deep, profound
lebela	wave	-lembelela v.i.	wave, vibrate, oscillate
leka	sleep well	-leka v.t.	sell
		leka v.t.	leave off, abandon, quit
lekeleke	white-feathered bird	ekelekele!	exclamation of surprise
		lekela imp.	stop!
lekula		-leula v.t.	stupify, anesthetize, cause to be faint, unconscious
lela		-lela v.t.	give birth to, bear a child
lele	disinclination to work	-lele past part.	born
lelema		-lelema v.i.	float on the surface of water
lelemesa	lubricate	-lelemesha v.t.	cause to float on water
lelu		lelu adv.	today
lema	forget	-lema v.t.	string a bow, stretch a skin over a drum
		-lèma v.i.	be lame, crippled, disabled
lemba	fish basket	-lemba v.t.	hunt animals, game
		-lèmba v.i.	sway, swing, move back and forth
lembeka	bewitch	-lembeka v.i.	be hanging down, drooping
lemu		mulemu n. sing.	lip, brim edge, spout
		mulemu n. sing.	bowstring; trigger of a gun
		mulèma n. sing.	a crippled person
lenda		-lenda v.i.	get weak, decay, fail
lende	mouse	-lende past part.	weakened, failed
lenga	personal name	-lenga adj.	good, beautiful, sound, worthy, wholesome
		-lènga v.i.	abound, be overwhelming
		-lenga v.t.	touch with the hand
		-lenga v.i.	be good, useful, secure
		-lènga v.i.	manner of dancing, swing the arms, waddle
lengela	personal name	-lengela v.t.	be good for, useful to, becoming to

		-lengele adj.	good, beautiful, useful, advantageous
leshe		-lesha v.t.	show, exhibit, demonstrate
lewesa	soften	-lepesha v.t.	pulverize, filter, sift
lewu		lewu adv.	feeble, exhausted, worn out
		dilewu n. sing.	weakness, physical exhaustion
li		ndi v. to be	I am
lifu		difu n. sing.	stomach, abdomen
lile		dile adj.	long
		dile n. sing.	a day
lima	cultivate	-dima v.t.	cultivate
limba	Liberian language	-dimba v.t.	fool, trick
lisha	feed	-disha v.t.	feed, nourish
litana	entangle	ditanu adj.	fifth
liya	to eat	diya v.t.	eat
liyata	tread on	-diata v.t.	step on, tread on
loka	to rain	-loka v.i.	rain
lole		lole n. sing.	species of tree
lolo	large	ndolo n. sing.	generosity, ethic, beauty, the good side of anything
lomba	to beg	-lomba v.t.	beg, demand, ask for
		lômbe n. sing.	manioc, starch paste
lombeyi		lombe n. sing.	iguana
lombo	patch	ndombo n. sing.	charm for easy childbirth
londe		-londe adj.	the following, the second
londi	peninsula	mulondi n. sing.	a follower
lonzo		lonzoo adv.	suddenly, unexpectedly, without warning
lotai		lotayi imp.	dream!
loti	a dreamer	ndotshi n. sing.	a dreamer
		ndoto n. sing.	a dream
		-lota v.t.	dream
lwaka	to arrive	lwaku imp.	come here!
luala	to be cut, wounded	lwala n. sing.	fingernail, claw
luayi	umbilical cord	lwayi imp.	come!

lubambu		lubambu n. sing.	magic preparation which gives power to steal unobserved
ludi		ludi v. to be	it is
		ndudi n. sing.	marksmanship, good aim
luha		lupapa n. sing.	scabbard, sheath, case for knife
luila	ant's nest	-luila v.i.	come for
luina	perspiration	luinu n. sing.	child who cuts upper teeth first
lukata		lukata n. sing.	circlet, bracelet used as charm
lukaya	leaf paper	lukaya n. sing.	incantation for ceremonies for harming someone
lukusu		lukusu n. sing.	louse
lulule	personal name	-lulula v.t.	excite, cause to bubble
		-lulule past part.	excited, bubbling
luma	to emit semen	-luma v.t.	have sexual intercourse with a woman
lumbu	stockade	lumbu n. sing.	wall, enclosure, harem
lumingu	Sunday	lumingu n. sing.	week
lunga	day	-lùnga v.t.	poison, kill by poisoning
		-lunga v.t.	season food, cook with seasoning
		-lunga v.t.	stretch, lengthen, make an effort to reach or attain
lunza	to ache	lunzanguila n. sing.	pestering, persistent nagging
lusa		lusha n. sing.	antelope
lusala	plume, feather	lusala n. sing.	feather
		lusala n. sing.	bed, mat to sleep on
luse	forehead, face	luse n. sing.	love, pity, mercy, compassion, emotion
lute	fishy flavor	lute n. sing.	saliva, spittle, expectoration
luwa	manufacture, beg	-luwa v.t.	covet
		-luwa v.t.	hurry, make haste, press on
luwadi	squirrel	luwandi poss.	his, her

luwanga	a small abscess, frog	luwanga n. sing.	sweat, perspiration
		luwanga n. sing.	bush with fruit that gives coloring matter
luweso	disobedience, contempt	luweso n. sing.	cooking pot
luwila	relationship, family	-luwila v.i.	come for, come around
luzemba	the sling upon which an infant is carried	luzembe n. sing.	corner of a piece of cloth
		luzembo n. sing.	frog

M

madimba	musical instrument	madimba n. sing.	xylophone
madiya	food	madiaka n. sing.	glutton, selfish person; one who "eats" the dowry of a daughter due to be used for the son of another member of the family
maget	old	majetete n. pl.	regrets, troubles, sufferings
magonge	small, thin, short	mangonge n. pl.	rhinocerous beetles (common folk saying: Wakudia mangonge lelu, you've eaten beetles today, done something you shouldn't)
mahaya	kingship	mapaya n. pl.	razors
makaiya		makayabo n. pl.	dried, salted fish
makanya	tobacco	makanya n. pl.	tobacco
makaya	leaves, foliage	maka.ya n. pl.	shoulders
		makaya n. pl.	act of going through ceremonies for harming someone, make "medicine" against someone
makene	obscene expression	makane adj.	good, beautiful, wholesome
makinu	dame	makina n. pl.	acts of hate, harming another person

makishi	Angola folklore	mukishi n. sing.	ancestral spirit, ghost
makongo	deformity	makongo n. pl.	calluses, corns
makoto		makote n. pl.	witchcraft remedies for self-protection
		makotà n. pl.	species of ant
maku	arms	maku- makudia makufulu	disparaging prefix terrible food dowdy hats
makumba	chains, fetters, earrings	makumba n. pl.	sows
		makumbu n. pl.	boastings, braggings
mala	corn beer	mala n. pl.	native beer
malasa	rock salt	malashi n. pl.	perfume
malawu	palm wine	maluvu n. pl.	palm wine, any alcoholic beverage
male		male adj.	long
		malela n. pl.	movements for enlivening a song or a dance
malemba	ethnic group in Angola	malemba n. pl.	weaknesses
		malemba n. pl.	fogs, mists
malo	rice, hippopotamus	malu n. pl.	affairs, business matters, reasons, responsibilities, circumstances
malonga	plates, dishes	malonga n. pl.	plates, dishes, bowls
malunda	grandparent	malunda n. pl.	friendships, federations, companionships
malundi	ashamed	malundu n. pl.	hunting prowess, qualities of a great warrior
mambu	talks, affairs	mambu n. pl.	palavers, matters of consequence
mametu	our mother	mametu n. sing.	our mother
mana	be perfect, be finished	-mana v.t.	finish up, use up, complete
mande	language group in West Africa	Mande	very common personal name
mane		-mane adj.	finished, completed
manene	much-used path, high road	manène adj.	large
		mane.ne n. pl.	lower part of abdomen
		mane.ne n. pl.	fogs, mists

manika		-manyika v.i.	be well known, recognized
manisa		-manyisha v.t.	cause to use up, dispose of
manji	killer of adversary	manji n. sing.	murderer, killer of adversary in battle
masa	king, chief	masa n. pl.	winnings, gain, profits
masanga	beer, wine	masangu n. pl.	crossroads, intersection
masi	the human race	mashi n. pl.	blood
matama	faces, cheeks	matama n. pl.	cheeks, jowls
mawu	God	mau n. sing.	mother
mayi	water	mayi n. pl.	water
mbazimene	tomorrow morning	mbajimine	they are lost
mbila	summons	mbila, n. pl.	cries, shouts
mele	breasts	mabele n. pl.	breasts, teats
mema		-mema v.t.	take, lift, carry, transport
meme	delicate, refined	meme pron.	I, me
mena	to sprout, spring up	-mena v.t.	sprout, spring up, grow
mene		mene adv.	exactly, very, actual, just, identical, same
mene mene	early morning	mene mene adv.	really, truly, verily
menesa	cause to grow	-menesha v.t.	cause to grow, sprout
menga		menga n. pl.	seeds of wild olive tree
menya		menya n. pl.	urine
mesa	python	mesa n. sing.	table (Portuguese)
mesu	eyes	mesu n. pl.	eyes
miando	there, yonder	mianda n. pl.	business, affairs, reasons, responsibilities, causes, matters
miangu	tumult, bluster	miangu n. pl.	landmarks, boundaries, limits
miawa	the left wing of an army	miawu n. pl.	yawns
mika	wool, fur, hair	mika n. sing.	species of bird
mikolo	ropes	mikolo n. sing.	legs
mina	African from Elmina or Accra (Ghana)	-mina v.t.	drink, swallow
mise		misele n. pl.	gonorrhea
moko		moko n. sing.	umbilical cord
mole	man	mole n. sing.	species of tree

momo	a Hausa guitar	momo adv.	yes, exactly, that's right
mona	to see	-mona v.t.	see
mone		-mone past part.	seen
mongo	a hill, plateau	mongo n. sing.	spine, backbone; thorn, fishbone
mota		-mota v.i.	clot, coagulate
moyo	spirit, life	muoyo n. sing.	life
mu	to stagger	mu prep.	in, inside
muana	offspring, seed	muana n. sing.	child
mubidi	shepherd, herdsman	mubidi n. sing. muibidi adv.	body, form, shape, color second
muhika		muhika n. sing.	slave
muhatu	woman	mupatu n. sing.	wild olive tree
		mupata n. sing.	a fat person
mukajina	second or third wife of polygamist	mukajiana n. sing.	a certain woman
mukila		mukila n. sing.	animal's tail
mukite		mukite n. sing.	one who dares, shows audacity
mukongo		Mukongo n. sing.	a person from Kongo
		mukongolo n. sing.	swarm, flock of birds or insects
muku	smell of hot food	muku n. sing.	husband's father-in-law or mother-in-law
mulambu	offering, tax, tribute	mulambu n. sing.	offering, tax, tribute
mule	to harden	mule adj.	long
mulonga	edible winged ant	mulonga n. sing.	winged ant
		mulongo n. sing.	row, file, series, rank, line, procession
mululu	great grandchild	mululu n. sing.	white-barked spirit tree
mulunga	inside of an egg	mulunga n. sing.	inside of an egg
		mùlùnga n. sing.	shriek, howl
mumo	spirit, breath, life	muma n. sing.	python
mumu	deaf and dumb	mume n. sing.	dew
muna	raise livestock, tame	-muna v.t.	raise livestock, tame

munda	our, own, ours	munda n. sing.	inside, belly, womb, stomach
muni	the art of anointing	munyi int.	why? how?
munse	suger cane	munsa loc.	alongside, the length of, outside
munini	meat	munyinyi n. sing.	meat, flesh
mungu	tomorrow	munga adv.	elsewhere, somewhere else
musa	Moses	musa n. sing.	kernel of a nut
musangu	personal name	musangù n. sing.	person with a congenital birthmark
		musangu n. sing.	time, period, epoch, turn
		musangu n. sing.	poling stick for a boat
museki	cluster of bananas on the stalk	museki n. sing.	cluster of bananas on the stalk
		museki n. sing.	one who laughs
mushiba	gun barrel, pipe	mushiba n. sing.	gun barrel; pipe, tube; flute, whistle
mushima	heart	mutshima n. sing.	liver; heart, soul, mind, will, spirit
musonding	personal name, girl	musondi n. sing.	sloppy woman, negligent, poor housekeeper
musoti	the woman	musote n. sing.	mudimu wa musote: unrecognized labor, unconsidered toil
musu	woman	musu n. sing.	one who loves
muta		mutua n. sing.	pygmy, dwarf
mutombo	personal name	Mutombo	common proper name, Luba ancestor
mutudi	blacksmith	mutudi n. sing.	blacksmith
mutumba	boundary limit	mutumba n. sing.	quarter of a village; boundary, limit, border
mutwe	head	mutu n. sing.	head, source, summit, top
muzumbu	official	muzungu n. sing.	chief, official
mwana		mwana n. sing.	child, baby, offspring
mwene	the same	mwena n. sing.	person of, citizen of, native of, owner of, inhabitant of, member

mwinda	a candle	mwinda n. sing.	lamp, light, candle
mwula	rain	mvula n. sing.	rain

N

nai		-nayi num.	four
nana	grandparent	nana n. sing.	grandparent
		nana n. sing.	glue, latex, paste
		-nana v.t.	stretch, lengthen
		-nana v.t.	dun, reclaim payment for a debt
nange		-nanga v.t.	admonish, discipline, scold
		-nanga v.t.	love, desire
		-nànga v.t.	roast, grill, toast by fire
		-nanga v.t.	surpass, exceed, be too much
nano		nanu	picture word indicating length, continuity
nasa		nasha adv.	no
natu		netu conj.	with us
nawa		nawu conj.	with it
ndeda		ndedi n. sing.	the cause
ndungu	pepper	ndungu n. sing.	pepper
ne	tongue	ne conj.	and
nege	desire, envy, a metal	-nenga v.t.	elapse, intervene, tarry, be late, tardy
nema	happiness, affluence	-nema v.i.	be heavy, weighty, important
nene	large, famous	-nene adj.	great, big, large, immense
nesi		nishi n. sing.	electric fish
nganga	doctor, diviner, priest	nganga n. sing.	doctor
ngebe		ngebe	it is yours
ngimbidi		ngimbidi n. sing.	ways of singing
ngo		ngo dem.	here it is
ngombe	ox, cow	ngombe n. sing.	ox, cow
nima	back, rear	nyima n. sing.	back, rear

nimisa	misfortune	-nemesha v.t.	add weight, make important, cause to respect
nina	flogging, a gift	-nina v.t.	evacuate the bowel
nkidi		nkindi n. sing.	story, legend, folktale
nkishi	charm, medicine	nkishiabendi n. sing.	afterbirth, placenta
nokonoko	nothing-nothing	nankunanku adv.	so-so, fair
noni		nonu n. sing.	munu wa nonu: sixth finger
nono		-nòna v.t.	be greedy for, avaricious
		-no.na v.t.	sharpen, grind, make keen
nowa		-nowa v.t.	reap, harvest
nowisi		-nowesha v.t.	cause to reap, harvest
nsole		nsolo n. sing.	chicken
		nsolo n. sing.	talk, conversation
nsoye		nsonyi n. sing.	shame, embarrassment
ntama		ntama adv.	for a long time
ntelu		ntelu n. pl.	jokes, stories to laugh at
nukisa		-nunkisha v.t.	cause to smell, cause to emit an odor
nuna	to increase	-nuna v.i.	increase, become great; glisten, shine
nunga		-nùnga v.i.	sway, swing back and forth
		-nùnga tulu	doze, snooze
		-nunga v.t.	weave; season, give zest or relish to
nunka	emit an odor	-nunka v.i.	smell, emit an odor (either good or bad)
nunu		-nunu adj.	old, aged
nya		nya adv.	slightly, softly, lightly
		nyaa adv.	quickly, in great haste
		-nya adj.	small, petite
		nya n. sing.	friend
nyam	personal name "ugly"	nyama n. sing.	animal
nyamuna		-nyamuna v.t.	pull up, extract, uproot
nyana		nyânà n. sing.	friend, companion, mate
		-nya.na v.t.	grow thin, weak emaciated
		-nya.na v.t.	insist

nyanda		nyandu n. pl.	papyrus, papyrus mat
nyege		nyeka v.i.	stoop over, bend over, weigh down
nyema	to run away	-nyema v.i.	run, flee
nyeta		nyeta n. sing.	leggings
		nyi adv.	tightly, in a constricted way
nyiki	pyorrhea	nyiki n.s.	pyorrhea
nyimbidi	a singer	nyimbidi n. sing.	bird, singer
nyimi	to tread upon	nyimi n. sing.	ruler, king (Bushongo)
nyina		-nyi.na v.t.	evacuate the bowel
		-nyina v.i.	turn aside, step out of the way
nyo		nyo	picture word for dryness, drought
nyoka	snake	nyoka n. sing.	snake
nyoma		nyoma adv.	in disorder, in a state of teeming unrest
nzala		nzala n. sing.	hunger
		nzàla n. pl.	fingernails, claws

O

oba		-oba v.i.	score, win a point in a game
ombela	rain	-ombela v.i.	swim
omeka		-omeka v.t.	impose upon, lay a burden on, charge with
ona	a louse	-ona v.t.	snore
		-ona v.t.	cause to go bad, spoil, waste, pollute, desecrate
osa	to produce	-osa v.t.	do, accomplish, make, shape
oshe		-oshe adj.	burnt, charred, consumed
osho		-osha v.t.	set on fire, ignite, burn; hurt, pain, burn, smart
oshuka		-oshika v.i.	burn up, be consumed
otu	waterside, shore	-ota v.i.	warm oneself (by fire, in the sun)

owo	money, trade	-owa v.t.	hang a person, kill by hanging
		-owa mayi v.i.	bathe
oya		-oya v.t.	finish, complete, put the last touches to

P

pakasa	buffalo	-pakisha v.t.	have a charm made, cause to make witchcraft, "medicine"
pakata	carry under the arm	-pakata v.t.	suspend, hang from the shoulder, carry under the arm
pakolo		-pàkula v.t.	empty contents out of a deep container, horn, mortar
pala	to grind	-pala v.t.	clear away, sweep, clean up
		-pa.la v.i.	be crazy, demented, deranged
		-pala v. t.	refuse to give, be stubborn
pali	place crosswise	pale adv.	far away, at a great distance
		pa.le adj.	crazy, demented, deranged
paloti	drunk, pride	-palata (ku tshibi) v.i.	scratch at the door (as a dog); strive in vain
pama		-pama v.i.	settle, dwell, inhabit an area
pambi	a red handkerchief	mpamba n. sing.	nursing mother, taboo to her husband until child is weaned
		-pamba v.i.	be sterile, childless
pana	distant	-pana v.t.	sell, barter
panda	husk, approach	-panda v.t.	split, cut open lengthwise
		-pànda v.i.	escape from danger, be rescued, saved
panda	divination	mpanda n. sing.	savior, guardian, keeper; name of charm against lightning or enemies wishing to do one evil
pando	a city in Togo	mpandu n. pl.	wooden tongs used in forge

pange	brother	panga adv.	elsewhere, somewhere else
		-panga v.t.	fail, break down, forget, make a mistake, be exhausted
		-pànga v.t.	make, invent, determine, decide
pangu		mpangu n. pl.	fences, enclosures
pani		panyi int.	where? whereon?
pansa	dry, uncut calabash	-panza v.t.	borrow with intention to return
		mpanza n. pl.	metal cups, containers
pantu	a large bottle	pantu adv.	at a place, on the spot
papayi	father	papayi imp.	be sterile, barren! (a curse)
pashi	pain, misfortune	mpashi, n. sing.	pain, agony
pasoka	remove the debt	-pasuka v.i.	cut, lacerate oneself
patamo	shark	-patama v.i.	be held fast, caught, squeezed in
pato	broad	patu adv.	outside, outdoors
pawo	loss, sadden	pawu loc. adj.	on its (head, etc.)
paya	strength, powerful	-paya v.t.	pack, place in a container
payula	to beckon	-pawula v.t.	loot, pillage, plunder, spoil
pela	puberty	-pela v.t.	grind, mash, crush
		-pèla v.i.	be poor, indigent
		-pè.la v.t.	give to
pele	tribal marks on the face	-pele adj.	poor, indigent
pemba	become white	lupemba n. sing.	whitewash, chalk
		-pemba v.t.	blow the nose
pemuna	trim the hair, shave	-pempumuna v.t.	cut, shave
penda	personal name	-penda v.t.	insult, curse, abuse, revile
pende	delay	pende intensive pron.	yeye pende: he himself
peng		-penga v.t.	seek, search for a place
peni		penyi int.	where?
pepe	wind	-pepa v.i.	blow, shake with the wind
pepi		pepi adv.	near

peshi		peshi adv.	perhaps, possibly, maybe
		mpeshe	please give me
petu		petu loc. poss.	pa mutu petu: on us
		petu intensive pron.	tuetu petu: we ourselves
peya		-peya v.t.	scrape, scour, rub, scrub
pidi	throw, shoot	mpidi n. sing.	clothing worn during period of sexual taboo
		-pidia v.t.	refuse, revolt, rebel
pilula	to turn	-pilula v.t.	turn, roll (as the eyes)
pime	run	-pime adj.	weighed, measured
pinda	a bird resembling a canary	mpinda n. sing.	small bird, siskin
		-pinda v.i.	accumulate, multiply
pinda	ground nut	kabindi n. sing.	peanut
pindi		mpindieu adv.	right now
pingi		mpinga	after pains
pita	pass	-pita v.t.	pass on ahead, go before; surpass, excel, exceed
		mpita n. sing.	bitterness, resentment
pitshi		pitshi adv.	further on, beyond
po		po adv.	open (kushiya buashi po)
poi		Mpoi	common proper name
poko	a knife	mpokò n. sing.	cut, slash, gash, notch
		mpoko n. sing.	frankness, sincerity
		-po.ka v.i.	be cast, be shed (as fruit, teeth, leaves, etc.)
pola		-pòla v.i.	be calm, at peace, gentle; be cool, damp, moist
		-pò.la v.t.	harvest, pick, gather
poma	corpse	-poma v.i.	be troubled, fearful
ponga	fatness	-panga v.t.	fail, break down, be exhausted; forget, make a mistake
pongo		mpongo n. pl.	valleys, vales, hollows
popo	principality in Dahomey	mpopò n. pl.	tips of grass blades
		mpobò n. pl.	topknot, crest, headfeathers of bird, chicken

posi	coffin	mpotshi n. sing.	palmnut without kernel
poso	a trap for catching small animals	mposo n. sing.	ration
puja		-puja v.t.	blow the fire
puka	a string of beads	-pù.ka v.i. -pù.ka v.t.	rain in torrents not to care, take no interest, be indifferent
puku	rat, fieldmouse	mpuku n. sing.	rat, mouse
pula	drive off	-pù.la v.t. -pula v.i. -pula v.t.	move out of the way, turn aside be exhausted, fatigued thrash out grain
pulule	open air	-pulule adj.	scraped, rubbed, scaled off
pusa	to wash the face	-pusha v.t. -puisha v.t.	winnow, fan, blow the fire hush up, quell, silence
pusu	the mbadi palm	mpusu v.t.	itch, skin disease
puyi	short	mpuya n. sing. -puya v.i.	breath, respiration breathe
pwita	a dance	-pwita v.t.	sip, puff (water pipe)

S

sa		sa adv.	in motion, spurtingly, flying off, shooting off
saba	play, foment	-saba v.i.	play; boil, bubble
sabala	Saturday	-sabila v.t. nsabula n. sing.	have fun with, play with, amuse kingfisher
sadaka	a concubine	-sadika v.t.	multiply, make increase
sake	a climber	kuenda nsake	sound of walking in the mud
saki	bunch, cluster	nsaki n. pl.	branches
saku	large blade knife	nsaku n. sing.	flintstone used for grinding, sharpening
sakula		-sakula v.t. -sàkula v.t.	sakula tshisalu: go marketing put out of tune, harmony
sala	mix	-sala v.t.	do, make; mix well

squirm		-sa.la v.i.	wiggle, squirm, stir about, beat about (as hunters in the bush)
tattoo		-sàla v.t.	tattoo, vaccinate
salala	itch	-salala v.i.	itch
salama		-salama v.t.	tickle, titillate, have the urge to
		-salama v.i.	be shallow, have no depth
		-salama ne v.i.	dissipate, waste
salo	feast	nzalo n. pl.	tattoo marks
		nzala n. pl.	hunger
		nsàlà n. pl.	woven palm-rib mats
saluka	be lukewarm	-saluka v.i.	be in disorder, mixed up, helter-skelter; be lukewarm, tepid
salulula	repeat a performance many times	-salulula v.t.	do, make over and over again
sama	to be ill	-sa.ma v.i.	be sick, suffer, have pain
	to crow	-sàma v.t.	sing, shout, crow, cry
	place the head on a pillow	-sà.ma v.t.	pillow the head
samba	be merciful toward	-samba v.t.	cheer, console, comfort, soothe, solace
		-samba v.t.	run here and there, jump about
sambala	a syphilitic malady	-sambila v.t.	pray, worship
sambi	worshipper	nsambi n. sing.	small drum beaten with palm of hand
sambo	disgrace; shameful	nsambo n. sing.	kosa nsambo: settle a dispute, prove guiltless
sambu	prayer, good fortune	nsambu n. pl.	palavers, law cases for trial, judgments
samina		-sa.mina v.t.	covet, long, yearn for
		-sàmina v.t.	scold, reproach, rebuke, admonish, control, reprove
samo	dried leaves	nsamu n. sing.	state of invisibility
		buanga bua nsamu	charm for making one invisible
sanda	to look for	-sanda v.t.	look, search for; stalk (an animal)
sanga	assemble, intermingle	-sanga v.i., v.t.	unite, assemble, mix
		-sanga mayi	remove taboo after birth of a child

		nsangà n. sing.	joiner, uniter, assembler
		nsànga n. sing.	sole survivor of twins
nsange		nsangi n. sing.	hand of bananas
sanji	hen	nsanji n. sing.	cage
sanko	baldness	nsanki n. sing.	pepper
sansa	providence	-sansa v.t.	sprinkle, scatter by hand
		-sansa v.t.	invoke the spirits of the dead, pray to the departed ancestors
		nsànzà n. sing.	second of twins
		nsànzù n. pl.	firewood
		nsanzu n. sing.	malice, guile, cunning; craftiness
sanzala	lying-in-state of a great chief	-sanzala v.t.	appease, placate, calm down; chant the name of someone while beating the drum
sasa		-sasa v.i.	be sour, acid
		-sasa v.i.	sprout, bud
		nsasa n. sing.	quickness, alertness
sase	earth goddess	-sase adj.	spoiled, sour, rancid
satu	three	-satu num. adj.	three
sawo	name given to the first of twins	nsawu n. sing.	edible watercress, water moss, freshwater kelp
saya		-saya v.t.	carve, cut up
se	say; taste	sè conj.	saying that (invariable particle used to introduce direct discourse in first person)
		nse n. sing.	flavor, good taste
sebe		tshisebe n. sing.	leather, hide, skin
		-sebe v.t.	winnow
		-sebe adj.	winnowed, sifted
seje		-seja v.t.	put aside, carry off, cause to move
sejima		nsènjì n. sing.	young man
		nsenji n. sing.	mammiferous rodent
seka		-seka v.i.	laugh
seke	anchor	nsèke n. pl.	leftovers, siftings of corn, grain
		nseke n. pl.	sides, edges
sela	to cohabit	-sela v.i.	grow up, increase in size, swell up, expand

		-se.la v.i.	move sideways, sidle along
		-sèla v.t.	marry, pay dowry on a wife
sele	fringe	-sèle adj.	engaged, dowered
		nsele n. sing.	corn-shuck "ball" bounced on palm of hand
sema	a large tree	-sema v.i.	climb by grasping with arms and legs
semuna	speak incorrectly; mispronounce	-semuna v.t.	carry, transport on head or shoulders
senda	the act of digging, cultivation	-senda v.t.	dig up roots of edible plant, leaving others to grow, as in manioc cultivation
		nsendà n. sing.	sarcasm, disdain, scorn, contempt
		nsende n. sing.	blacksmith, carpenter, artisan
senga	mourn someone, mentioning the deceased by name	-sènga v.t.	mourn for, lament
		-senga v.t.	sift, shake, move about
seni	to cultivate	nsenè n. sing.	vine carried by pregnant woman to help her deliver without aid
		nsenià n. pl.	young corn for drying
sensa	to cut into small pieces	nsènsè n. sing.	beginning, origin
		nsense n. sing.	grasshopper
sesa		-sesa v.i.	jog, trot, run with small steps
sese	to worship	nsese n. pl.	radiance, glory, rays of emanating light
seya	adjust; agree	-seya v.t.	carve, cut up, dissect
shikama	to sit down	-shikama v.i.	sit down, be seated
shilu		nshilu n. sing.	promise, memento, something willed to someone
shima		-shima v.t.	lie, deceive, trick, be false, fabricate
shina		-shina v.t.	smear on, spread on, as oil or mortar
shingu	neck	nshingu n. sing.	neck

shinisa		-shinsa v.t.	catch, surprise, overtake someone in flagrant wrongdoing
shisha		-shisha v.i.	be last, be late, be behind, be in the rear
shita	to close tightly	-shita v.t.	to close tightly
siha		-shipa v.t.	kill
sobo	the god of thunder	nsobo adv.	in disorder, haphazardly
sodi	the heart of a horse	-sodia v.i.	click the lips, throat to express disapproval, anger; grumble, show offense
soka		-soka v.t.	call, scream, warn
		-soka mvita	begin a fight
soke		nsoke n. sing.	anger, contention
solo	leopard	nsolo n. sing.	talk, conversation
somba		-sòmba v.i.	sit, be seated
		-somba v.t.	borrow, contract a debt
sona	an African plant	nsona n. pl.	grass, gramineous herb
songa		-songa v.t.	sharpen to a point, file, carve
		-songa v.t.	excite, instigate a fight
		-songa v.t.	cohabit with, have intercourse with
songo	personal name	nsongo n. sing.	helpfulness, even-temperedness, pleasantness of manner or attitude
soni	sacrifice	nsonyi n. sing.	shame
sonsa		-sonsa v.t.	mash, pulverize, crush
		-sonsa nyama	hunt animals
soso		nsonso n. sing.	nail
		nsonso n. pl.	pleats, gathers, frills
sudi		nsudi n. sing.	leprosy
suka		-suka v.i.	get out of a tight spot, be loosed, unbound
suki		nsuki n. pl.	hair
suku	haunch	nsuku n. sing.	bowl, head of pipe
sumbi		nsumbi n. sing.	buyer, purchaser
sume	an ant	nsume	that I may bite
sumika		-sumika v.t.	draw blood, bleed

sunga	to mediate	-sùnga v.t.	intervene, mediate, reconcile, separate quarrelers, stop a fight
		-sunga v.t.	choose, select
sungila	to visit by night	-sungila v.t.	defend, save, deliver, rescue
suni		nsungi n. sing.	moon, moonlight
swanga	evil; lascivious	-swanga v.t.	hull, husk, shuck

T

taba		ntàbà n. sing.	one who is wakeful, alert even in sleep
		ntaba n. sing.	species of rat
tabu	a boundary, place on the edge of a river	tabu adv.	wide awake
tadi		tadi conj.	but
tafo	residents of Nta	ntafa	I am cutting
		ntafua n. sing.	sharp point of grass
takula	trap for birds	-takula v.t.	drive, shove, push; lift up, raise up
tala		-tala adj.	childish, immature
		-tala v.t.	swell up, crack open, swell like a boil
talo	member of Sanda Society	ntalù n. sing.	excellence, gain, profit
		ntalà n. sing.	wise, alert person
		ntàlà n. sing.	drake, rooster, male pigeon
tama	to measure space, distance	ntama n. sing.	long distance, long time
	to be extended	-tama v.i.	be tall, long, drawn out, extended
tamba	surpass	-tamba v.t.	go ahead, be first, surpass, vanquish, overcome, exceed
tambe	thorny, rattan	ntambe	that I may win, overcome
tambi	footmark, track	ntambi n. sing.	one who surpasses, wins, overcomes
tanda		-tanda v.t.	give birth to, bear
		-tanda v.t.	argue, quarrel with, fuss at
		ntande n. sing.	spider

tanga	to read	-tanga v.t.	do someone a wrong, make sad, cause someone to grieve
tangingika	spread out, open	-tangidika v.i.	spread out, open out, extend
tangisa		tangadisha v.t.	scatter, strew, disperse
tangu	branch	ntangu n. sing.	circle, ring
tani	a native of Nta	ntanyi n. sing.	anonymous, unnamed person
tanu	five	-tanu num. adj.	five
tapo	twenty cowries	ntapu n. sing.	instrument for making incisions, tattooing, cutting
tata	to be annoyed	-tàta v.i.	be worried, annoyed, troubled, provoked
		-ta.ta v.t.	urinate, strain, sift, filter
		ntata n. sing.	instant, moment, second
tati	alert	-satu num. adj.	three
tatu	father	tatu n. sing.	father, title of respect
tawa	forehead	tawu or tau n. sing.	father
taya	throw down	-ta.ya v.t.	lay down, put down on the ground
		-taya v.t.	crack, shell, hull; hatch
te	to go away	nte n. pl.	foam, slaver, slobbering
		-nte adj.	light, fine, slight, airy
tebe	plantain	-teba v.t.	test, trap, seek to discern how one is thinking inside
		-teba v.t.	require restitution
tela	add; climbing	-te.la v.t.	mention, name
		-tela v.t.	sew, stitch
telo		ntelo n. sing.	large kingfisher
telu	we	ntelu n. pl.	jokes, tales, jests
tema	to pause; to remain stationary	-tema v.i.	be lighted, kindled, shine
		ntema n. sing.	attention, alert listening
tembe		-temba v.t.	boast about, take pride in another
		-tèmba v.t.	pluck, pick, pinch off
temuna	to open wide	-temuna v.t.	speak of, mention name of someone not present
teta	to peel	-teta v.t.	attempt, strive, try, test, make an effort

tete	bundle, sheaf	ntètè n. sing. ntete n. pl.	sore, blister, ulcer grain, seeds
tewa	to spread the hand	-tewa v.t.	present with a welcoming or parting gift
tima	excavate	-dima v.t.	dig
tita		ntita n. sing.	official, person not of royal line who assists in inducting chief or burying him
to		to adv.	no, not all (emphatic negative)
		too adv.	constantly, on and on, without a break
toba	to be spotted	-toba v.i. ntobo n. pl. ntoba n. sing.	be spotted half gourd, bowl digitalis
todi	expenses	ntodi n. pl. kupa muntu ntodi	siftings; minute details put someone on their guard
toko		-toka v.i.	be or become white, bright, light
tola		-tola v.t.	pare, peel
tombola		ntombolo n. sing.	colobus monkey
tonda		-tonda v.t. -tonda v.t.	abhor, despise, be weary of, disgusted with confess, avow, reveal
tonya		-tonya v.t.	fold, bend, curve (as a wire)
toto		-tota v.i. -to.ta v.t.	be greasy, thick, syrupy give a loud report (as a gun), resounding slap, smack
to to to		to to to adv.	on and on, incessantly, over a long period of time or distance
toya		-toya v.t.	burst shell, crack, hatch
tsham		tshiamu n. sing.	iron, metal
tshama		-tshama v.t.	prevent, put an obstacle across the path
tshebi		tshiebe poss. adj.	your (thing)

tshema		tshiema n. sing.	albino
tshiboli		tshibodi	I may not get wet
tshika		-tshika v.t.	turn or bend the neck
tshina		-tshì.na v.i.	menstruate
		-tshì.na v.t.	fear, be afraid of
		tshi.nà n. sing.	hole, pit, excavation
tshitshi		tshitshi n. sing.	kosa tshitshi: break a stick as a sign that trade has been closed, wager been laid, taboo been removed
tu		-tu n.i.	always, habitually to be
tuba	to throw	-tuba v.i.	speak Tshituba
tubu	prison, custody	tubu adv.	gapping, wide open
tufina	pus, matter	tufina n. pl.	pus, matter
tukila	fall into the hands of	-tukila v.i.	fall into the hands of, happen upon
tukuna	rub	-tukina v.i.	be absorbed in doing, be persistent, be a slave to
tula	put down a burden	-tù.la v.t.	put down a burden
	forge	-tùla v.t.	forge (metal, iron)
tulante	a title of nobility	ntulentule n. sing.	remedy against miscarriage
tulu	slumber, repose	tulu n. pl.	sleep, slumber, repose
tulula	take down, let down	-tulula v.t.	take down, let down, put down
tuma	send	-tuma v.t.	send
tumba	be famous	-tumba v.t.	be famous, prominent, noble, influential
		Ntumba n. sing.	proper name for man or woman
tumina	send to	-tumina v.t.	send something to someone
tumpa	parboil, stew	-tumpa v.t.	parboil, stew
tuna	disobey, be indifferent	-tuna v.i.	turn aside in anger, disobey, be indifferent
tunga	to sew	-tunga v.t.	sew
tungi	inhabitant; builder	ntungu n. sing.	tip, recompense
		ntunga n. sing.	lassitude, exhaustion
tuniya	whiteness, cleanness	-tunya v.t.	fold, turn up (as a garment)
		tunya tshianza	clench the fist

tupula	pierce	-tupula v.t.	pull out or up with a jerk, draw out, swing up
tuta	to carry	-tùta v.t.	carry an object from one place to another
	punish	-tu.ta v.t.	hit, strike, beat, punish, chastise, discipline
tutu	title of respect for older brother	tutu n. sing.	title of respect for older brother
tuwa	bail out	-tuwa v.t.	dip out water, bail out
tuwi		tumvi n. pl.	excrement
tuwiya		tupiya n. pl.	fires
tuyi		-tuya v.i. mvula watuyi	cease, be calm, subside storm has subsided
twala		-twala v.t.	carry, transport, conduct

U

udi	grave	udi	he, she is
ukese	mashed manioc	mukese adj.	small
ula	be full	-ula v.i. -ula v.i. -ula v.t.	be full, be complete be distended, swollen buy, purchase
ulalu	lounging, personal name	bulalu n. sing.	bed
ulume	man, husband	mulume n. sing.	man, male
una	that one	unua pres. part.	drinking
unene	renown, greatness	munene adj.	big, great, important
unu (hunu, wuna)	you	wenu poss. adj.	your
		nuenu pl. pron.	you, you all
		wenu henu poss.	your very own
ununu	old age	mununu adj.	old, aged
upa	to remove	-upa v.t.	row a boat, pull an oar, paddle
		-upa v.t.	fan
		-upa munda v.i.	have diarrhea

V

valuka		-valuka v.i.	remember
vanda		-vanda v.t.	give someone a beating, thrashing, trouncing
vila	deny a charge	-vila v.t.	deny a charge
vilula		-vilula v.t.	complete, finish; be in control of, master of
vimba		-vimba v.t.	fashion, form, make
vinda		-vinda v.t.	clean off, rub off, scrape off (as a plate)
vula		-vula v.i.	become many, abundant
		-vù.la v.t.	peel, pare, remove husks
vule		-vule adj.	much, many
vulula		-vulula v.t.	bring to mind, cause to remember, remind
		-vulula v.t	escort someone home, go off with someone
vuluja		-vuluija v.t.	cause to remember, remind

W

wa	novelty; good	wa prep.	of
wa	to fall, to spring	wa-	prefix for subjunctive, polite imperative: "may you . . ."
wabo	broad, wide open	wabo poss. adj.	their
wadi	small fish	wadi poss. adj.	its
wafu	he died	wafu	he is dead
wai		wayi	he has gone
walaye	to be alive	walaye imp.	may you promise
waluka	to go; distance	waluka imp.	may you return
wamiya	embrace	wamanya imp.	may you know
wana	counter; four	wana imp.	may you menace, curse
		wanua imp.	may you drink
wanda	a net	wanda imp.	may you throw down violently; set a trap
wandaji	thunder and lightning	muandaji n. sing.	one who beats up, gives a trouncing to
wande, wandi		wandi poss. adj.	his, her

		wende poss. adj.	his, her
wanga	charm, witchcraft	buanga n. sing.	medicine, charm, fetish, witchcraft
wangula	mutilate; talk	wangula imp.	may you find, gather, pick up, harvest
wani	removal	wanyi poss. adj.	my, mine
wanina	to give	wanyina imp.	may you admire, praise, speak of with admiration
wanyika	to put on one's shoulder	wanyika imp.	may you spread out to dry in the sun or by the fire
wasa	bushy; tufted	wasa imp.	may you make, do, build, construct
wau		wau poss. adj. muau n. sing.	its yawn
wawa		wawa dem. adj. mwamwa dem. adj.	that (at a distance) over there, yonder
wawula	to separate	wawula imp.	may you disclose a dream, talk in your sleep; reveal, tell the meaning
waya		waya imp.	may you go
welasha	to sow; broadcast	welasha imp.	may you cause to pour, cast, throw, sow
wema	to prowl about	wema imp.	may you tap a tree, draw sap for palm wine
wendesha	to miss the mark	wendesha imp.	may you cause to move, go
wengula	grasshopper	wengula imp.	may you skim off, remove scum
wenu		wenu poss. adj.	your, yours
wenza		wenza imp.	may you do, make, invent
wewela	to flutter in the wind	wewila imp.	may you work over lightly, scratch the surface
wila	to listen to	wihila imp.	may you hoe, cultivate, till, dig up weeds
wiluki	a penitent	mvuluki n. sing.	one who remembers
wilula	to reverse	-vilula v.t.	complete, finish up; be master of, in control of

wimba	to smell	wimba imp.	may you dig; may you sing
winda	candle, any light	muinda n. sing.	lamp, light
wisa	authority, mastery	muisa n. sing.	testicle
wishi	smoke, vapor	mwishi n. sing.	smoke, vapor
wita	war; to fight	mvita n. sing.	war, fight, battle
wiwi	dishonesty, theft	mwivi n. sing.	thief, stealer
wobole		wobola imp.	(you) acquire, draw to yourself, gain
wofi	conception in womb	muofo n. sing.	navel
wole		muole n. sing.	species of tree
wolesha	cause to decompose	-bolesha v.t.	cause to get wet, rot, decomposed, soaked
wondesa		-bondesha v.t.	cause to soak in water
wosha		wosha imp.	may you burn, burn up, cause to be consumed, by fire
wota	mash, knead	wota imp.	may you get warm by the fire or strip in the sunshine
woye		woye imp.	may you complete, finish up, bind off, saw the edge of
wula	rain	mvula n. sing. wula imp.	rain may you buy, purchase, barter
		wula imp.	may you dry up, decrease, diminish, abate
wule	sing	-vule adj.	many, much, abundant
wulula	to rescue from great danger to life	-vulula v.t.	bring to mind, make remember
		-vulula v.t.	escort someone home, go with
wuluza	rescue	-vuluija v.t.	cause to know, remember
wumbe	a soup made with blood	-vumbe adj.	saved, put aside for later use
wumbisa	to let out water	wumbisha, imp. wambisha, imp.	clench (fist), screw up (face), wince in pain awaken me, wake me up
wumina	to defame	wumina, imp.	dare, venture
wumisa	cause to dry	wumisha, imp.	cause to dry, heal a sore

wumuna	to breathe	wumuna, imp.	venerate, reverence, revere
wungisha	ashamed; shame	wungisha, imp.	cause to gather, collect, accumulate (wealth)

Y

ya	ready, early, quick	ya imp.	(you) go
yabi	infused	yabi poss. adj.	their, theirs
yako	odd	yaku! imp.	go there! get gone!
yala	to spread	(idi) yala	they are lying in wait
yalamuna		(idi) yalamina v.t.	they expect, wait for, lie in wait for
yamba	hard to please	(idi) yamba	they are saying
yambidisa	to commit adultery	-ambuluisha v.t.	help to lift, hasten, hurry, assist
yanda	to spread; stretch	(idi) yanda	they are throwing down, bringing to earth, hauling down violently (animals)
yande	personal name	yende poss. adj.	his, her, its
yandi	sensual	yandi poss. adj.	his, her, its
yanza	to tear to pieces with the teeth	-anza aux. v.	first do (followed by infinitive)
yase	first	(idi) yasa nyatshi n. sing.	they are building sneeze
yawo	name given a child born on Thursday	nyawo n. sing.	syphilis
yaya	title of respect for older sister	yaya n. sing.	older sister
ye, yeye, yeyi, eye		yeye pron.	he, she, it
yela		(idi) yela	they are pouring, casting, throwing, blowing
yelesha		(idi) yelesha	they are causing to pour, cast, throw, blow
yemaja		(idi) yemaja	they are tapping, drawing sap
yende		yende poss. adj.	his, her, its
yeye		yeye pron.	he, she, it

yiba	to steal	(idi) yiba	they are stealing, cheating
yidisa		-idika v.t.	name, say, tell the name
yika	to talk about	-yikila v.i.	converse, talk about
yila	shut; boil	-yila v.t.	learn
yilo	can; to go	nyilu n. sing.	attitude, manner of walking
yima	to bear fruit	nyima n. sing.	back
yimba	to fire a gun	(idi) yimba	they are singing, playing an instrument
yina	complaint	-nyina v.t.	evacuate the bowels
yinisa	complaint	-nyinisha v.t.	cause to evacuate, have a bowel movement
yipada	to turn over	-ipata v.t.	drive out, rout, put to flight
yiya	quick	-iya v.i.	come
yoba	falsehood	-yoba v.i.	suffer; -yoba ne nzala: suffer hunger
yoka		-nyoka v.t.	chastise, punish, deny, denounce, censure, disown
		nyoka n. sing.	snake
yomba	clarity; delicious food	-yomba v.i.	become thin, emaciated, starved, weak because of hunger, disease
yonga		nyonga n. sing.	snail shell, used as container for witchcraft preparations
yowo		-yowa v.i.	become emaciated, grow weak with hunger or sickness
yoyo	talker; noise; tumult	diyoyo n. sing.	noise, tumult
yoyoyo	talkative	yoyoyo! excl.	word used when crying out either for sadness or joy: Miadi yoyoyo!
yukuta	to be satisfied	-ukuta v.i.	be full, satisfied, no longer hungry
yuya	to burn with a roar	-yuyakana v.i.	be versatile, widely traveled, have had a variety of experiences

Z

zakama	shake, be agitated	-zakala v.i.	shake, shiver, tremble, quake

zala	hunger, appetite	nzala n. pl.	hunger
zambi	God	Nzambi n. sing.	God
zambu	a monkey	-zambuka v.i.	bounce, stride along; zambuka mei: "bounce words," give false, incomplete testimony
zanga	soil; defecate	nzangu n. sing.	hemp seed
zanza	to cause to fall heavily	nzanzu n. sing.	artfulness, tact, finesse, dexterity, astuteness
zaula	to take up with a scoop	-zauka v.i.	be startled, scared
zaza	bill; beak	-zaza v.t.	chop, mince
		-zaza v.i.	be acid, rancid, bitter
zazaza		nzazanza adv.	long ago
zeji		nzeji n. sing.	flash of lightning
zekezeke	boring beetle	njekunjeku n. sing.	longicorn beetle
		nzenzeku n. sing.	profuse thanks
zela	to be pale	-zela v.t.	expose, tell all, bring to light
		-zelela v.i.	be viscous, gooey, like cooked okra
zemba		-zemba v.i.	cease to move, come to a halt, be powerless
		-zemba v.i.	hover (as a bird), hang around
zenji	a judge	nzenji n. sing.	one who judges, a judge
zenza	to be sweet	-zenza v.i.	talk incessantly, tell in detail, chatter, babble
zoka		nzoko n. sing.	indiscretion
zola	long; to long for	-zola v.t.	sketch, draw, design, decorate
zonza	quarrel; strife	nzonza n. pl.	insect bites, thorn pricks
		-zonza v.t.	prune, strip off branches, trim a tree
zozo	joy; merriment	nzonzo n. sing.	quail
zuka	to be inflamed	-zuka v.t.	be belligerent, inflamed, looking for a fight

Two

BLACK NAMES IN THE
UNITED STATES

AFRICAN NAMES IN COLONIAL AMERICA

Scholars searching for linguistic Africanisms in African-American names have not been successful in establishing a direct relationship between African and black American naming practices. Turner, *Africanisms in the Gullah Dialect* (1949), is the exception. Other scholars who have searched for Africanisms and focused on the phonology, morphology, semantics, and syntax of Black English in relation to African languages include Herskovits (1941), Stewart (1967), Baratz and Shuy (1969), Labov (1970), Wolfram (1969), and Dillard (1972).

This chapter explores the historical relationship between African and African-American naming practices and the search for Africanisms in black names. It begins by examining runaway slave advertisements for possible Africanisms. The focus is on African names in Colonial America, Africanisms in black naming practices, and African-American nicknames. At the end of this chapter is a list of African words of Bantu origin from Puckett, *Black Names in America* (1975), as identified by Winifred Vass.

In the Colonial period, African linguistic survivals were numerous because the memory of the African past was still present. Planters were very aware of African ethnicity and attempted to prevent a continuation of African culture and customs on the American plantations which they controlled. This actually accelerated the acculturation process among house servants, who were forced to learn English as the only medium of communication with one another and the planters. The level of English proficiency among enslaved Africans was generally related to the slaves' jobs. House servants, because of their close contact with the planters in the "Big House," learned English more rapidly than field slaves, who had little contact with European-American culture and remained unacculturated for a longer period. African acculturation in South Carolina took place at two levels, in the house and in the field.

The first Africans in North America were not completely unaware of English and other European languages. For instance, Africans arriving in South Carolina from the coastal communities of Africa generally spoke some form of pidgin or creole

English prior to coming to America. Many Angolans coming from the Congo-Angola area spoke Portuguese. Le Jau reported in 1710, "I have in this parish a few Negro Slaves . . . born and baptised among the Portuguese,"[1] and an account in 1739 declared that "amongst the Negro Slaves there are people who spoke Portuguese."[2] Some "Spanish Negroes" were mentioned among the runaways in the *South Carolina Gazette* as heading toward Spanish Florida, while others attempted to seek out other Spanish-speaking slaves.[3]

Peter Timothy's "Negro named Pierro" could speak "good English, Chickasaw, and perhaps French."[4] A runaway mulatto, Antoine, could speak "very good French and English," whereas Clase spoke "good English, and a little Spanish." Phobe spoke "French and English" and Jupiter could speak "good English and some French."[5] In 1772 Finda Lawrence, the Gambian slave trader in West Africa who came to the American South as a tourist, must have had some knowledge of English to move around the South as she did.[6] Obviously these Africans who spoke multiple languages had prior contact with Europeans on the western coast of Africa.

A brief survey of advertisements of runaway slaves revealed that in some cases Africans were speaking creole or pidgin learned on the coast of Africa. An advertisement read that he or she spoke "good English," a sign of acculturation; if the enslaved African spoke "bad English" it was a sign the African had been in the colony for only a brief period and was probably an adult at the time of arrival.

During the Colonial period African ethnicity played a strong role initially in the development of plantation life. The *South Carolina Gazette* revealed that the majority of "New Negroes" arriving in South Carolina spoke little or no English unless they had been imported from the West Indies or Central Africa. A sale advertisement in the *Gazette* read as follows: "A likely Negro Boy about 13 years of Age and speaks good English to be sold."[7] That he spoke good English meant that he was probably "country-born"—raised in the colony and acculturated. Africans born and raised in the colony had little trouble learning the language. For example, a fourteen-year-old Angolan spoke "pretty good English,"[8] a seventeen-year-old Angolan spoke "broken English,"[9] and a nineteen-year-old spoke "good English."[10] An Angolan by the name of Cordelier, having been in the colony since he was a boy, spoke "good English"; an Angolan woman, two Gambian men, and an Igbo man could speak "pretty good English."[11] Obviously, acculturation and the learning of English among younger Africans was quite rapid, whereas older Africans learned English with greater difficulty.

An example of older and unacculturated Africans can be found in this advertisement: "Ran away from the Plantation farm belonging to Capt. Douglas, near Dorchester, a tall Negro fellow named Tower-hill and talks bad English."[12] Many of the Charleston newspapers revealed this slow progress in learning English. Four new Negro men were reported in the *Gazette* of January 22, 1737, out of the ship *Shepherd* from Angola in the beginning of November as "speaking no English and not knowing their master's name." Four others could speak "no English," and an Ebo runaway could "speak no more English other than his name is Jack."[13]

Thomas Wright advertised that his slave Paul "had been one year in my plantation near Silk Hope" and still spoke "little English."[14] Another African could not speak any English when he ran away almost a year earlier,[15] and three Angolan men had been in Carolina three years and still spoke "little English."[16] But "country-born" Africans such as Jacob could speak only English.[17]

African cultural and linguistic acculturation into the American culture took several generations. In each generation less and less of the African culture was retained. After about eight generations of country-born Africans, successful Americanization had taken place. But the linguistic exchanges were mutual and reciprocal: the process also brought about the Africanization of the South. Generations of interaction with African speech patterns produced the distinct white southern accent. Edward Kimber, a traveler in the South in 1746, noticed the impact of Black English on white southern speech, writing that "one thing they are very faulty in, with regard to their Children, which is, that when young, they suffer them too much to prowl amongst the young Negroes, which insensibly causes them to imbibe their Manners and broken speech."[18]

Africans arriving in Colonial America, especially South Carolina, continued to give their children African names well into the nineteenth century. In the seventeenth and eighteenth centuries African-American slaves had retained Africanisms in their naming practices. The greatest percentage of African names occurred among male slaves in the eighteenth century, when the majority of the black population was still unacculturated. African names gave them a sense of cultural integrity and a link to their African past and heritage.

While learning English the Africans did not at first forget their traditional naming practices. During the Colonial period the practice of naming children after the days of the week, months, and seasons was retained. In some cases the African Americans retained the original African versions of their day names, but as generations passed they substituted the original African name for their English equivalent. The following table lists Akan day names found in the South Carolina Gazette.[19]

Also found in the Gazette and other publications are such temporal names as January, April, May, June, September, November, March, August, Christmas, and Midday. There are numerous examples of English equivalents of African day names such as Monday, Tuesday, or Friday. According to Cohen, male names derived from the seasons are Spring (Ebo or Calabar) and Winter. Moon and Thunder are names connected with the state of the weather at time of birth. Other names which are probably English equivalents of African words are Arrow ('of the Pappa country'), Boy (Guiney), Huntsman (new), Little One (Ebo), Plenty (Gambia and Mandingo), and Sharper (Bambara).[20] This Akan naming was practiced in the Sea Islands of Georgia and South Carolina until the 1930s. Actually, Cohen is incorrect in listing Little One as the English equivalent of Spanish pequeño niño. Pickanniny, meaning "very little one," survives from the Spanish trade.

After the first and second generation, Africans began to substitute African day names for the English translations. Paul Cuffee, a wealthy shipbuilder, came from this African naming system. Cuffee, the seventh of ten children of Paul and Mary Slocum, was born on January 17, 1759, on Elizabeth Island near New Bedford, Massachusetts. When he was nineteen years old, nine of the children dropped the slave name Slocum (the surname of their father's master) and adopted their father's

TABLE 5
**Days of the Week with Corresponding
African Names**

Day	Male Name	Female Name
Monday	Cudjoe	Juba
Tuesday	Cubbenah	Beneba
Wednesday	Quaco	Cuba
Thursday	Quao	Abba
Friday	Cuffee	Phibba
Saturday	Quamin	Mimba
Sunday	Quashee	Quasheba

slave name, Cufle.[21] This word is Ashanti, meaning "male child born on Friday," and comes from *Kofi*. Dillard pointed out that female day names followed practices similar to the male day names and that Cuba was among the most common names given to female children born on Wednesday. The name often given to a female child born on Friday was Phibba, which was later translated into Phoebe. Abby came from Abba, the female day name for Thursday. According to Dillard, the name Benah, from Gubena (Tuesday), was frequently misanalyzed as "Venus." Cudjoe, the male day name for Monday, might be Monday in one generation, then Joe in the next.[22]

The Georgia Writers' Project during the 1930s found that among the Georgia coastal blacks, a number of people had been named for week days or the month in which they were born. One ex-slave who was interviewed in regard to this practice, Thursday Jones, explained:[23]

> Dey name me dat way jis cus uh happen tuh be bawn on Tursday, I guess. Sech things seem tub be in our fambly. I had ah uncle who name tis Monday Collins. It seem tuh come duh fus ting tuh folks' mine tuh name duh babies fuh duh dey is baw on.

Here we see how the English equivalent of African day names were being used. By the nineteenth century the African day names often had lost their meaning, but African Americans continued to give day names after their parents.

Quaco, the male day name for Wednesday, was also commonly found during the Colonial period. But later Quaco became Jacco, Jacky, and Jack. There was the case of Martin Jackson of Texas who decided to become Jackson because one of his relatives had a similar African name:[24]

> The master's name was usually adopted by a slave after he was set free. This was done more because it was the logical thing to do and the easiest way to be identified, than it was through affection for the master. Also, the government seemed to be in an almighty hurry to have us get names. We had to register as

someone, so we could be citizens. Well, I got to thinking about all us slaves that was going to take the name Fitzpatrick. I made up my mind I'd find me a different one. One of my grandfathers in Africa was called Jeaceo, and so I decided on Jackson.

By 1734, when the *South Carolina Gazette* was established, names of African origin included Bowbaw, Cuffee, Ebo Jo, Ganda, Quaquo, Quomenor, and Quoy for male Africans and Auba, Bucko, Juba Mimba, Odah, and Otta for females. African names common in the eighteenth century were Sambo, Quash, Mingo, and Juba. The most widely used day names were Cuffee (Kofi) and Cudjoe for males and Abba and Juba for females.[25]

According to Cohen, African day names and their English counterparts existed side by side. Two male slaves named Friday, one of them "this country born" and the other from the "Angola Country," and two male slaves named Monday, one from "Bomborough" (Bambara?) and the other "A Barbian (Bambara) Negro," are mentioned in the *Gazette*.[26]

Blanche Britt supplied Mencken with this list of African names taken from southern newspapers from 1736 to the end of the eighteenth century: Annika, Boohum, Boomy, Bowzar, Cuffee, Cuffey, Cuffy, Habella, Kauchee, Mila, Minas, Monimea, Pamo, Qua, Quaco, Quamina, Quash, Warrah, and Yonaha.[27]

Cohen gives a list of African names found in the *Gazette* between 1732 and 1775 (table 6).[28]

A list of slave names from a 1656 land patent record suggests that these slaves came from the "Bight of Guinea" to Virginia on a Dutch ship, the *Wittepaert*, by way of New Netherlands. The Virginia importer was Edmund Scarburgh. The names are given in table 7.[29]

AFRICANISMS IN AFRICAN-AMERICAN NAME CHANGES

Names are of great importance in West and Central Africa. Names are given at stages in an individual's life and, as among all people for whom magic is important, the identification of a real name with the personality of its bearer is held to be so complete that this real name, usually the one given at birth by a particular relative, must be kept secret lest it come into the hands of someone who might use it in working evil magic against the person. That is why, among Africans, a person's name may in so many instances change with time, a new designation being assumed on the occasion of some striking occurrence in that person's life. When the person goes through one of the rites marking a new stage in his or her development, a name change also occurs to note the event.[30]

Stuckey, in *Slave Culture: Nationalist Theory and the Foundations of Black America* (1987), noted that black naming practices were African in origin, in that African Americans changed their names just as Africans did, corresponding to major changes in the life of the individual. This name shifting is clearly demonstrated by

TABLE 6
African Names from *South Carolina Gazette*, 1732–1775

Male Names

Ankey	Folee	(Kuamania)*
Asam (Asame)*	Footbea	Quaow
Assey (Ase)*	Gamone (Ngamone)*	Quash (Kuashila)*
Bafey (Bofe)*	Goma (Ngoma)*	Quaw
Balipho	Gunnah (Kuna)*	Rente
Banjoe	Haloe (Halue)*	Saffran
Beay (Mbiya)*	Homady	Sambo (Shamba)*
Beoy (Beya)*	Hughky (Huki)*	Sandico
Bobodandy	Jamina*	Sango (Shanga)*
Boo (Mbo)*	Jellemy	Santry
Boswine	Jobny	Saundy (Shanda)*
Bram	Ketch	Savey
Bury	Mahomet	Sawney
Chopco (Tshikapu)*	Mallay	Serrah
Claes	Mambee (Muambe)*	Shampee (Tshambi)*
Clawes	Mamena (Maminu)*	Sirrah
Chockcoose	Manso	Sobo (Nsobo)*
(Tshikusa)*	Marmillo	Sogo (Soko)*
Congo*	Massery	Stepney
Crack	Mingo (Minga)*	Tokey (Mutoke)*
Cudjoe (Kudia)*	Mobe (Mumpe)*	Tomboe (Ntambue)*
Cuff (Kufa)*	Mollock (Muluka)*	Wabe (Webe)*
Cuffee (Kufi)*	Monvigo (Muvinga)*	Whan
Culley (Kule)*	Morrica	Wholly (Hola)*
Cumin (Kumina)*	Musce Jack	Woolaw (Ulama)*
Dago	Mussu (Musue)*	Yanke
Dembow (Ndembu)*	Okree	Yanki
Dibbie	Pherco	Yonge (Nyanga)*
Donas	Fouta (Futa)*	Zick (Tshika)*
Doney	Quacoe (Kuaka)*	Zocky (Nzoko)*
Easom	Quammano	Zoun

Female Names

Aba (Aba)*	Camba (Kamba)*	Juba
Abey	Choe (Njo)*	Juda
Affrey	Cuba (Nkuba)*	Mabia (Mambiya)*
Agua	Dye (Ndaye)*	Mamadoe
Arrah	Eley (Elayi)*	Mawdlong
Banaba (Ban' Aba)*	Embro	(Walongo)*
Binah (Bena)*	Famtame (Patane)*	Minda (Minda)*
Body (Mbudi)*	Fortimer	Nea (Neaye)

Plaeby   Rynah   Sibby (Tshibi)*
Quant (Kantu)*   Sack (Seka)*   Tinah (Tshina)*
Rino   Sard   Windy (Wende)*

*Luba words identified by Vass.

Names Listed on the Dutch Slave Ship *Wittepaert*

Tony
Ufoler (uhola-harvest)*
Aiquera
Ambe (let him tell)*
Aura
Assone (Asune, let him bring water)*
Ay (Aye, let him go)*
Ottome (Atume, let him send)*
Monafunke (Mona nfunke, see, I'm pointing)*
Eare
Messon (Mesu-eyes)*
Roundells
Wortells
Johney
Angora (A Ngola)*
Margarretta
Monque
Veco
Ogombe (Ngombe-cow)*
Werrye
Ottonco
Tubuno (Tubu'enu, your hole)*
Tabortha
Janna (Tshiana, fat child)*
Ommo
Jihur
Curmer
Dondo (Ndondo, ritual term, depths)*
Tary
Jonara
Jomora
Sango (Sanga, unite)*
Croila
Jurna
Rommo
Wingoe
Elloren

TABLE 7 *(continued)*

Corle
Murrom
Angoe (Angue, let him seek)*
Dony

---

*Luba words identified by Vass.

the experience of Frederick Douglass, who, soon after escaping slavery, began a series of name changes.[31]

> On the morning after our arrival at New Bedford, while at the breakfast-table, the question arose as to what name I should be called by. The name given me by my mother was Frederick Augustus Washington Bailey. I, however, had dispensed with the two middle names long before I left Maryland so that I was generally known by the name Frederick Bailey. I started from Baltimore, I found it necessary again to change my name. . . . I gave Mr. Johnson, Mr. Nathan Johnson of New Bedford, the privilege of choosing me a name, but told him he must not take from me the name of "Frederick," I must hold on to that a sense of identity.

Sojourner Truth, a crusader for black emancipation and feminine equality, was known as Isabella until about age twenty, when she was freed and left her master's plantation. She had a vision in a dream that told her about her new name and her mission to free her people. And Malcolm X, through various stages of his life, was known as Malcolm Little, Homeboy, Detroit Red, Big Red, Satan, Malcolm, El-haji, and Malik El Shabazz.[32]

Such name shifting is common throughout West and particularly Central Africa. In many parts of Africa every man who leaves his traditional setting and family is given or takes a new name when he turns or walks away from home. This situation parallels that of slaves who were brought to the Americas, away from their ethnic group, but who remained in contact with others who shared a similar ethnic background.[33]

Nowhere is this tradition so vivid as in the jazz world, where name shifting is common, signaling a major event in the life of the musician: Jelly Roll Morton (Ferdinand La Menthe), Satchmo (Louis Armstrong), Yardbird (Charles Parker), Lady (Billie Holiday). The story of these name changes follows the African pattern of using a new name to adapt to new circumstances and changes in the person's new life.

AFRICANISMS IN AFRICAN-AMERICAN NICKNAMES

A more direct African survival is the use of nicknames. Almost every black person is known by two names: a given name and a name used only within the family circle.

Turner found a dual naming system among the Gullahs in the Sea Islands of South Carolina. This system consists of an English (American) name given at birth and a more intimate name used exclusively by the family and community. Turner was surprised that previous scholarship had failed to note this practice or the importance of Africanisms in Gullah nomenclature. Slaveholders recognized this dual naming practice among enslaved Africans in the eighteenth century. In their advertisements of runaways in the *South Carolina Gazette,* owners always included "proper" (given) names and "country names," the African names retained.[34]

This naming practice still exists among the Gullahs and in the general black population. In African-American naming practices every child receives a given name at birth and a nickname that generally follows the individual throughout life. Some examples of these nicknames are Jo Jo, June, Tiny Baby, O.K., Jon-Jon, Mercy, Baby Sister, "T," Sunny Man, Main, Bo, Boo, Bad Boy, Playboy, and Fats.

Among enslaved Africans this practice was also evident in names used by slaves, such as Pie Ya, Puddin'-tame, Frog, Tennie C., Monkey, Mush, Cooter, John De Baptist, Fat-Man, Preacher, Jack Rabbit, Sixty, Pop Corn, Old Gold, Dootes, Angle-eye, Bad Luck, Sky-up-de-Greek, Cracker, Jabbo, Cat-Fish, Bear, Tip, Odessa, Pig-Lasses, Rattler, Pearly, Luck, Buffalo, Old Blue, Red Fox, Coon, and Jewsharp.[35]

Turner found that Gullah-speaking people preserved their language and nicknames by what they called basket names or day names. Their children always had two distinct names, an English one for public use and an authentic African name for private use by the extended family alone. Here are a few examples of Gullah basket names which are also straight, unchanged, present-day Tshiluba names:

Ndomba is the name given a Gullah child whose hand protrudes first at birth. It means "I am begging (with my outstretched hand)." Mviluki has a Gullah meaning of "a penitent." Its Luba source word is Mvuluki, a rememberer, one who doesn't forget his sins. The basket name Sungila means "to save, help, deliver," while Kamba, a very common Luba name, comes from Munkamba, meaning "ancestor." The Gullah meaning of Kamba is "a grave." Anyika, a Gullah name meaning "she is beautiful," is related to a Luba word, spelled exactly the same, meaning "to praise the beauty of." Sebe, a Gullah name meaning "a leather ornament," comes from the Luba word for hide or leather, *tshisebe.* Tulu (sleep), Tuma (send), Pita (pass by), Mesu (eyes), Kudima (to work or hoe), and Kudiya (to eat) are all Gullah day names, exactly the same in Gullah and Luba.[36]

In the Sea Islands, children sometimes have not only their given names and basket names but also community names. The community gives the child a name that characterizes or is characteristic of the individual, i.e., Smart Child, Shanty (show off).[37] This practice parallels Bantu naming practices in Zaire. Georgetown University's former basketball center Dikenibo Mutombo from Zaire illustrates this point. His full name is Dikambe Mutombo Mpolondo Munkamba Diken Jean-Jean-Jacque wa Mutombo. In order, these names are his uncle's name, his family surname, his grandfather's name, his nickname given by his village, his name given at birth, and his hometown village, wa Mutombo (which means "from the village Mutombo").[38]

Other creolized Gullah pet names (nicknames) so typical of Bantu naming practices are names of animals or fish: De Dog, Doggie, Kitty, Fish, Yellowtail, Croker, Frog, Spider, Boy, Gal, Jumper, Tooti, Crocki, Don, Cuffy, Akebee, Dr. Buzzer, Dr. Eagle.[39]

In Gullah naming practices, as in African naming practices, children are named after parents because they are believed to be the parent spirit residing in the children. The same name might appear in several generations in a family. In the Sea Islands the name Litia appeared in four generations of female children.[40]

An integral part of Bantu culture is the unchanging secret "spirit name," something that the individual has which is uniquely his or her own from the past and is carried on to the next generation, given to a new baby so that it may remain incarnate. Thus by a strange interweaving of religion and language, the "inner soul" of the speech of a cultural group is preserved. As Munday reported,[41]

> Investigation brings to light the fact that the Africans of these parts, whether man or woman, have two classes of names: (a) spirit-names and (b) names of manhood or womanhood. Each has one (a few have two) of the names of the first class, and one or more names from the second class. It is by these names of manhood or womanhood that they prefer to be called; some are traditional African names of these parts, some are debased European words, some are European given or family nicknames, some are nicknames, given owing to some peculiarity, some are names given at baptism. All of these names of manhood and womanhood (except the last) can be, and are, changed for any and no reason, and according to who is changed, once it is finally given. It is of this spirit-name that the Lala aphorism says: *The name is the Spirit.*
>
> Officials now prefer the African to be registered under his spirit-name, owing to its never being changed, but there are two practical disadvantages which weigh against its being used for registration purposes: An African of tribes with which we are concerned is very shy of using it for himself or another, and in some parts, the spirit names are so few in number that the majority of persons in one area may share half a dozen names. However, as has been said, *the spirit name is never changed from the mother's back to the grave.*
>
> The giving of the spirit-name (literally, "of birth" or "of the navel") is regarded as an event of the greatest importance. *Every child born is regarded as the "come back" of some dead person, either of the same or of the opposite sex. The person has to be given the spirit-name of the dead person.*

Munday points out that the spirits of the dead are immortal only as they become incarnate again in another human being that bears their name. If a name is forgotten so that it cannot become incarnate, it wanders through the world as a ghost.[42] As one becomes more and more familiar with the inner "creole" world of the African American, one becomes more and more aware of the deep currents of relationship that still exist with the African mother continent.

The following Bantuisms are found in Puckett's *Black Names in America: Origin and Usage* (1975). The asterisk indicates that the word is listed in Guthrie's *Comparative Bantu* (1967) and thus is common to Bantu languages throughout sub-Saharan Africa.[43]

aba v.t.*	apportion, distribute goods, special honorary task of tribal official designated to succeed the present chief
aku dem. loc.	there, thence, thither, yonder
aka v.t.	harvest, reap
aka!	exclamation of surprise
ala v.t.	spread out
ala v.t.	lie in wait for, await
alakana v.t.	crave, covet, desire keenly
alakana v.i.	be proud, haughty, vaunt oneself
amba v.t.	speak, tell, say, proclaim
anika v.t.	dry by the fire, dry in the sun, roast, toast
asa v.t.	hit, shoot (an arrow), lance (a spear)
asa v.t.	construct, build, undertake
bala v.t.	open out, unfold, spread out
bala v.t.	read, count
mbala n.	menses
mbale n.	pnuemonia (ribs)
bamba v.t.	sew a patch, put a ridge on a house, stretch a hide on a drum
bamba v.i.*	lie down in order to hide, crouch down, keep oneself hidden
bamba n. (mamba)	poisonous snake
bana n. pl.	children
bano n.	arrowshaft
basha v.i.	fear, cringe, cower, be afraid
bata v.t.*	walk flatfooted, stomp on dirt, earth
bata v.t.	examine in detail, pay attention to
mbata n. sing.	fist
mbata n. sing.	species of fern
bata n. sing.	duck
baka v.i.	exaggerate, go too far
bela v.t.	warn, admonish, reprove, correct
bemba v.t.*	stalk, creep up on
bena n. pl.	the people of
benda v.i.*	curve, bend, be crooked, skewed
beta v.t.*	pack down, beat, pound, hit, strike
bila v.t.*	call, scream, yell
mbila n. pl.*	cries, calls, shouts, proclamations, announcements
binga v.i.*	to be acquitted, be declared innocent, justified, vindicated
bisha v.t.	lift up, raise up, cause to stand up
bosa v.t.	crack, burst, shell, hull
bulalu n. sing.	bed
bumba v.i.	determine to, decide to, make up one's mind
bumba v.t.*	put away, store
bumba v.t.*	mold pottery

mbumbu n. sing.	borer, insect
bunu n. sing.*	buttock
bunu n.	drunkenness
bunga (tulu) v.t.	doze, sleep
bunga v.t.*	gather up
a bungi adj.	many (of muchness)
kafi n. sing.	rectum
nkofi n. sing.	oar, paddle
kafi neg. imp.*	"Let him not die" (spirit name given to protect a baby)
kaji n. sing.*	woman, female
kalolo n. sing.*	goodness, kindness, integrity
kama v.t.*	squeeze, wring out, compress
kama v.i.*	evaporate, dry up
kana n. sing.	small child
kana v.t.	threaten, menace
nkasa n. sing.	foot
nkata n. sing.*	pad, circular coil for head
kavuamba n. sing.	bad impression, reputation, report
tshila n. sing.	cry of amazement (chila)
tshima n. sing.*	heart, liver (chima)
tshina v.t.*	fear (china)
tshita n. sing.	trap (chitta)
koba n. sing.*	skin
koba n. sing.*	strap, belt
koka v.t.*	drag, pull, stretch, draw
koka v.i.	yield, be submissive
kola v.t.	be strong, well, vigorous, grown
nkole n. sing.	strong, powerful man
koma v.t.*	smooth out, press, hit with hammer
komba v.t.*	sweep, brush
nkombo n. pl.*	dregs, scrapings
nkonge n. sing.	African otter
nkusu n. sing.	parrot
nkutshi n. sing.	pigeon
kuta v.t.	wrap up, roll up, fold
kota v.i.*	come, go in, enter
nkoyi n. sing.	arrow with blunt wooden point for killing birds
nkoyi n. pl.	fit, spasm, convulsion
kuba v.t.	care for, take care of, oversee
nkuba n. sing.	flash of lightning
nkudu n. sing.	turtle, terrapin
kula v.t.	dislocate, disjoint, pluck
kula v.t.	grind, masticate, pulverize

kula v.i.	endure, last a long time
nkumba n. sing.	toilet
nkumba n. sing.	a barren, sterile, childless woman
nkumbi n. sing.	large, wedge-shaped drum
ndela n. sing.	man with many children
dema v.i.*	become tired, heavy, too difficult for
ndeshi n. sing.	nurse, caretaker of children
dia v.t.*	eat, consume, devour
dia dem.*	that, those
diba n. sing.	sun, time, hour
dila v.i.*	cry, weep, wail, mourn
dima v.t.*	cultivate, hoe, work
dima n. sing.*	clay, earth used in making pots
dime n. sing.*	tongue
dina n. sing.	name
dina v.t.*	dive, sink, drown
ndolo n. sing.	generosity, bounty, esthetic beauty
ndondo n. sing.*	pact, treaty, covenant; great depth
duba v.i.*	become lost, make a mistake
ndubi n.*	tomorrow, yesterday
duka v.i.*	vomit, get rid of something
ndugu n. sing.*	friend
dula v.t.*	undress, remove clothing
duma v.t.*	bite, seasoning
ebe poss.*	your, yours
elela v.i.	hint at, speak with irony
elawu v. imp.	pour it in
Elele! or Ekelekele!	exclamation of surprise
ena v.i.*	not to be
ewo	this
enzeka v.i.	be done, be made
fina v.t.	press, squeeze out, throw down, as in wrestling
fuka v.t.	create, form, make, shape
futa v.t.	pay, remunerate, award, compensate
ngabu n. sing.*	shield
ngamba n. sing.*	an eloquent person
ngambi n. sing.*	speaker, orator
ngondo n. sing.*	moon, month
hadisha v.t.	make drunk, crazy, intoxicate
hala v.i.	be or become insane, crazy, deranged
hana v.t.	sell, trade, barter
hata v.i.	be stopped up, full, constipated
hila v.i.	be guilty, be convicted, condemned

hoka v.i.	be cast, shed, as leaves or fruit from a tree
huka v.i.	rain in torrents
huka v.t.	step aside, avoid, draw away from
hula v.i.	move out of the way, turn aside
husha v.t.	quell, cause to be silent
iba v.t.	steal, cheat, defraud
ika v.i.	bear, bring forth, yield, produce
ika v.i.	get down, descend from
ila v.i.	used with *butuku* (night), to grow dark, night is coming
imana v.i.	stand erect, upright
ina v.t.	put to soak, immerse, dip in water
ina n. sing.	mother (ine'be, your mother)
isatu	cardinal numeral three
nzala n. pl.	hunger, famine
jamisha v.t.	stick fast in, make steady, firm
njana n. sing.	one who criticizes, complains
njanda n. sing.	witch, sorcerer
joba v.t.	plait, weave, braid
njiu n. sing.	peril, danger, accident
njolo n. sing.	crack, fissure, chapped skin
kanka v.i.	tremble, shake
Kanku	personal name for younger of twins
nkanza n. pl.	*muele wa nkanza:* long knife with four points
nkanzu n. pl.	*muntu wa nkanzu:* nimble, quick, fast-moving person
kaula v.t.	remove charm or medicine
kata n. sing.	venereal disease
kata n. sing.	a large number
nkotshi n. sing.	coveralls, dungarees
ke-ke adj.*	little, young, small
ke neg.-part.	no, not
kisa v.t.	be cruel to, hate
nkeke collective n.	sun's rays, sunbeam, glow of fire, of phosphorus
keke v.t.	scorn, disdain, despise
keka v.t.	cut up into pieces
kela v.t.	strain liquid through a cloth; perspire freely
kela v.t.	train, instruct, educate
nkela n. sing.	a sneer
kesa v.i.	to be happy, rejoice
kesha adv.*	tomorrow, yesterday
keta v.t.*	cut or lower price
nkete n. sing.	stomach wrinkle
nketo n. sing.	native pepper
kia v.i.*	dawn, grow light, get bright

kia! excl.	what! amazing!
nkila n. sing.	dam in a stream, dike
nkima n. sing.	monkey
kina v.t.	hate, be mean to
kina v.i.*	dance, gambol
kisa v.t.	be cruel to, torture
kishi n. sing.	small insect, bug
kita v.i.	dare, be audacious
nkita n. pl.	graves
koma v.t.	smooth out, straighten, iron, press
koma v.t.*	fasten, hit with a hammer
nkoma n. sing.	tree whose fruit is used to flavor palm wine
komba v.t.*	sweep, brush
nkombo n. sing.	dregs, scum
nkondo n. sing.	bend of the knee
kondo n. sing.	banana, plantain
Kongolo	Luba ancestral name, hero of folklore
kongolo biuma v.t.	return the dowry, break the marriage relationship
kosa v.t.	cut, sever, chop off
nkose n. sing.	house rat
nkoshi n. sing.*	neck
nkosolo n. sing.	cough
kuba v.t.	care for, guard, take care of, oversee
kuba v.t.	wait for, wait
kumbana v.i.	be enough, be sufficient

Three

AFRICANISMS OF BANTU ORIGIN IN BLACK ENGLISH

This list of Africanisms was compiled by Winifred K. Vass, *The Bantu Speaking Heritage of the United States* (Los Angeles: Center for Afro-American Studies, UCLA, 1979), 105–122. The list is reproduced here by permission. Column one gives the Africanism, column two its English meaning, and column three its Bantu equivalent and meaning.

A

ameela[1]	word used repeatedly in prayers	*-ambila:* tell someone, say to someone

B

bamboula[2]	small cylindrical drum covered on one end with hide, held between knees	*-bambula:* beat, hit, strike surface
bamboula[3]	African drum used by New Orleans Creoles, covered with cowhide, made of a length of bamboo; name of dance, derived from the drum[4]	
bakalinga[5,6]		*bakelenge:* masters, overlords, authorities chiefs
ballahoo[7]	spectral dog of African-American folklore	*mbua wa lufu:* dog of death
ballyhoo[8,9]	publicity, blatant advertising	*balapu:* read about it
banga[10]	medicine, a voodoo charm, talisman	*buanga:* medicine, fetish
boackum[11]	medicine, home remedy for illness	

banjo, banjore[12,13,14]	stringed instrument	*mbanza:* stringed instrument (cf. also Latin, Greek, Spanish, English: bandore)
barra, barrafou[15]	xylophone	*bala:* xylophone
batra, battra, batten[16]	clothes, beat clothes on a block to launder	*-bata:* beat, pound something on a hard surface
battling[17]	stick, laundry stick for stirring clothes in a washpot	
battuta[18]	beat, measure in music	*batuta:* they are beating, keeping time
batuque[19]	Brazilian round dance of African origin	*batukue:* they that have become perturbed, excited, wrought up
belambi[20]	objects requested in formal prayers	*bilamba:* clothing
bele[21]	dance of chanted, spur-of-the-moment improvisation	*mbele:* I am reproving, rebuking, admonishing (someone in song)
Beluthahatchee[22,23]	legendary, blissful state where all is forgiven and forgotten	*bilota mpatshi (bilota bia mpatshi):* blissful dreams, visions
bidibidi[24]	small bird	*bidibidi:* small, yellow bird
biddy[25,26]	baby chick, chicken, fowl	
bolim-belum[27]	Florida cooper's chant while beating barrel hoops over staves	*mbole bilamba:* my clothes are wringing wet with perspiration
bonki[28]	he-goat	*mpongo:* he-goat
booboo[29]	blunder, error	*mbubu:* stupid, blundering way of acting
booboono[30]	circular house	*-bulunga:* be round
boody[31]	sex	*bwedi:* act of emission
booger[32]	ghost, spirit	*mbuka:* divination, consultation of the spirits (cf. Scottish *bogee, bogey*)
boogaboo[33]	imaginary cause of fear, worry; nemesis	*-buka lubuka:* conjure, enchant, divine, consult a medicine man
boogie-woogie[34]	form of instrumental blues for the piano, using melodic variations over a constantly repeated bass figure	*mbuki-mvuki:* I take off (in flight), I shuck off (all clothing that hinders my performance)
bowdacious[35]	extremely, exceedingly (cf. Uncle Remus)	*-botesha:* pulverize, grind to a fine powder, reduce to the absolute minimum

bozo[36]	big, strong, stupid fellow	*-boza:* be a stumblebum, one who smashes things, knocks things over in passing
branzobo[37]	voodoo password	*banzoba:* strong people
brinjer, brinjin[38]	cold, extremely cold	*mbinda:* pneumonia
brawtus, broadus, broatus, brotus[39]	something extra thrown in for good measure	*mbata:* something given on credit, without payment (Mbatas! would be the slang form, with s added)

C

caffuffle[40]	confuse, fluster	*kufufula:* to blow on strongly, beat the air with wings, create confusion
cahootin, callihootin,[41] gallihootin	go along at high speed, at a great rate, lickety-split	*kuhuta:* to trail along, pass along, stretch out to a great length, drag
cala[42]	creole rice cakes	*kala:* rice
calinda, kalinda[43]	a voodoo dance	*kalanda:* renown, fame, notoriety
catawampus, caliwampus,[44] kittywampus	askew, awry, diagonally	*-katakankulu:* hang unevenly, one side long, one short
c'dear! chu-dear![45]	exclamation	*kokya-kodya:* adv., pell-mell, in complete disorder
chance[46,47]	a certain number, several	*tshianza:* hand, handful
cheweeka[48]	insignificant, puny little person	*njeku:* dwarf, runted, deformed person
chikama,[49,50,51] chimecrow, chick-mah-chick, mah craney crow	children's game	*-shikama:* sit down, sit here
chinch, chinch bug[52]	bug, bedbug	*tshinji:* insect, bug (tonal pattern: glide, high)
chinchy[53]	stingy, cheap; impatient, irritable person	*tshinji:* anger, irritability, impatience, unwillingness to listen (tonal pattern: high, high)
churray[54]	spill, discard, throw away	*tshiupulayi:* throw it away, discard it (act supposed to remove the effects of death of husband or wife)
Conga[55]	a dance; drums	Congo, Kongo
congeroos[56]	dancers	*Kongolo:* traditional Luba ancestor

coob[57]	hutch, pen, coop for fowls or small domestic animals	-kuba: care for, watch over, take care of
cool-do[58]	wood ibis	nkundulula: ululating cry of bird or human being (made by clapping hand rapidly over mouth)
colly[59]	understand, comprehend	(bi)kole: well, absolutely (a response to "Do you understand?")
counjai, coonjine,[60,61] counjaille, koundjo	bodily motion used to lighten or hasten labor, such as unloading cotton bales	konyayi: bend, bend over (plural imperative)
cooter[62]	turtle	nkuda: turtle
cooter-grass	purslane	
cooter-backed road	sloped for drainage	
cooter-log	place for chronic idlers to sit in the sun	
box-cooter	close-mouthed person, uncommunicative person	
count-aquil[63]	expression used in slave songs	kutuakuila: to speak on our behalf, intercede for us
covess ding[64]	derogatory term for a black woman, used by African Americans	kupesha ndinga: to give red dirt (red clay used to smear body, according to custom of being taboo to husband till child is weaned)
cubbage[65]	small cooking pot	-kupesha: make small, diminish
cullah-cullah[66]	wild duck	nkolonkolo: a large fowl
cupla[67]	remembered African vocabulary in Savannah, Georgia	kupola: to reap, harvest
cymbi[68,69]	spirit, water sprite	tshimbidimbidi: indescribable, shapeless object; something vague, undefined, deformed, misshapen, having neither head nor tail

D

day-day, da-da, du-du[70,71]	that-there	dia-dia: that there, that over yonder (demonstrative for distance)
de monkey[72]	exhaustion, fatigue	dipungi: exhaustion, fatigue
diddle[73]	cheat, swindle	-dinga: deceive, trick, cheat

diddy-wa-diddy[74]	legendary place of plenty to eat	*wadia-wadia:* you eat and eat
diffy[75]	fire	*-fia:* to burn up; *didi difia:* it is burning up
dinge[76]	a black-skinned African American	*mudingi:* rascal, hypocrite (name jokingly used to call each other; never to be used by an outsider)
doney-gal[77]	sweetheart, girlfriend	*doni, ndondi:* burden, load (to be carried by the woman)
dunger[78]	cultivated area, former site of a dwelling	*ndungu:* pepper plants, always planted on site of former dwelling
duppy[79]	apparition, ghost	*nduful:* it is death!
duppy-dust[80]	graveyard dirt	
Duppy[81]	the devil, a malicious spirit	
Duppy-agent[82]	undertaker	

E

eagle-quarter[83]	expression heard in slave songs	*ikala ukuata:* be holding, prepared, ready and waiting for some event

F

flap-doodle[84]	nonsense, bosh	*-papa ndulula:* give back dispute, vehemence, loud talk
fofie-eyed[85]	bad eye, covered with blue-white pigment	*mufofo:* a blind person
foofaraw[86]	fuss, disturbance about very little	*-fufula:* blow on strongly, beat the air with wing, create confusion
foo-foo[87]	a new person, an outsider; disliked person, one not accepted	*mufufu:* a glutton, greedy person disliked by all

G

Gabe Staggers[88]	voodoo incantation: "Bring Gabe Staggers back to me!"	*-keba nsadika:* seek out the sacred, spared chicken (used in animistic ritual)
gall, gaul[89,90]	swamp	*ngala:* an embankment, low dam built in shallow water

gam[91]	participate in a social visit; have a gam with someone, talk with	(ndi) ngamba: I say . . .
gee[92]	agree, get along with, accept another's viewpoint	-itshija: accept, agree with, get along with
geech, gooch[93]	tickle the ribs	kuisha: row, paddle (poke the ribs with finger paddle); nkeshilu: reason for laughter
giffy[94,95]	cloudy, damp	ngifenyi: sniffings, nasal stuffiness (perhaps associated with humid weather)
gigi, gi-gi, gee-gee[96]	child's favorite toy; object toyed with by an adult	njiji: objects to dance about, agitate, play with
Ginny-Gall[97,98]	black legendary place of want and suffering	Ntshina Kalunga: I fear the Place of the Dead
gombay[99]	cow	ngombe: cow
gombre-work[100]	conjuring, make evil, negative charms	kuomba: to pulsate, beat (as the heart), shake, quiver; Kuomba ngoma: beat the drum
goober[101]	peanut	nguba: peanut
goofer[102]	voodoo charm	kufua: to die
goofer-bag	charm, fetish	
goofer-dust	graveyard dirt or ground-up bones	
goofer-doctor	witch doctor	
goola,[103] goola-box[104]	a piano	ngula: strength, might, power, force
gooly[105]	good, strong, powerful	ngula: strength, might, power, force
grin' salt[106,107,108]	said of a hawk or vulture circling aloft	kuanzama: float, swim in the air
guff, guffer[109]	baloney; empty, foolish, misleading talk	nkufukila: inventions; made-up, created stories
gula mu-antu-mu-la[110]	Obeah worship formula used in Florida	ngula muandamuka: the life force has changed, altered (become something else by its own force)
gumbo[111]	southern dish of okra, corn, butterbeans, etc.; gumbo soup, gumbo ball, gumbo file, gumbo French	kingumbo, tshingombo: okra
gunger[112]	gingerbread, ginger pone	kanja: ginger root
guyascutus[113]	imaginary monster	kuyisakula: make trouble, be deranged, out of order, out of tune; pull at something,

shake and buffet at the
same time, "worry" in
dog-fashion

H

haberdidie[114]	turkey buzzard	*nbabididi:* first one to arrive on the scene, one who takes the lead (to the carrion?)
han[115]	magic charm worn for good luck	*-handa:* escape, be rescued from death or danger
hershel[116]	call coaxingly, as a dog	*-hotesha:* coax, entice, allure
hinkty, hincty[117]	a white person; snobbish, pompous, overbearing, aloof person	*mpingi:* one who curses, damns
holla ding[118]	expression used in work songs	*halua dinga (dituku):* when another (day) comes
hulla-balloo[119,120]	noise, uproar, disturbance	*halua balualua:* when come those that are coming
hully-gully, hull da gull[121]	children's game of guessing how many nuts, stones, etc. are hidden in the closed hand	*-halakala:* compare; set one alongside the other for comparison
hunnah, [123,124] hoonah[122]	you, you-all	*henu, wenu-henu:* you, you-all, your, yours

I

ile me bade[125]	grease my mouth! (folklore expression)	*ela mbedi!* me first! pour me some

J

jambalaya[126]	Creole dish of tomatoes, onions, shrimp, etc.	*tshimbolebole:* dish of tender cooked corn
jazz[127]	music originating with blacks in New Orleans	*-jaja:* cause to dance, make dance
jazz-bo[128]	fancily dressed, "hep," sharp person; male black	*kujabo:* they dance
Jenipee[129]	name of voodoo spirit addressed in prayer	*ntshina mpidi:* I fear mourning; I fear widowhood
jiffy[130]	in a moment, in a short time	*(mu tshitupa) tshipi:* in a short time, in just a moment
jiga, jigger[131]	flea, sandflea	*njiga:* sandflea

jiggaboo, ziggaboo[132]	an African American (derogatory, disparaging, and offensive word)	*tshikabo:* they bow the head servilely, give in docilely, assent too readily (an "Uncle Tom")
jit[133]	a black person (derogatory)	*tshita:* shackles, handcuffs, manacles, symbols of slavery
jive[134]	baloney, bull, insincere talk, anything to be ignored; misleading talk	*tshivuma:* noise of talking, sound of loud voices (cf. Wolof: jev)
joggling-board[135]	see-saw	*-jukula:* to lift again, pick up again
janky-board, jinky-board		*-juka:* rise up, ascend, go up high
"John de Conqueror"[136]	root used for medicinal and conjuring purposes	*tshianda:* place where evil spells are cast, place for sorcery; *-kankila:* tremble with fear
jovy[137]	"let's we be jovy," let's get along, be of one accord	*tshiovo:* an accord, a pact; a friendly gathering, convention
juba, jubilee[138] pat juba	black dance; clap hands in time	*diuba, juba:* pat, beat the time, the sun, the hour
juba-haltuh[139]	water bucket	*ntshuba hatupu:* I draw water without end, indefinitely, on and on

K

kah! kah![140]	laughing exclamation	*ka ka!:* exclamation of surprise
kalinda, calinda[141]	voodoo dance	*kalanda:* renown, fame, notoriety
kalunga[142]	the sea; place of the dead	*kalunga:* the sea; death, the grave, destruction, fate[143]
kangaroo[144]	word used in voodoo incantations in connection with cat rituals	*kangalu!:* purr, growl (imperative)
kia, ki, kiyi[145,146]	exclamation of surprise	*kia!:* exclamation of mild surprise
kook[147]	an unusual, peculiar, insane or very stupid person	*(tshi)kuku:* tree stump; dolt, blockhead

L

lackashoola[148]	word used by Mississippi blacks	*luakajuula:* it put in danger, caused a dangerous accident
lahgin[149]	assume self-importance, put on airs	*-laka:* be boastful, proud, a braggart
lallygag[150]	be idle, loaf	*-lalakana:* wander about aimlessly, be a vagabond
limus-cooter[151]	a small malodorous black terrapin, held in contempt by both races[152]	*-lamuisha nkuda:* set (this) turtle aside, detach, separate it from other turtles
loblolly[153]	thick gruel, cornmeal mush mixed with meat	*-lambulula:* cook and cook and cook
loll[154]	lie around, recline	*-lala:* lie down, recline
Lulla Negro talk[155]	special type of slave speech known for continuing to use Africanisms	*Lulua:* river area of Zaire from which many slaves were taken
luluh[156,157]	a respected woman, nurse, understanding, mother-confessor, faithful wife ("My Luluh")	*-lulamatu:* uprightness, faithfulness, integrity, loyalty

M

maaii[158]	the "prophets of maaii" who use water in worship, which takes place beside a creek; patient's clothes doused in running water, which destroys demons (Florida)	*mayi:* water
maduba[159]	mistress	*muena ndumba:* a prostitute
mafoobey[160]	exclamation of amazement	*mufuba:* a bone; *mufube:* lazy bones!
mahaba[161]	used in Savannah area	*mahamba:* special charm for good harvest; spirit trees planted to bring good luck to newborn child
mahoola[162]	silly talk, "hooey," baloney	*mahula:* divulged matters, indiscretions, secrets
malafee, mulafo[163,164]	whiskey	*malafu, maluvu:* palm wine, fermented drink
maldosher[165]	dumplings made of spring onions, cooked with a hambone	*madiaka:* foreign food

mamba[166]	arboreal snake	*mamba, mambamba:* arboreal snake
Mandy, Mande, Monday[167,168]	personal name common in the South	common personal name: *Mande*
marimba[169]	xylophone	*madimba:* xylophone
maulin a bumba[170]	thunder	*mulenda wa mbumba: mulenda,* sorcery, evil spell; *mbumba,* instant, immediate
maum, mauma[171,172]	name for elderly woman, used by children	*mau, mama:* mother, woman
Meta[173]	female personal name	*Meta:* female personal name among Baluba
mojo, carry a mojo[174]	charm, amulet	*muoyo:* life, life-giving power
Moke[175]	generic term for Cameroonian	*Moko:* group of Bantu languages in the Cameroun
mooch[176]	pilfer, acquire by petty thievery	*-umusha:* remove from its place, take away
moola[177]	money	*mulambo:* tax money, offering money, tribute money; gift of an inferior to a superior
mosey, mosey about,[178] mosey along	amble, stroll, saunter	*muonji:* long, trailing vine, winding forest creeper
musojo[179]	deep cooking pot	*musonji:* sauce, juice, gravy
musungo[180]	tobacco	*musungu:* tobacco; water-filled gourd pipe for smoking

N

nana[181]	grandmother	*nana:* grandmother
nanigo, words of nanigo[182]	prayer addressed to Zambi	*-nanyina:* pray to, ask for a debt, make a request of
neighbo[183]	I disagree; no, don't! don't do it; refusal to accept	*ngeba:* I chase away, put to flight, have nothing to do with
nenine[184]	grandmother	*nyinka:* grandmother; *nyina:* his mother
nuka-nuka[185]	enjoying poor health, so-so	*nanku-nanku:* so-so, fairly well, pretty good
nya mpinga[186]	words used in worship formula	*nya mpingu:* (these things) are of the idols, belonging to the fetishes

O

ooanga, wongah[187]	voodoo charm	*buanga:* medicine, charm, fetish
oofus[188]	oaf, blundering person	*ufuas!* drop dead! (slang form)
oonah[189,190,191]	you, your	*wenu:* you, your

P

paluka, palooka[192]	inferior prizefighter; stupid person, oafish hoodlum	*-paluka tshiseke:* have a fit, seizure, convulsion, spasm
pampah, pamper[193]	scolding words: "I'll catch you and make you pamper!" (scare the livin' daylights out of you!)	*-pampa:* be worried, afraid, upset, disquieted
penepne[194]	wild plum, hog plum of the low country	*penyapenya:* grimace, show the teeth with distaste, sourness
peola[195]	a very light-complexioned black girl	*-peula:* peel off, remove the outer skin, make bald
peruse[196]	conduct someone along the road, escort	*-peluja:* move along slowly, deliberately; *peluja njila:* sweep the path, wielding the broom in a regular pattern of extensions
piggin[197]	small cedar pail with one panel extended for a handle	*mpika:* measure quantity by means of a container
pinda, pindar[198]	peanut, ground nut	*mpinda:* peanut, ground nut
plat-eye, plat-eye prow[199]	animal-like quality of the ghost that scratches at the door; malevolent supernatural being thought to haunt the Georgetown area of South Carolina	*palatayi:* scratch like a dog at the door
"play the dozens"[200]	slander one's or another's parents	*mpala disonguela:* I refuse the slander
poke[201]	bag, sack, wallet, purse pocket	*(tshi)poko:* sack, deep bag; cavity, socket
pompasset[202]	ostentatious person	*mpampa:* I have mastery over; I am the ruler of, in charge of
poon tang[203]	sexual intercourse with a black female or a mulatto	*mu ntanga:* under the bed
poots[204]	"you young poots won't listen to nothing!"	*-putuka:* to be a worrywart, cause trouble

proaged[205]	proaged on through the woods	*-pokola*: furrow through, make a path through, channel, dig through
pull fodder[206]	give birth to	*-pula mfunda*: lay down, put down the small, round box always carried by woman in childbirth
pyo[207]	admonitory cuff or slap	*piol*: sharply, exceedingly hard, stingingly

Q

| Quananmina[208] | personal name in Georgia Sea Islands | *kuanamina*: remain a long time in the same situation, circumstances |

R

| ruckus[209] | informal, noisy commotion, rumpus | *lukashi*: sound of applause, loud cheering, clapping shouts |

S

segashiate, segaciate[210]	fare, do, get along	*-sakisha*: get along, push along, make progress; be in harmony, put in tune
semolia[211]	a stupid, idiotic person	*-zemuna lute*: slobber at the mouth
shag-lag,[212] shack-alack-alack	social talk, conversation	*tshiakulakula*: social talk, conversation, chatter
shulalay[213]	July 4 celebration in Charleston, South Carolina	*tshilele*: custom, habit, usual practice; pleasantries, cutting up, clowning
"si-maye a mans of monkeys"[214]	Daddy Cudjoe's incantation while making a charm	*Tshimunayi manza mukishi!*: put the spirit to flight with all haste!
sisure[215]	a chicken	*nsusu*: a chicken
stepney[216]	hunger	*nsheti*: shuffle, drag or slide the feet because of hunger, exhaustion, or weakness
swanga[217]	conceit, self-love	*-sua*: love, desire, esteem; *kudisua*: self-love, conceit
swobble[218]	eat hurriedly, gulp down one's food	*-zabala*: stuff the cheeks, cheeks protruding, bulging with food

syllabub,[219],[220] sillabub	foamy, frothy drink	*nshila-mbuba:* leave me the bubbles; *mbuba:* substance beaten soft by whipping

T

tabby, tabi[221]	building material composed of oyster shells, lime, sand, and salt water	*ntaba:* muddy place from which mud for building walls is taken
tchombe, chombo[222]	beat a drum	*tshiomba:* beat it (the drum)
tiguili-tigewala[223]	words of a voodoo song, sung by the charm-maker	*tshikudi:* charm used by sterile women in hopes of conceiving; *tshikuata:* take hold of it, grab it!
ting and ting[224]	exactly alike	*tshintu ne tshintu:* each thing
toby, tobe[225]	amulet, charm, talisman	*ntobe:* in order that I not worry, that I be not fearful
too-la-loo[226]	words of a song	*tulualua:* we're coming!
tote[227]	carry, pick up	*-tota:* lift a burden down from one's head without help; carry, pick up
Tumba walla,[228] Bumba walla!	words of voodoo chant, sung during ceremony	*Ntumba walua! Mbombo walua!:* Ntumba come! Mbombo come! (Luba ancestral names)
tush[229]	malicious, dangerous person; wealthy, influential person; mulatto, light-skinned African American	*-tuisha:* cause to have power over, make efficacious

U

unnah[230]	to drink	*-unua:* drink
une, unna, wunna[231]	you, your	*wenu:* you, your

V

vip a vop[232]	"Don't vip a vop till I say so!": don't say a word, don't move	*-fipa:* breathe, suck in, draw in a breath

W

wallay-wulloss[233]	exclamation of poignant grief, extreme sadness	*waleulas!:* make me cease to feel such anguish! (from *-leula*, stupefy, anesthetize, cause to be without feeling)
wampus,[234] wampus-cat, wampusjawed, whampus-jawed	imaginary monster; mythical cat with occult powers	*wapampas!:* be troubled, afraid! (from *-pampa*, be afraid, fearful, hesitant, irresolute, perplexed)
wongah, ouanga[235]	charm, fetish; medicine, remedy	*buanga:* charm, fetish; remedy, medicine
wunnuh[236]	for you	*wenu:* you, yours (singular)

Y

yackety-yak, yakitty-yak yakked, yakking[237]	voluble talk, gab, chatter	*yakula-yakula, yakulakula:* gabbing, talking, chattering
yam[238]	red sweet potato	*nyambi:* sweet potato
yatata yatata[239]	idle chatter, monotonous talk	*ya ntata ya ntata:* of the passing moment, only temporary
yeddy[240]	to hear	*nyidi:* I am learning
yent[241]	negative of the verb "to be": is not, are not, was not, did not	*kena:* is not; *kayena:* are not
yinner, yoona, yunner,[242] yunna	you, your, you-all	*yenu:* your, yours (plural)

Z

zanze[243]	musical instrument, finger-piano	*tshisanji:* musical instrument, finger-piano
zombi[244]	supernatural force that brings a corpse to life; ghost, phantom, walking corpse	*Nzambi:* God
ziggaboo, jiggaboo[245]	a black (derogatory, disparaging, offensive word)	*tshikabo:* they bow the head servilely, give in docilely, assent too readily (an "Uncle Tom")

Four

BANTU PLACE NAMES IN NINE SOUTHERN STATES

African place names found in the American South have been largely unexplored in the search for New World Africanisms, yet they are essential to tracing and documenting linguistic Africanisms. In the search for Bantu language retentions, the category of place names is especially important. The distribution of Bantu place names throughout the American South is a testament to the lasting influence of a people, a nation, and their legacy. These place names are widely distributed along coastal areas and rivers, at ports of entry, and in centers of population (see map 5). They represent possible areas of Bantu influence and settlement and provide possible clues to the location of early plantation sites. Their predominance suggests a critical mass of Central Africans serving as the vehicle of language transmission, dispersal, and acculturation.

The number of African place names in the American South originating from Zaire and Angola in Central Africa are as follows: Alabama 28, Georgia 18, Florida 31, Mississippi 14, North Carolina 26, South Carolina 104, and Virginia 26. That the largest number of Bantu place names are found in South Carolina suggests that more Bantu-speaking Africans were enslaved in South Carolina.

African Americans are known for a propensity to name all of the places with which they associate, including streams, hills, small communities, even alleyways. Stewart, in his historical account of place naming in the United States, says frankly and pointedly:[1]

> Pinder Town in South Carolina preserved the Kongo *Mpinda* (peanut), but white men probably did the naming after the word had become current in local speech. Doubtless many hundreds of small streams and swamps were named by Negroes, but their meanings cannot be distinguished.

Reference to this trait is found in *Names in South Carolina,* a periodical publication of the Department of English of the University of South Carolina. An unusual

This material is from Winifred K. Vass, *The Bantu Speaking Heritage of the United States* (Los Angeles: Center for Afro-American Studies, UCLA, 1979), 41–65, with revisions by Vass. Used by permission.

instance of Edisto Island nomenclature was brought to Vass's attention by Chalmers S. Murray, author and native of the island. Murray noted that the Sea Island Negro was most fertile in naming everything, giving particular names even to the narrow saltwater drains or gutters interlacing the marshes when they are dry at low tide.[2]

A second factor meriting consideration is that Native American place names differ in kind and form from African-American place names. The research necessary for uncovering this body of data began with no preconceived ideas, but as more and more Bantu place-name possibilities came to light and were compared with their Indian counterparts, the distinctive character of the Indian and the African-American names became excitingly apparent.

Native American place names deal almost totally with nature, whereas African-American place names deal consistently with human or social situations. William Read, author of Indian place-name studies for the states of Louisiana, Alabama, and Florida, says:[3]

> The vocabulary of Indian placenames is limited in scope, consisting largely of designations of animals, birds, fish, soil, reptiles, watercourses, plants, trees, settlements, and prominent features of the landscape. Some popular elements, for instance, in Choctaw placenames are *bok* or *bog* (creek), *hacha* (river), *oka* (water), *chula* (fox), *kinta* (beaver), *sinti* (snake), *tala* (palmetto), *tali* (rock), and *ushi* (cane).

Read points out a second distinctive feature of Native American place names: the use of several elements, often a qualifying adjective which follows its noun. Examples are the Chickasaw-Choctaw term *okalusa* (black water)[4] and the name of the Mississippi town of Nittayuma, originally *Nit-a-yum-ma* (bear yonder).[5]

The map of Zaire indicates a very different trend in place naming. Rather than using objects of nature, society-oriented Africans name their towns with verbs or verbal nouns commemorating significant human experience, emotion, or action. Many place names begin with the grandiose class prefix *tshi-*, which indicates a marked or memorable experience of the action of that verb. Representative, random examples of Bantu place names are Tshifuaka (the great dying, many successive deaths in a short period), Tshimbundu Tshibue (the stolen bundle of cloth), Mudiandambo (ate a small portion), Mulonda Mbuji (followed the goat), Kolema-shika (it really got cold), Kanyinganyinga (sadness), and Bululu (bitterness).

One of the strongest arguments for the authenticity of southern place names as Bantu retentions is that they connote vivid, true-to-life commentary. Many are starkly revealing of the uncertainty, indignity, and backbreaking toil performed by enslaved Africans, while others throw light on the horrors of the remembered enslavement experience. Indicative of Bantu place names is the Angolan town of *Ambuila*, where the decisive Portuguese battle against the Bakongo was fought. This name is the applied form of the verb *ambula* (pick up, lift up a burden *for someone else*), implying the forced labor of a slave situation. A few place names, if read closely, disclose the rare African-American gift for character discernment that sees through sham and is capable of enjoying a bit of sly, camouflaged fun-poking at the "master."

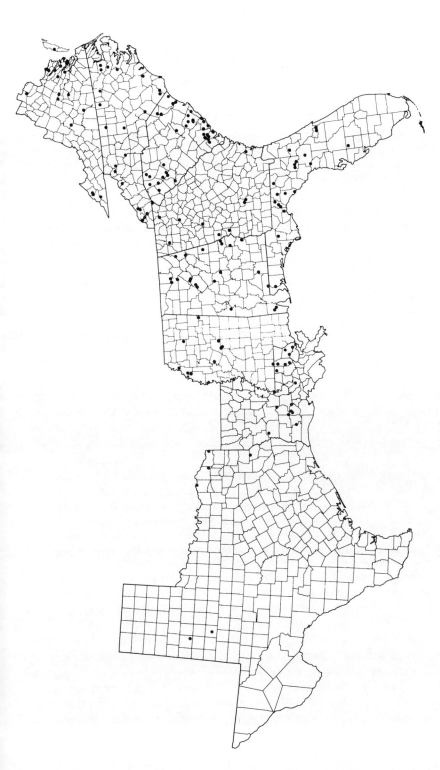

Map 5.   Location of Bantu Place Names in Nine Southern States

A third factor that supports the Bantu origin of southern place names is the historical fact of extremely close black-Indian relationships. It is possible that this physical amalgamation was accompanied by some linguistic amalgamation. Some words thought to be Native American may have had Bantu origins. This is especially possible in the Florida among the Black Seminoles.

Many of the places bearing names of Bantu origin are very small towns, according to the list of unincorporated towns in the 1947 edition of *Hammond's New World Atlas*.[6] Responses from a questionnaire mailed to 125 of these small towns having possible Bantu place names indicated that many had lost their United States Post Office status within the past twenty-five years. Such a change would be expected, given trends that have seen a shift of much of the southern rural black population to the urban North. The loss of post offices may support the contention that these towns were originally plantation communities of almost totally black population, perhaps named by a slave still fresh enough from his or her African background to have retained some of the Bantu lexicon.

ALABAMA

The number of place names in each state varies greatly because each state has had a distinctive pattern of slave importation. Alabama provides a happy hunting ground for Bantu place names (see map 6) because of Read's *Indian Place Names in Alabama* (1934a), indicating names of dubious Indian origin, and because of the comparatively recent slave arrivals in that state. Like the Sea Island area of Georgia and South Carolina, Alabama continued to smuggle slaves long after abolition because they were essential to the economy. According to an Alabama guidebook,[7]

> At Plateau is Africky Town, a settlement of Negroes, descendants of the last shipload of slaves brought to the South. Though the importation of slaves had become illegal after 1807, a brisk smuggling trade continued. The War Between the States was threatening when the ship, *Clothilde,* arrived in Mississippi Sound from the Guinea Coast with a cargo of Negroes. Under the direction of Captain Tim Meaher, wealthy slave trader, she was run up the Mobile River at night, the Negroes hidden in the delta marshes, and the ship burned. But Meaher found it difficult to dispose of his cargo. A few were sent to upriver plantations and some were put to work on the fortifications at Mobile, but the rest were left to shift for themselves. From this group has developed the present community.

The majority of the *Clothilde* group settled in Pritchard, Alabama. The town was known by whites as Pritchard but was also called Africatown because of the large African community. Today in the heart of Africatown there is a statue of Cudjoe, a member of the *Clothilde* cargo, who died in 1958 close to 130 years of age. Today Pritchard's name has been officially changed to Africatown USA in honor of those Africans from the *Clothilde* who settled the area and their descendants, who still live there.[8]

MAP 6.   Alabama

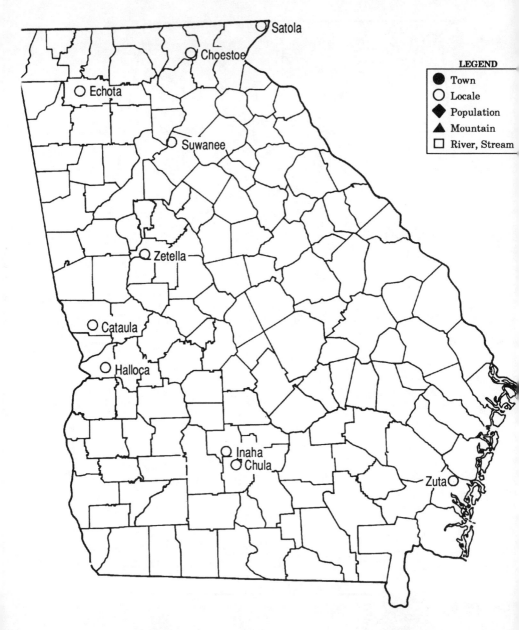

MAP 7. Georgia

GEORGIA

The present state of Georgia was the only one of the British colonies to prohibit slavery during any part of its early history. Founded as a military colony, it prohibited slavery "since it was desired that all men brought into the colony should bear arms and no Negro slave was ever allowed a gun." Thus no slaves were imported during the first twenty years after the founding of Georgia as a colony.[9]

When the importation of Africans did begin in 1755, the proportion of Africans brought directly from Africa increased with the passage of time. Between 1755 and 1798 Georgia imported directly from Africa via Savannah Harbor a total of only 5,369. The ethnic makeup of the Africans imported into Georgia did not follow the South Carolina market as speculated by Curtin.[10] Ethnically and by culture groups the breakdown was as follows: Mande 2,584, Akan 1,087, Bakongo 810, unknown origin 606, Mano River (Liberia), 282, and Ovimbundu 257.

The Mande, Akan, and Bakongo represent the largest groups imported into Georgia. The Bantu arrived between 1750 and 1767, the Mande primarily between 1765 and 1797; the Liberian groups entered in substantial numbers only in 1768. The Mande made up the largest percentage, 45.9, followed by the Akan with 19.3 percent and the Bakongo with 14.4 percent; 10.8 percent were of unknown origin, 5 percent were of Liberian origin, and only 4.6 percent were Ovimbundu.

Georgia prohibited all importation of slaves direct from Africa in 1798, just a decade before the United States passed similar laws. "From that time," Wightman and Cate have written, "all Negroes from Africa were smuggled into the country and kept in hiding until they could be disposed of to plantation owners. The winding creeks and waterways of coastal Georgia afforded ideal landing places for such cargoes."[11]

The conditions under which illegal traffic was carried on were described in the *Savannah Republican* of December 11, 1858: "Corrie . . . went up the Congo and took on a cargo of 750 young Negroes between the ages of thirteen and eighteen. He made another fast crossing and, by prior arrangement, met Lamar on Jekyll Island, at the mouth of the Little Satilla River near Brunswick, Georgia. Lamar had paid $15,000 to the owners of the island for permission to land the cargo. . . . The human cargo was soon disembarked and placed under the charge of old rice-field Negroes, who were nearly as savage as the new importations."[12] This was the famous yacht *Wanderer,* some of whose cargo were still around in the 1930s. The contributions of these more recently arrived slaves to Georgia place names does not seem to have been as well documented as in South Carolina. Map 7 shows place names in Georgia of Bantu origin.[13]

FLORIDA

Florida is unique, with its history of large communities of black freedmen as well as escaped enslaved Africans, all living in happy and close proximity with the Seminole Indians during the years before Florida became a state. As Garvin stated,[14]

Florida first acquired free Negroes in the seventeenth century. In 1704 the Spanish governor, Zuniga, opened the territory to fugitive slaves from the British plantations to the north. Thus established, potential liberty across the border tempted Carolina blacks and tormented their white owners. Georgia was colonized in the hope that it would serve as a buffer region to prevent the escape of slaves to Florida. Carolina benefitted but Georgia, once slaves had been imported, found the runaway problem its biggest nuisance. . . . Spanish correspondence of the period reveals a regular flow of Negroes to Florida. Once in the region, the blacks lived as free subjects of the Bourbon king. They were soon numerous enough to be formed into companies to aid in the defense of the territory. . . . At the same time in the Western parts of Florida, Negroes were immigrating with those fractious Creek Indians, called Seminoles (runaway). Spanish law extended its protection over them and gave the right of land ownership. . . . The Indians had obtained slaves as gifts from the British government or had purchased them for prestige value in imitation of the slave-owning whites. What to do with them once the novelty wore off posed an insuperable problem for the Seminoles. The Negroes, therefore, were allowed to build their own farms and had only to pay a moderate rent in kind to their Indian masters. A type of democratic vassalage was created completely devoid of feelings of racial superiority. Intermarriage was common. Some who possessed a knowledge of English or Spanish became useful interpreters. The most astute gained the confidence of the Indians and served as valued councillors of much influence. When necessary, the males willingly fought alongside the braves for the protection of their homes and their independence. Being free from annoyance, the Negroes worked harmoniously near the Indians. They settled on good land along the Apalachicola and Suwanee Rivers, many owning large flocks and herds.

This was the happy setup until 1816, when the fort built by the British for the protection of the blacks against slave-catching raids was destroyed at General Jackson's command. This was the beginning of the Seminole Indian Wars, which lasted for seven years and finally forced the migration of the Indians, together with their black allies, to Arkansas, Oklahoma, Texas, and Mexico in 1837.

Three Florida place names offer especially interesting opportunities for analysis in the light of the history of the farming and building activities carried on for years by the Black Seminoles, many of them escaped enslaved Africans from South Carolina. The river and the town of Aucila, near the site of old fort, appear on the Taylor War Map of 1838. As with many place names, the spellings vary from map to map. Aucila is spelled variously Assile, Agile, Axille, Aguil, Ochule, Ocilla, and Asile. In *Florida Place Names of Indian Origin,* Read groups Aucilla with place names of unknown origin and meaning. The Bantu verb *ashila* (to build or construct a house for someone else) is a fitting place name for this community of many homes of black settlers and their Indian masters and friends. *Ashile* means "let him build!"

Of the well-known Suwanee River, Read says that "it cannot be translated with certainty, the lack of historical data rendering futile all guesses at the etymology." The large Black Seminole settlement built along this river was destroyed in 1818 in the Seminole Indian Wars. It was called Old Suwany Town on an 1822 map,

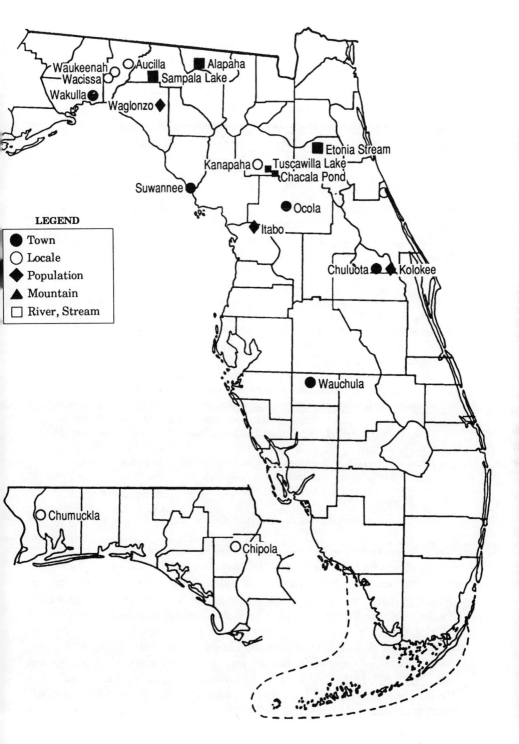

Waukeenah
Wacissa
Wakulla
Waglonzo

Aucilla
Sampala Lake
Alapaha

Etonia Stream

Kanapaha
Tuscawilla Lake
Chacala Pond

Suwannee

Ocola

Itabo

Chuluota
Kolokee

LEGEND
● Town
○ Locale
◆ Population
▲ Mountain
□ River, Stream

Wauchula

Chumuckla

Chipola

MAP 8.   Florida

Suahnee and Suanee on an 1836 map. A suggested solution to the mystery of this name could be the Bantu *nsub-wanyi* (my house, my home).

A third Florida place name of unusual interest is the town of *Chumukla*. The origin of this place name is unclear, according to Read. The Bantu word *tshiumukila* (a motive for leaving, for getting out, for moving on to another place) might be an appropriate and thought-provoking name for a town inhabited by escaped slaves. Map 8 shows place names in Florida of Bantu origin.

MISSISSIPPI

Slavery was introduced into Mississippi by the French in the early eighteenth century. During the period of English control, both the soldiers who received land grants and the Tory refugees "were eager purchasers of slaves to add to the number which the latter group had brought with them," according to Wharton.[15]

> When the government of the United States established the Mississippi Territory in 1798, the region around Natchez, which held the bulk of the population, contained about five thousand whites and thirty-five hundred slaves. . . . There was never any considerable opposition to the continuance of the institution of slavery in either the territory or the state. Furthermore, Mississippi received slavery as a fully matured system and made no contribution of any importance to its theory or practice. The same is true of her reception of the plantation system, which, with its staple crop economy, was immediately established wherever the soil was suitable. . . . The Negro population, of course, was concentrated in the sections where the plantation was the predominant agricultural unit. There the Negro went, willy-nilly, under the pressure of slavery, and there, to a large extent, he remains to this day. This is the equivalent of saying that the best agricultural land of the state had always been cultivated by Negro labor. . . . In addition to the work in the field, the Negro performed the necessary mechanical work on practically all of the plantations. On a large estate, there was generally much specialization of labor, with skilled slaves devoting their time exclusively to carpentry, ironworking, weaving, or the manufacture of shoes, shingles, or bricks.

Mississippi turned up the least number of place names of Bantu origin, probably because of difficulty in locating good bibliographical material on state place-name studies. But several place names are of unusual interest. It was a visit to the Mississippi Delta town of Tchula that first aroused Vass's interest in the possibility of some Bantu mark having been left upon the southern map. Residents of Tchula said that the name of their town was the old Negro word for tadpole or frog, showing that it was not named after the Choctaw word *chula* (fox).

Another fascinating puzzle that the map reveals is a creek which Phelps and Ross (1952) mention in their study of place names along the Natchez Trace: "Bayou Why-i-a (bending white oak) is correctly interpreted, though the Choctaw words might more accurately have been written Baiya waiya, which has become *By WY Creek.*" The striking similarity of the name of this creek with a common Bantu folk

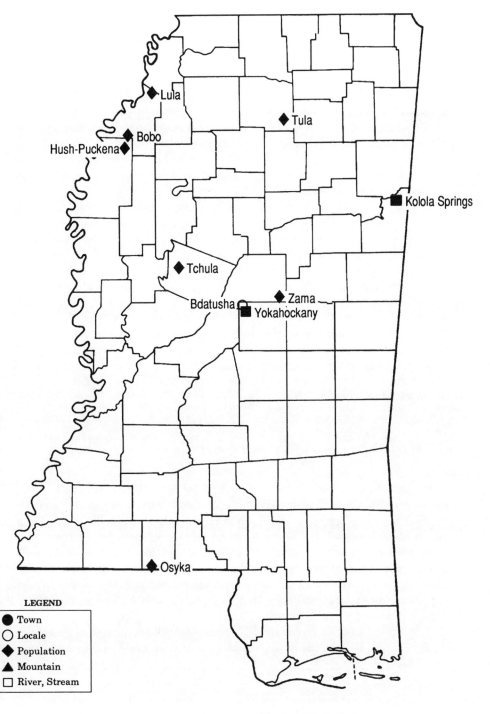

LEGEND

● Town
○ Locale
◆ Population
▲ Mountain
☐ River, Stream

◆ Lula

◆ Tula

◆ Bobo

◆ Hush-Puckena

☐ Kolola Springs

◆ Tchula

Bdatusha ☐ ◆ Zama
Yokahockany

◆ Osyka

MAP 9.   Mississippi

saying must be noted. *Baya-waya* (They go! You go!) is always said at a parting of the ways, when one person takes leave of another and goes in a different direction. This is so common a piece of Bantu folk culture that one cannot but wonder if it did not survive intact, perhaps through Choctaw-black relationships. At the time of the writing of the WPA guidebook to Mississippi in the 1930s, the population of Mississippi was 50.2 percent African American, a fact indicative of *some* black linguistic influence, at least![16]

The Natchez Trace study of Phelps and Ross offers another interesting place name: "In many Southern towns, the district where Black household servants live is *Shakerag*. Even though it does not appear on maps, it is as truly a place-name as Courthouse Square."[17] Remembering that the Bantu letter *a* is pronounced like *a* in *father,* it suggests that *Shakerag* is the Bantu word *tshiakalaka* (social conversation; getting together to talk and gossip). An interesting confirmation of this is found in Hurston's *Mules and Men,* when someone entering a group says, "Awright, lemme git in dis shag-lag." This means, "Let me get in on this conversation," *tshiakalaka* again being the Bantu word involved.[18]

Correspondence with an elderly resident of Zama, Mississippi, revealed that the small town was named for the beautiful young daughter of the white Franklin family, owners of a large sawmill operated in that area for many years.[19] As in the case of Chlota, Alabama, a town named for a Miss Clark, it may be suggested that Zama was Miss Franklin's original Bantu basket name given to her by her "mammy," which went with her through life. Whether from the Hausa root word *zama* (good luck), the Bantu-Kongo root word *-zama* (settle), or the Bantu-Luba root word *zama* (upright, erect), it is a good name. Map 9 suggests place names of Bantu origin found in Mississippi.[20]

NORTH CAROLINA

North Carolina does not offer as fertile a field for place-name searching as other southern states. The history of blacks in North Carolina must be constructed from meager and unsatisfactory materials, and to an even greater extent this is true of the history of its slave trade.[21] One characteristic peculiar to the North Carolina slave trade helps to account for this paucity of records. A large number of enslaved Africans were brought into the colony by land rather than by water, and for these there are no reports comparable to customs entries or naval officers' lists. Direct importation from Africa was comparatively light, possibly because of the lack of good harbors and a central port.[22]

Correspondence concerning the place name *Makatoka* is interesting because of the light it may shed on the process by which a comparatively recent Bantu name was acquired.[23]

> Your inquiry as to how *Makatoka* got its name was given to my mother for a reply. She was the last Postmaster at *Makatoka* before it was discontinued in the early

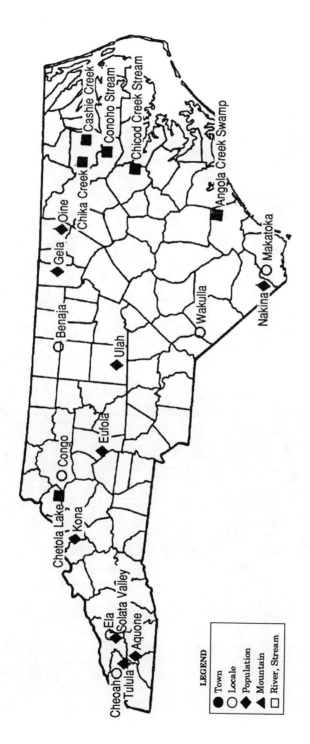

LEGEND

● Town
○ Locale
◆ Population
▲ Mountain
□ River, Stream

Cheoah
Tulula
Ela
Solata Valley
Aquone

Chetola Lake
Kona

Congo
Eufola

Benaja
Ulah

Gela
Oine
Chika Creek

Cashie Creek
Conoho Stream
Chicod Creek Stream

Wakulla

Angola Creek Swamp

Nakina
Makatoka

Map 10.   North Carolina

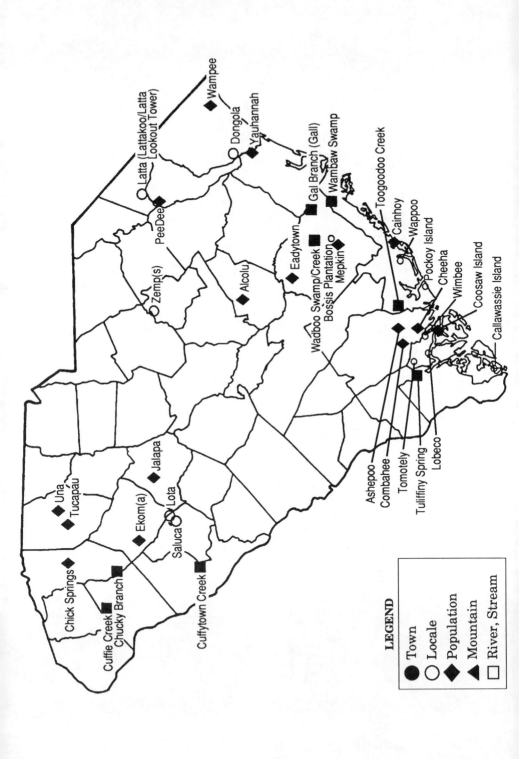

LEGEND

● Town
○ Locale
◆ Population
▲ Mountain
□ River, Stream

Wampee
Latta (Lattakoo/Latta Lookout Tower)
Dongola
Yauhannah
PeeDee
Zemp(s)
Alcolu
Eadytown
Gal Branch (Gall)
Wambaw Swamp
Wadboo Swamp/Creek
Bossis Plantation
Mepkin
Toogoodoo Creek
Cainhoy
Wappoo
Pockoy Island
Cheeha
Wimbee
Coosaw Island
Callawassie Island
Una
Tucapau
Jalapa
Ekom(a)
Lota
Saluca
Chick Springs
Cuffie Creek
Chucky Branch
Cuffytown Creek
Ashepoo
Combahee
Tomotely
Tuliffiny Spring
Lobeco

30's. We are at a loss to give you the origin of the name. We know the place was called Boston in the middle 1800's with the name *Makatoka* being adopted before 1900. Around the turn of the century most of the land in the area was purchased by a group of investors from New York. A small town was established for their logging operation. It was the typical setup with railroads through the swamp. . . . The town has disappeared with only pine trees remaining.

In Bantu we find the phrase *mua katoka* (in the little white man's town). If blacks were among those employed in the logging operations, a fact more than likely, their possible nickname for the small town established by the investors may have been heard often enough to be attached to it. Map 10 suggests place names of Bantu origin in North Carolina.[24]

SOUTH CAROLINA

Because of South Carolina's primary role in the slave trade it is not surprising to have found 104 Bantu place names. The search was aided by the University of South Carolina's *Names in South Carolina*, which provided a wealth of place-name material.

Remarks by Mannix describing the nature of the South Carolina slave trade are pertinent:[25]

There was an eager, at times almost frantic, demand for slaves in the rice colonies, and the total listed importation into South Carolina for the years between 1733 and 1785–only 45 years in reality, since the trade was suspended during the Revolution–was 67,769 Negroes. . . . Charleston as a busy port was visited by more of the big Liverpool Guineamen. That explains why so many of the imported slaves–about 36 percent–came from Angola or the Congo and hence were presumably Bantus. The Liverpool captains bought slaves where they were plentiful and sold them where they would bring the highest prices. Charleston prices were usually high, and the captains came to regard it as another West Indian island. The fact seems to be that Charleston, settled in part by Barbadians, long retained an island mentality; the rice planters of the neighborhood were more Carolinian than they were American. . . . The colonial import trade in slaves reached its climax in the ten years (1764–1773) that followed the French and Indian War. It was a time when rice and indigo were booming crops that required more and more labor. From November 1, 1772, to September 27, 1773, more than eight thousand Africans were landed in Charleston alone.

Map #11 indicates a clustering of Bantu place names in the Sea Islands along the coast of South Carolina as well as distribution throughout the state.[26]

VIRGINIA

Virginia was the first colony to acquire slaves, but it never imported them in the wholesale fashion of South Carolina. According to Donnan,[27]

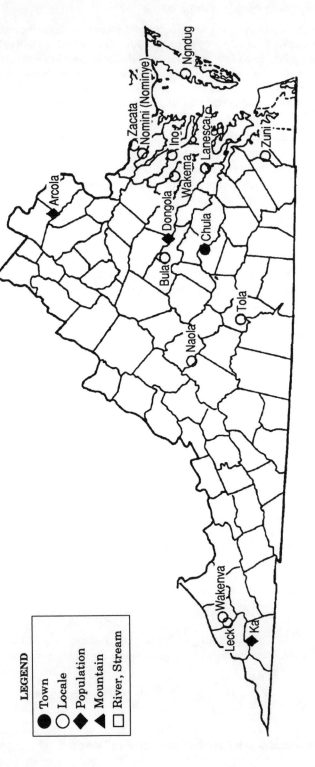

MAP 12. Virginia

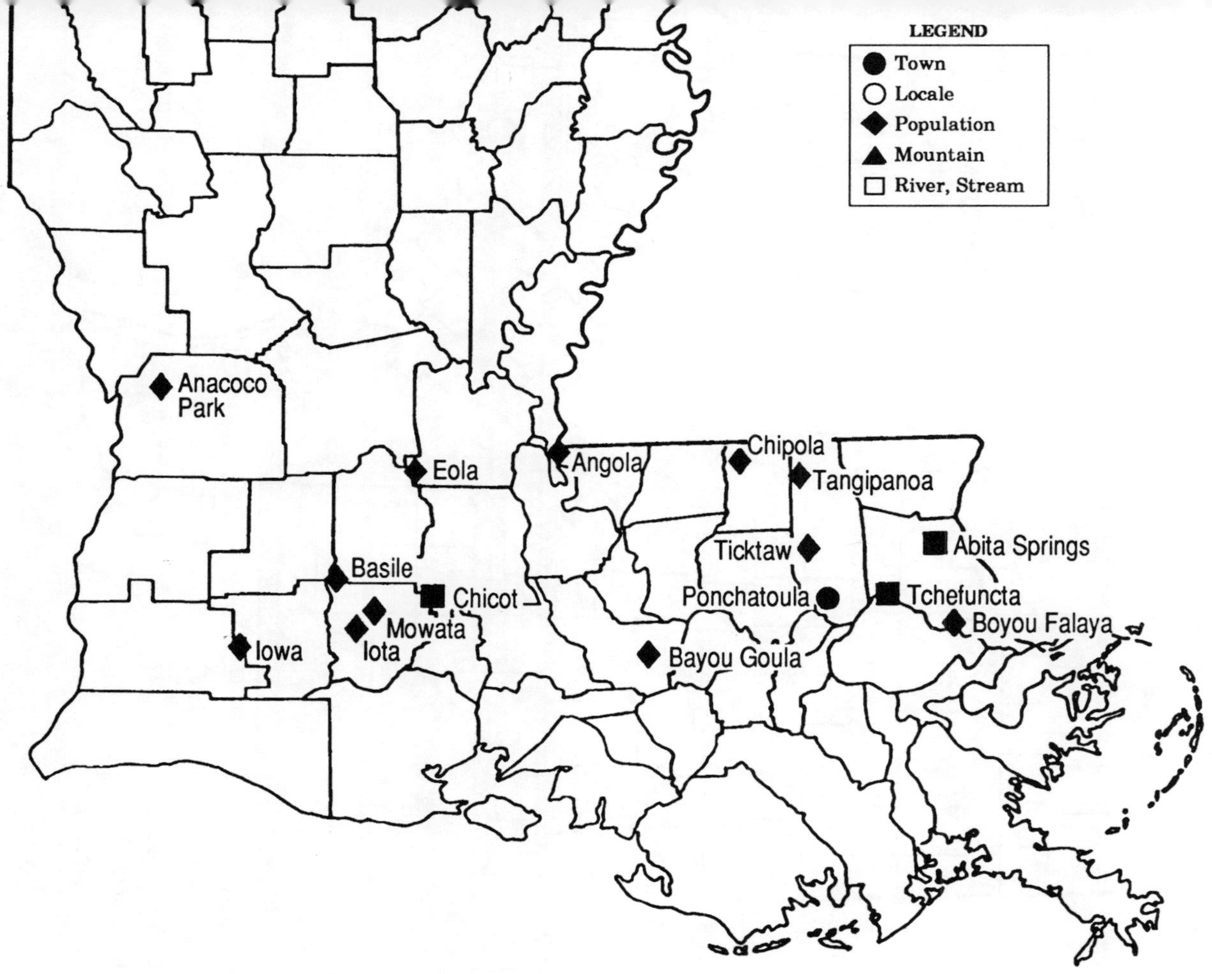

MAP 13. Louisiana

LEGEND
- ● Town
- ○ Locale
- ◆ Population
- ▲ Mountain
- □ River, Stream

Abita Springs
Tchefuncta
Boyou Falaya
Tangipanoa
Chipola
Ticktaw
Ponchatoula
Bayou Goula
Angola
Eola
Chicot
Basile
Mowata
Iota
Iowa
Anacoco Park

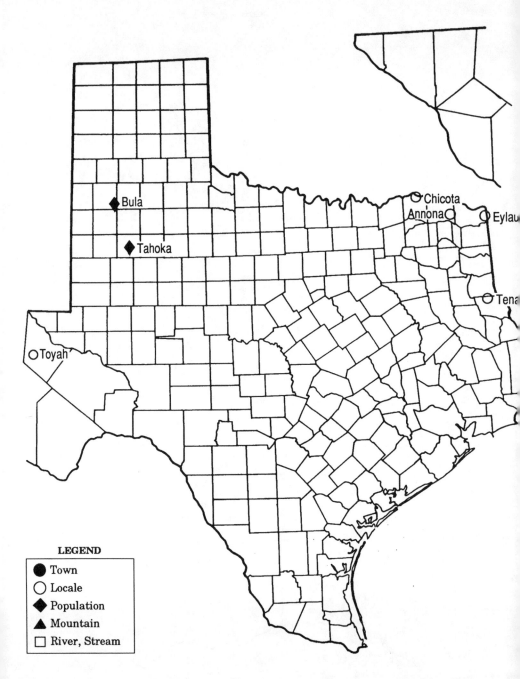

LEGEND

● Town
○ Locale
◆ Population
▲ Mountain
□ River, Stream

MAP 14.   Texas

Our knowledge of the first introduction of negroes into Virginia rests upon the concise, oft-quoted, and much-discussed statement of John Rolfe: "About the last of August (1619) came in a dutch man of warre that sold us twenty Negars." This brief record has been the subject of many conjectures, but little positive knowledge can be added to it. . . . There is today little chance of determining whether the landing of the first twenty negroes in Virginia was part of some abortive colonial project on the part of a group of Englishmen or merely the accidental venture of an unnamed Dutch trader. . . . The arrival of this group was not followed by immediate negro importation into Virginia, though abundance of laborers and large profits in tobacco may well have been connected in the minds of the planters. Not until after the Restoration, when England herself had actively entered the slave trade, did a Virginia importation large enough to be significant come into existence. . . . Despite the habitual neglect of the colony by English purveyors of slaves, the negro population of Virginia slowly grew. . . . That the history of the slave trade to Virginia has heretofore consisted in large part of an account of the efforts of the assembly to impose duties, prohibitive or otherwise, results partly from the fact that the acts of the Virginia legislature and the action of the Board of Trade was easily obtainable, while other significant material relating to the subject is elusive. A second reason is undoubtedly that many writers on this subject have been interested to demonstrate the early and persistent antipathy of Virginia to the trade.

Map 12 shows place names of Bantu origin to be found in Virginia.[28] Also see maps 13 and 14 for Louisiana and Texas.

A

Abita Springs, LA[29]	a bita	of handcuffs, manacles
Acca, VA[30]	aka!	common excl. of surprise
Akwetiyi, NC[31]	akuetu	from our place, just like home (Powell: "The meaning of the name is lost")
Alapaha, FL[32]	alue papa	let him come here (to a safe place) (Read: "Alapaha is obscure")
Alcolu, SC[33]	alakana	hope for, long for, desire exceedingly (freedom?)
Ambato, AL[34]	ambata	lie on top of each other, be piled up, packed one on top of the other, bodies crowded together (as in the hold of a slave ship) (questionnaire response: no idea of origin)
Ampezan, SC[35]	ampeje	let him give to me
Anacoco Park, LA[36]	anuekoku	let him drink here
Angola, LA[37]	Angola	African coast from which majority of Bantu slaves were shipped
Angola, NC[38]	Angola	African coast from which great majority of Bantu slaves were shipped
Annona, TX[39]	nona nona	be envious of another's possessions sharpen, file

	nona	
	mukaji	court a woman
	anone	3rd person imp., "let him be envious, etc."
Aquone, NC[40]	akuone	let him scrape, scrub, plane, shave off (sawmill or carpentry work)
Arcola, VA[41]	akula	talk, speak (imp.) (Hanson: derivation unknown)
Ashepoo, SC[42]	ashipe	let him kill
Attakulla, SC[43]	atuakuile	let him intercede for us, speak on our behalf
Aucilla, FL[44]	ashile	let him build, construct (a house) for someone (Read: "Its meaning is unknown")

B

Basile, LA[45]	bashile	let them build, construct for others
Bayou Ngula, LA[46]	ngula	strength, life force
Becca, SC[47]	beka	exaggerate, go beyond the bounds
Beetaw, SC[48]	bita	handcuffs, manacles, shackles used in slavery
Bena, VA[49]	bena	the people of (such and such a place) (Hanson: derivation unknown)
Benaja, NC[50]	benzaja	made to work, forced to labor
Bobo, MS[51]	bobo	they, them (Bobo was an early plantation settlement with a population of 110 in the 1930s; the disjunctive pron. was probably the only needed reference to the white masters and owners)
Bogue Falaya, LA[52]	falaya	to menace, threaten
Bolatusha, MS[53]	balua-tshisha	they make you, cause you to be dressed, wear clothing
Boyano, SC[54]	mbuy'enu	your friend
Boo-Boo, SC[55]	mbubu	imbecile, stupid person
Booshopee, SC[56]	bushipi	murder, killing
Bossis, SC[57]	botyshisha	be beaten down, trampled upon
Bula, TX[58]	bula, n.	open space in front of a house
Bula, VA[59]	bula, v.	peel (vegetables); husk (corn)
Buquo, NC[60]	buko	in-law relationship, wife's parents
By-Wy, MS[61]	baya-waya	They go—you go (common Bantu folk saying when parting)

C

Calwasie, SC[62]	kaluatshi	short battlefront, line formed for the chase
Caneache, SC[63]	kenaku	he isn't here
Canehoy, SC[64]	kenahu	he isn't here

Cash, VA[65]	Kasha	Kasai area of Zaire place name; species of antelope (Hanson: derivation unknown)
Cashie River, NC[66]	kashia	river eel
Cashua Neck, SC[67]	kashia	river eel
Cataula, GA[68]	katuulua	he never comes (absentee master?)
Chacala, FL[69]	tshia kale	from ancient times, of long ago (Chacala is a small pond near Payne's Prairie, Gainesville, a site of great prehistoric interest)
Chachan, SC[70]	tshiatshia-kana	not know what to do, where to turn for help
Cheaha, AL[71]	tshiahu	a working group, as a field gang or family group that works together as a unit (no Indian meaning is given)
Chebash, SC[72]	tshibasu	chieftain's seat (symbolic block of wood on which chief sits)
Cheeha, SC[73]	tshipa	make a vow, curse
Chennba, GA[74]	tshiema	an albino, a white
Cheoah, NC[75]	tshiowa	waterfalls; wild duck
Chepasbe, SC[76]	tshipese	any small portion, piece, bit broken off or taken from the whole
Chetola, NC[77]	Tshitola	place name in Lubilaji Valley, Luba-Kasai area of the Zaire (Chitola is also found in Florida)
Chetopa, AL[78]	Tshitupa	a Zaire place name; a small portion, a little bit
Chewacla, AL[79]	tshiwakula	whatever it is you are speaking (may be a reference to some difficulty in understanding English instructions; no Indian meaning is given)
Chiahao, SC[80]	tshiahu	working group, field gang; family that works together
Chichessa, SC[81]	tshitshenza	big doing, important event, happening
Chick, SC[82]	tshika	guard, keep a secret (imp.)
Chicod, NC[83]	tshikata	length of hippo hide, used as whip for disciplining slaves by caravan leaders and slavers (also found in North Carolina, Texas, and the southeast corner of Arkansas)
Chicot, LA[84]	tshikata	whip used by slavers
Chicota, TX[85]	tshikata	whip used by slavers
Chinch Row, SC[86]	tshinji	bug, insect
Chipola, AL[87]	tshipola	great harvest, abundant reaping (Read: "Chipola bears a formal resemblance to Choctaw *chepulli* [feast, great dance] but may be derived more plausibly from Creek *hachapala* [on the other side of the stream]") (also found in Florida and Louisiana)

Chipola, FL[88]	tshipola	great harvest, abundant reaping (Read: "I can think of no absolutely convincing etymology for Chipola")
Chipola, LA[89]	tshipola	great harvest, abundant reaping
Chiquola, SC[90]	tshikole	strong, well; grown, mature.
Chiska, NC[91]	tshisaka	large market basket
Chitola, FL[92]	Tshitola	place-name in Lubilaji Valley, Luba-Kasai area of Zaire (Read: "I connect this name very doubtfully with Choctaw")
Chlota, AL[93]	tshilota	a dream, important omen to all Africans (Read identifies the name of this town as "Pseudo-Indian." It was named for a certain Miss Clark. Since this is not a typical English name, it is suggested that this may have been the "basket-name" given Miss Clark by her "Mammy")
Choestow, GA[94]	tshiotu	an accord between differing ethnic groups; confederation, alliance
Chota, SC[95]	tshiota	the clan, extended family group
Chukky, SC[96]	tshuki	don't answer, don't reply, be close-mouthed (imp.).
Chula, VA[97]	tchula	frog
Chula, GA[98]	tchula	frog (chula is the Choctaw word for "fox")
Chuluota, FL[99]	tshilota	a dream (important omen to all Africans)
Chumukla, FL[100]	tshiumukila	a motive for leaving, for getting out, for moving on to another place (Read: "The origin of Chumukla, in spite of the late appearance of the name, is far from being clear")
Chunchula, AL[101]	tshutshulu-ka	to be held back, restrained, retarded (Read: "All attempts to trace this name positively to a Choctaw source will prove fruitless")
Coatopa, AL[102]	kuatupa	to give them to us (rations or supplies?) (no Indian meaning is given)
Cofitachequi, SC[103]	kufitshishi	don't allow to pass over, don't let cross over to the other side, go over the boundary
Colee, FL[104]	kole	strong, well, powerful (Read: "The name is modern and may not be Indian") (The imp. v. is often pronounced for emphasis with an elongated final syllable: Kolee! [become strong, powerful, great!])
Combahee, SC[105]	kombahu	sweep here (imp.)
Conecuh, AL[106]	kuneku	right here, to this very place (Read: "If Conecuh is Creek, it may be compound of koha [canebrakes] and anaka [near]. If Choctaw, it may be from Choctaw kuni [young canes] and akka [below])

Congo, AL[107]	Kongo	name of Bantu group that occupies the area where the Zaire River flows into the Atlantic
Congo, NC[108]	Kongo	name of Bantu group that occupies the area where the Zaire River flows into the Atlantic
Conoho, NC[109]	konoko	right here, to this place
Coosabo, SC[110]	kusabo	they shake their heads, say "no"
Coosa, SC[111]	nkusa	louse, lice
Cooterborough, SC[112]	nkuda	turtle, terrapin
Cotaco, AL[113]	kotaku	split wood (firewood, kindling, fence rails) (imp. form of Bantu v.) (Read: "May be a corrupted form of Cherokee *ikati* [thicket] and *kunahita* [long].")
Cotaquilla, AL[114]	kutuakuila	to intercede for us, speak on our behalf (Read: "May mean dead honey locusts, from Creek, *katowa* [honey locusts] and *ili* [dead]")
Cuakles, SC[115]	kuakulas	to talk, converse (slang form)
Cubee, FL[116]	kubi	don't wait, don't tarry (a swamp in Jefferson County; runaway slave hideout?)
Cuffee Town, SC[117]	kufi	don't die
Cuffie Creek, SC[118]	kufi	don't die
Cumbee, SC[119]	nkumbi	large, wedge-shaped, slit drum beat on both sides

D

Dibidue, SC[120]	ndubilu	it is quickness, speed
Dongola, VA[121]	ndongola	I fix, prepare, work on
Dongola, SC[122]	ndongola	I fix, prepare, work on

E

Eady Town, SC[123]	idi	they are (common form of v. to be)
Echota, GA[124]	a tshiota	of the clan; belonging to the extended family group
Ekoma, SC[125]	ekoma	finish up, come to an end
Ela, NC[126]	ela	cast, throw, pitch; pour, pour out
Elasie, SC[127]	elasha	cause to pour, pour out; cause to throw
Eola, LA[128]	ewila	to hoe, scratching only the surface
Etonia, FL[129]	itunua	that which we drink (a creek in northern Putnam County, on the Taylor Map of 1839 spelled It-Tunwah) (Read: "no support in Creek or in Choctaw.")

Eufaula, AL[130]	uhaula	loot, pillage, plunder (Read: "Eufaula cannot be translated") (Indian uprisings were common here in the early 1800s; the name, originally Irwinton, was changed when mail went to Irwinton, Georgia; the new name was taken from a branch of the Creek Confederacy that had, as Heard has shown, a large black population)
Eufola, NC[131]	upola	is calm, at peace, settled down
Eylau, TX[132]	elau	pour it out

F

Flouricane, SC[133]	mvula ikenya	a storm is threatening
Fulemmy Town, GA[134]	fulama	dry up, contract, wither (like tobacco leaves; perhaps a community of old people?)

G

Gall, SC[135]	ngala	an embankment; raised walk between two flooded fields; a dam constructed in a river or stream for fishing purposes (Horse Gall, Cane Gall, Spring Gall, Dry Gall all found in South Carolina)
Gela, NC[136]	ngela	(I am) casting, throwing, pitching, pouring
Gippy or Jippy, SC[137]	tshipi	short; *tshitupa tshipi*: in a short time, in a jiffy

H

Halawaka, AL[138]	halawuka	take the initiative, take the lead, proceed to act (questionnaire response: this is a small creek; the community no longer exists; no idea of origin)
Halloca, GA[139]	haluka	faint, be unconscious; have a fit, seizure
Hoot Gap, SC[140]	huta	drag, drag away something very heavy, such as trees from a cleared area (imp.)
Hulaco, AL[141]	huluka	have the skin rubbed off, hands scraped from lifting heavy burdens
Hushpuckena, MS[142]	husha mukana	blow on with the mouth, as coals for cooking

I

Inaha, GA[143]	hinaha	right here, at this very place
Ino, VA[144]	inanyi	my mother (Hanson: derivation unknown)

Iota, LA[145]	nyota	thirst
Iowa, LA[146]	yowa	to be thin, emaciated from hunger
Itabo, FL[147]	itaba	answer, reply, speak up (imp.) (Bloodworth: "perhaps a corruption of Creek *italwa* [tribe]")

J

Jalapa, SC[148]	shalapa	remain here (imp.)

K

Ka, VA[149]	ka!	common excl. of surprise
Kalona, AL[150]	Kalonda	place name in Kuilu area of Zaire, from which many slaves were taken (questionnaire response: no longer a community; no idea of origin)
Kanapaha, FL[151]	kena papa	he isn't here (Read: "Owing to the complete lack of any local information about Kanapaha, my translations of this name must be taken purely as guesses") (this area was often searched by owners of runaway slaves who met with little response or information about escapees from local residents!)
Katala, AL[152]	katala	a very common Luba-Kasai personal name
Kecklico, SC[153]	kekelaku	ignore, demean, deliberately snub (imp.)
Kemah, TX[154]	kema	be amazed, astounded
Kiowa, AL[155]	kuyowa	to be famished, weakened with hunger, exhausted.
Kissah, SC[156]	kisa	hate, be cruel, vicious, sadistic (imp.)
Kolokee, FL[157]	kuoloki	don't stretch out, expand, unfold (remain in your cramped position) (this is a settlement in Seminole County homesteaded by slaves)
Kolola Springs, MS[158]	kolola	to spread out, smooth out, open out, extend
Kona, NC[159]	kona	grind, file, plane, sharpen, scrape (imp., carpentry or metalwork).
Kushia, AL[160]	kushia	to leave, leave behind
Kushla, AL[161]	kushala	to stay, remain behind when others leave (Read: "This place name is considered locally to be of Indian origin, perhaps Choctaw *kusha-hieli* [standing reeds]")

L

Ladiga, AL[162]	ladika	lay down, cause to lie down (Read: "This name is said to be that of a Creek Chief, Ledagie")
Lanexa, VA[163]	langesha	cause to make even and smooth, as a foundation site for a house or a roadbed (imp.)
Lattakoo, SC[164]	luataku	get dressed, put on clothes (imp.)
Leck, VA[165]	leka	stop!
Loango, AL[166]	luangu	sweat, perspiration
Lobeco, SC[167]	lobaku	steal, take by stealth, nibble away at (imp.)
Loblolly Bay, SC[168]	lambulula	distill, extract (turpentine, liquor, etc.)
Lota, SC[169]	lota	dream (imp.)
Lula, MS[170]	lula	be bitter, refuse to obey, be refractory

M

Makatoka, NC[171]	mua katoka	in the little white man's town
Malpus Island, SC[172]	mapusa	gun wadding
Mamon, LA[173]	mamu' anyi	my mother
Mayna, LA[174]	mena	names
Mazyck, SC[175]	majika	finished, completed
Mepkin, SC[176]	mapeku	shoulders
Mobjack, VA[177]	mombejaku	beat the drum!
Mowata, LA[178]	mwata	chief
Muckawee, SC[179]	'muka wee!	get out! get gone! scram!
Mump Fuss Row, SC[180]	mumpas!	give it to me! (slang form)

N

Nakina, NC[181]	nuakina	hate, be cruel to, be mean to (pl. imp.); ngakina: I am hating, being cruel to
Nandua, VA[182]	nendue	I will come
Naola, VA[183]	neulue	you will come
Nenemoosha, AL[184]	nenumushe	you will remove, take somewhere else
Nominye, VA[185]	numanye	that you may know, be warned
Nyota, AL[186]	nyota	thirst

O

Ocala, FL[187]	okola	drag off, drag out, haul (terminology of heavy labor) (Read: "Ocala cannot be translated")

Occola, GA[188]	okola	remove, extract an object from the fire (as baked yam from the coals, or metal object being forged)
Oine, NC[189]	wine	soak, immerse, dip; dye (imp., work with cassave, indigo, or plants requiring soaking)
Onemo, VA[190]	unema	be weighted down, be heavy to bear, have a burden to bear
Oniseca, SC[191]	anyishaku!	traditional Luba-Kasai greeting
Oshila, SC[192]	oshila	set fire to, burn up for someone else
Opopome, SC[193]	apopome	let him be blind
Osyka, MS[194]	oshika	burn up, catch on fire

P

Palachocolas, SC[195]	palua tshikole	when the strong one comes
Palawana, SC[196]	palua wanyi	when mine comes
Parachucla, SC[197]	palua tshikulu	when the old one comes
Peedee, SC[198]	mpidi	dark cloth worn during mourning, during time that all sexual relations are banned
Picola, GA[199]	mpikula	redeem me from slavery, free me
Pindar Town, SC[200]	mpinda	peanut
Pockoy Island, SC[201]	mpoko	frankness, truth, sincerity
Ponchatoula, LA[202]	pa tshitulu	a burden carried around the neck or astride the shoulders
Pooshee, SC[203]	mpuishi	one who always completes his tasks

Q

| Quaqua, NC[204] | kuakua | there, over yonder |
| Quocaratchie, SC[205] | kuokolatshi | to remove a heavy object, such as a log, from the forest |

S

Saluca, SC[206]	saluka	be in disorder, society all disrupted, upset, in turmoil
Sampala, FL[207]	sampula	to splash, splash water at, play in the water (a lake in Madison County) (Read: "Sampala may be connected with Seminole *sampa* [basket], but this etymology seems to me to be very uncertain")
Satolah, GA[208]	sotola	extract, pull out from where inserted (terminology of heavy labor, as pulling up tree roots during road construction)

Sauta, SC[209]	saula	weep, cry aloud
Shakerag, MS[210]	tshiakalaka	social conversation, gossiping, talking together
Shiminally, SC[211]	jiminayi	get lost, disappear from sight (imp.)
Shongalo, MS[212]	jonguela	eat your fill, have plenty to eat
Solola, NC[213]	solola	talk, converse together (imp.)
Suwanee, FL[214]	nsub-wanyi	my house, my home (Read: "The name Suwanee, however, cannot be translated with certainty, the lack of historical data rendering futile all guesses at its etymology")
Suwanee, GA[215]	nsub'wanyi	my house, my home

T

Tahoka, TX[216]	tauka	be cast off, shed, as leaves off a tree
Talloka, GA[217]	taluka	be troubled, distraught, without peace of mind
Talucah, AL[218]	taluka	be troubled, emotional, grieved, worried (Read: "I have not been able to obtain any reliable data on this name of modern application")
Tangipapo, LA[219]	tangila papa	look here!
Tchifuncle, LA[220]	tshifuku	clan, family
Tchula, MS[221]	tchula	frog
Teckle-gizzard, SC[222]	tukulukaji	numbness in limbs from circulation cut off by tight bindings, ropes, chains
Tenaha, TX[223]	tendaha	wail, cry, mourn here
Tichkfaw, LA[224]	tukupa	we give you
Tola, VA[225]	ntola	species of antelope; tribal totem and personal name among Bena Lulua, Kasai area of Zaire
Tomoka, FL[226]	tumuka	let's get out, let's leave
Tomotely, SC[227]	tumutele	let us name him, mention his name
Toobedoo, SC[228]	tub' etu	our dialect, language, our "Kituba"
Toogoodoo, SC[229]	tukuta	we are satisfied, filled (with food)
Toyah, TX[230]	toya	shell or husk, as rice or corn
Tucapau, SC[231]	tukupau	we give it to you
Tula, MS[232]	tula	forge, beat out iron, shape or make metal by hammering
Tullifinny, SC[233]	tula mfinu	pull off, pluck off undeveloped ears of corn, undeveloped peanuts in farming
Tulula, NC[234]	tulula	take down, put down, let down (imp.).
Tuscawilla, FL[235]	tusawila	let us pay tribute to, render homage to (to Seminole chieftains?)

U

Uceta, FL[236]	usheta	walk with heavy feet, trudge along as in a slave caravan (Read: "The meaning of Uceta is unknown")
Ulah, NC[237]	ula	buy, purchase, barter (imp.)
Una, SC[238]	unua	drink, drinking
Untsaiyi, SC[239]	utusadila	serve us, be in servitude to us; wait on us
Upatole, GA[240]	upatule	haul out, shove out, push outside (terminology of labor for moving heavy objects, such as tar barrels or bales of cotton)

W

Wacissa, FL[241]	wakisha	cause to light, catch fire, as a lamp, a pipe (Read: "Its meaning is unknown")
Wadboo, SC[242]	wandapu	place of joking, teasing, relaxed conduct, indiscretions (black community)
Wakema, VA[243]	wakema	be amazed, astounded, wonder at (polite imp.)
Wakenva, VA[244]	wakunvua	you have heard, you have understood
Wakina, FL[245]	wakina	hate, be cruel, be mean to (imp.) (Read: "This is a perplexing name.")
Wakulla, FL[246]	wakula	talking, speaking (Bloodworth: "Another of the Florida names whose original meaning has been lost")
Wakulla, NC[247]	wakula	talking, speaking
Wambaw, SC[248]	wambau	say it
Wampee, SC[249]	wampe	give to me
Wantoot, SC[250]	wa ntutu	place of the elder brother
Wappoo, SC[251]	wapu	give it
Wappaoolah, SC[252]	wapaula	lay waste, pillage, loot (imp.)
Wataccoo, SC[253]	wataku	be naked, without clothing
Wauchula, FL[254]	waujula	raise it up, pitch in, take initiative (Read: "Wauchula is an obscure name. . . . I must admit finally that my translations of Wauchula are not based on sufficient data to be considered authoritative")
Waylonzo, FL[255]	walonza	kill, shoot to kill (imp.)
We Creek, SC[256]	we!	hey, you!
Wedowee, AL[257]	wetu wee	our very own; common Luba expression of greeting used when meeting takes place between long-separated relatives or friends

Weeboo, SC[258]	weba	chase, put to flight, make a fugitive of someone
Weetaw, SC[259]	wetau	ours, our very own
Welona, AL[260]	walonda	follow (polite imp.), follow behind me (Read: "The origin of this name is not clear")
Wende, AL[261]	wende	his (poss.; the master's?)
Wimbee, SC[262]	muimbi	a singer
Wosa, SC[263]	wosa	do, make, produce, prepare (general v. for all types of work; imp.)

Y

Yampanika, TX[264]	ya mpanyika	places for spreading things out to dry in the sun, such as clothing, peas, peanuts, rice (name of a street in Vernon, TX)
Yauhaney, SC[265]	ya uhane	go that you may sell; barter
Yeka, SC[266]	yika	talk, converse, have conversation with
Yoa, SC[267]	yowa	be thin, emaciated, weak from hunger
Yockanookany, MS[268]	yaku nukana	go make a fetish (voodoo charm against someone)

Z

Zacala, VA[269]	zakala	shake, tremble (with fear or because of the cold)
Zacata, VA[270]	zakata	strike against, hurl violently (as in beating an anvil in a forge)
Zama, MS[271]	zama	upright, erect; settled
Zanoni, VA[272]	(mu) sononyi	one who grimaces, has the habit of baring or show his teeth.
	(mu) Jiananyi	my criticizer, my accuser (Hanson: derivation unknown.)
Zemps, SC[273]	zemba	come to a halt, be immobile, paralyzed, unable to do or act for oneself
Zetella, GA[274]	jetela	be languid, have slow bodily movements
Zuni, VA[275]	(mu) sunyi	water-carrier
Zuta, GA[276]	zunta	wring off, wrench off (reference to traumatic break with motherland?)

Five

AFRICANISMS IN CONTEMPORARY AMERICAN ENGLISH

GENERAL VOCABULARY

A

adobe[1]	Twi (Akan), a palm tree, leaves or grass used for roof covering.
ananse[2]	Twi (Akan) and Ewe, spider; Bambara *nansi*, chameleon.

B

bad[3]	Very good, used esp. in emphatic form, *baad*. Cf. Michael Jackson's "I'm baad!" Similar are *mean*, in sense of satisfying, fine, attractive; *wicked*, in sense of excellent, capable. Cf. African use of negative terms, pronounced emphatically, to describe positive extremes: Mandingo (Bambara) *a ka nyi ko-jugu*, it's very good! (lit. "it is good badly!"); Mandingo (Gambia) *a nyinata jaw-ke*, she is very beautiful! Also West African English (Sierra Leone) *gud baad*, it's very good!
bad-eye[4]	Threatening, hateful glance. Common African-American colloquialism. Cf. Mandingo *nyejugu*, hateful glance (lit. "bad eye") and similar phrases in other West African languages.
bad-mouth[5]	In Gullah, slander, abuse, gossip; also used as v. Cf. Mandingo *da-jugu* and Hausa *mugum-baki*, slander, abuse (in both cases, lit. "bad mouth"). See *fat-mouth*.
bambi	Bantu *mubambi*, one who lies down in order to hide; position of antelope fawn for concealment (cf. Walt Disney, *Bambi*).
bamboula[6]	African drum, used in New Orleans, nineteenth century. Vigorous style of dancing there, early twentieth century. "Drum" in early jazz use. Cf. Bantu *bambula*, beat, hit, or strike a surface, a drum. Similar terms in other African West Coast languages.
banana[7]	Wolof for the fruit. First recorded 1563; entered British English in seventeenth century via Spanish and Portuguese.

banjo[8]

Kimbundu *mbanza*, stringed musical instrument; whence also Jamaican English *banja* and Brazilian Portuguese *banza*.

be with it[9]

Mandingo expression, to be *à la* (lit. "to be with it, in it"); to be in fashion.

big eye[10]

Igbo *anya uku*, covetous, greedy (lit. "big eye"). Cf. West African and Caribbean English *big yay*, big eye. Same in Gullah and Black English.

bo[11]

Temne and Vai (Sierra Leone), friend; informal term of address for an equal. West African and Caribbean English *bo, ba*.

bogue, bogus[12]

Hausa *boko, boko-boko*, deceit, fraud. West African English (Sierra Leone) *bogo-bogo*, Louisiana French *bogue*, fake, fraudulent, phony. (Could ending of *bogus* have an analogy with *hocus pocus*?)

booboo[13]

Bantu *mbubu*, stupid, blundering act; error, blunder. Common nickname found in Black English.

boody[14]

Bantu *buedi*, act of emission, sex. Cf. black American slang: "Give me that booty."

booger[15]

Bantu *mbuka*, divination, consultation of the spirits; ghost, spirit.

boogaboo[16]

Bantu *buka lubuka*, conjure, enchant, divine; consult a medicine man; imaginary cause of fear, worry; nemesis.

boogie (-woogie)[17]

Bantu *mbuki-mvuki*, to take off in dance performance. Hausa *buga* (*bugi* after n. object). Mande *bugs*, to beat, to beat drums. West African English (Sierra Leone) *bogi*, to dance. To dance fast blues music, eight beats to a bar; *boog*, to dance.

bowdacious[18]

Bantu *botesha*, pulverize, grind to powder; extremely, exceedingly, to the nth degree. Cf. Uncle Remus usage.

bozo[19]

Bantu *boza*, knock things over in passing; a strong, stupid person, a stumblebum. Common in black American slang: "Don't be a bozo!"

bree, breigh[20]

Girl, young woman in a number of West African languages: Akan *(o)-bere, bre*, female; Yoruba *obirti*, woman, female; Temne *(o)-bera*, woman, female. See *chick, mat, mouse, pharaoh*.

brer, buh[21]

Mandingo *kçkç*, elder brother; title used before animal names in fables, folk tales. Cf. Uncle Remus usage.

buckaroo, bucker[22]

See *buckra* (2) and section on Cowboy Culture.

buckra (1)[23]

Efik and Ibibio *mbakara*, master. Used by enslaved Africans to refer to and address their masters. By 1730s, enslaved Africans and colonists used it to mean "white man." Often pronounced and spelled *buccara* and *boccra*, by 1775 it had come to mean "gentleman" and even, by 1860s, the color "white."

buckra (2)[24]

Poor or mean white man, now rare in U.S. except South Carolina Sea Islands. Still current in Jamaican English. Convergence with Spanish *vaquero*; hence *buckaroo, bucker* (cowboy).

bug (1)[25]

Mandingo *jito-bag*, enthusiast; Wolof *hipi-kat*, man, fellow. Mandingo *-baga* and Wolof *-kat* are agentive suffixes, indicating persons. The compound words, denoting a person as the final element, have become *jitterbug* and *hepcat*. Cf. also West African English *baga*, fellow. Cf. convergence with English *bug, bugger, cat*. See *jitter-(bug)* and *hep, hip*.

bug (2)[26]   Mandingo *baga*, to offend, annoy, harm (someone); Wolof *bugal*, to annoy, worry. Note also West African and Caribbean English *ambog*, to annoy; this form pronounced in eighteenth century with stress on second syllable, may reflect the nominal prefix *m-* in Wolof *mbugal*, hindrance, annoyance. The same element may be contained in British and American English *humbug*, to hoax, impose upon.

bug (3)[27]   Mandingo *baga-baga* and Susu *bog-bogi*, termite, white ant, insect. Cf. West African English (Sierra Leone) *bog-bog*, (Liberia) *bug-aboo*, termite; also black Jamaican English *bug-aboo*, insect. The African term, recorded on West African coast by European mariners in seventeenth century, appears to have converged with English *bug(aboo)* or *bogy*, thus stimulating its shift in meaning to "insect." *Bug*, meaning "insect," is more commonly used in U.S. than in England.

C

calenda[28]   Voodoo dance performed in New Orleans in nineteenth century. See section on Dance.

cat[29]   Person, man, fellow, "a cool dude." See *hep, hip*.

chance[30]   Bantu *tshianza*, hand, handful; a certain number, several.

chickama[31]   Bantu *shikama*, sit, sit down; *shikamaku*, sit down here. Cf. song that accompanies children's game: "Chikama, chikama, chime crow! Chick-ma-chick, mah craney crow!"

chick[32]   Girl, pretty young woman, one especially "hip," or attractive. Cf. Wolof *jigen*, woman. Note convergence with English *chicken*. See *bree, mat, mouse, pharaoh*.

chigger[33]   Wolof *jiga*, insect, sand flea. Recorded 1743, via Caribbean. Originally pronounced and spelled *chigo, chego*, or *chiego*.

chinch-bug[34]   Bantu *tshishi*, bug, bedbug, insect, worm, fly, caterpillar.

chinchy[35]   Bantu *tshinji*, anger, wrath, meanness. Cf. "chinchy person," someone irritable, impatient, and stingy.

Congo[36]   A person from the Kongo region of Central Africa. First used in North America 1790.

coob[37]   Bantu *-kuba*, care for, take care of, watch over; a hutch, pen, or coop for fowls or small domestic animals: a chicken "coob."

cool[38]   Mandingo cool, slow and *gone not;* hence fast. Terms applied to music and dancing: calm, controlled, slow tempo and the opposite, hot, fast, and energetic. Corresponding terms found in other African languages.

cooter[39]   Kongo *nkuda*, a box turtle. Also West African *kuta*, turtle, use recorded 1832. Came into southern U.S. dialect via Gullah heard mainly in Georgia, South Carolina, Alabama, and Louisiana.

cuffy, cuffee, cuff[40] — Akan *Kofi*, a common personal name for any male born on a Friday. "Black man," used as greeting among Charleston, S.C., African Americans. See chap. two on Akan day names.

D

dashiki — Yoruba *danshiki*, a loose, colorfully patterned, buttonless pull-on shirt. Garment and word were introduced during civil rights movement of 1960s, when young black men wore dashikis to reassert their identity with African culture.

day-clean[41] — Bantu *kutoka kulu*, dawn, "clean sky"; Wolof *ba set na*, it has dawned (day is clean); Mandingo *dugu jera*, it has dawned (day has become clean, clear). Found in Gullah, West African and Caribbean English *do-klin*, day-clean, and black Caribbean French *ju netye* (lit. "day-cleaned").

dig[42] — Wolof *deg, dega*, understand, appreciate, pay attention to. Convergence with Black English to "dig," understand.

dinge[43] — Mandingo *den, din*, child, young person, younger than the speaker. *Den-ke*, male child, young man. A black person, *dingey*; a black child, *dinkey*. (Baltimore, now obsolete?)

dirt[44] — Akan *dôte*, earth, soil. Common in U.S., as in "dirt road" or "dirt track." West African and Caribbean English *doti*, dirty, earth. Convergence with British English in its original sense of "filthy."

doll-baby[45] — Yoruba *omo langidi*, little child; *oyedeji*, wooden images. Southern dialect idiom common in Black English, distribution mainly along Atlantic Coast.

do one's thing[46] — Mandingo *ka a fen ke* (lit. "to do one's t'ing"), to undertake one's favorite activity or assume one's favorite role.

done[47] — Wolof *doon*, past completive marker, "he done go"; Mandingo *tun*, past completive marker. Cf. also black West African English *don*, as past completive marker. Convergence with English *done*.

F

fat-mouth[48] — Mandingo *da-baa*, excessive talking (lit. "big, fat mouth"). See *bad-mouth*.

foo-foo[49] — Akan *foforo*, new, fresh, strange. An outsider, a newcomer, one who does not belong or is not accepted, a fool, a worthless person. Convergence with English *fool*. Cf. black Jamaican English *foo-foo, fool-fool*, credulous, easy to take advantage of, stupid.

fuzzy[50] — Wolof *fas*, horse (*fas wi*, the horse, *fas yi*, the horses). "Horse" in two specialized senses: "range horse" and "sure bet at a horse race." Hence, perhaps, *fuzz, fuzzy*, policeman, from an earlier use of horse patrols. Convergence with English *fuzzy-tail*.

G

gam[51]	Hausa *gama,* boastfulness, showing off.
geechee[52]	Liberian county called Kissi. Mende *gidzi.* Originally meant an African from the Guinea coast. Later it meant a black who was not yet acculturated in American culture. In 1789, applied to Africans brought to Ogeechee River plantation under coercion to become acculturated as southern Americans.
goober[53]	Bantu *nguba,* peanut; use recorded 1834. Another word for peanut is *pinder,* or *pindal,* from Congo *mpinda,* peanut; use first recorded in Jamaica 1707, South Carolina 1848.
goofer-bag[54]	Bantu *kufwa,* to die; v. common to all Bantu languages. A charm to protect from death.
goofer-dust[55]	Bantu *kufwa,* to die. Refers to grave dirt. In Congo (Zaire), earth from a grave is considered at one with the spirit of the buried person. Used by root workers on American plantations.
goose[56]	Wolof *kus,* anus. To nudge someone in the anus. (Originally from Arabic?)
gris-gris[57]	Object worn as protective charm against evil, or used to inflict harm. An amulet in place of and with the power to remove voodoo curses. Associated with voodoo rites in Louisiana. Used by Marie Laveau, noted voodoo queen. She concocted a *gris-gris* of salt, gunpowder, saffron, and dried dog dung. A *gris-gris* that protected from evil or brought good luck was a dime with a hole in it, worn about the ankle. Mende in origin, via Hausa.
gullah[58]	Bantu *Ngola,* an ethnic group in Angola. Refers to African Americans living in the Sea Islands and regions of South Carolina, Georgia, and northern Florida. Also refers to their language.
guff, guffer[59]	Bantu *nkufukila,* inventions, made-up stories, tall tales. Empty, foolish, misleading talk; "baloney." One who talks in this manner.
guy[60]	Wolof *gay,* fellows, persons. Used as a term of address, including "you guys," addressed even to a single man or woman. Convergence with English personal name Guy.

H

he (1)[61]	Undifferentiated third-person sing. pron., he or she. Similar usage is found in most West African and in all Bantu languages, as well as in most forms of black West African and Caribbean English. In Gullah, *he* remains undifferentiated, referring to either a male or a female. For reverse African influence in differentiation between second-person sing. and pl. pron., see *you-uns.*
he (2)[62]	Mandingo *a bolo,* his hand (lit. "he hand"). Undifferentiated poss. pron. for "his." Cf. similar lack of differentiation in other pron. usage and lack of genitive after n. Similar constructions are found in a number of West African languages.

hear[63]

Mandingo *n mu a men,* I didn't understand (lit. "I didn't hear it!"), hearing in the sense of understanding. Cf. similar application of v. meaning "to hear" in other West African languages.

hep, hip[64]

Wolof *hepi, hipi,* to open one's eyes, to be aware of what is going on. Hence *hipi-kat,* someone with eyes open, aware of what is going on. See *bug* (1) and *cat.*

honkie[65]

Wolof *honq,* red, pink; color used to describe white men in African languages. Cf. also *pink,* a white man, and *redneck,* a poor white farmer, in U.S. In black slang, *honkie* referred to whites who would come to the black community, park, and honk their horns for their dates. Evidence is required of use of this term for "white man" before 1960s.

hoodoo[66]

Hoodoo, as opposed to *voodoo,* is less centrally organized as part of voodoo religious practices. It generally connotes the mystic and magical aspects, usually evolved for negative purposes. "To hoodoo someone" implied that an individual was made to do something against his will by the use of various concoctions, which could be drunk, eaten, or worn, in order to make someone fall in love or to cause a death.

hulla-balloo[67]

Bantu *halua balualua,* when those that are coming arrive. Hence noise, uproar, racket of greeting.

hully-gully[68]

Bantu *halakala,* compare (the hands, to ascertain the one holding the rock). Children's game.

J

jam[69]

Informal gathering of jazz musicians, playing for their own entertainment. Same element may be contained in *jamboree,* noisy revel, celebration, a full hand of cards, first recorded in 1860s. Possible convergence of Mandingo and black West African English *jama* (from Arabic), crowd gathering, and Wolof *jaam,* slave (in U.S., a gathering of slaves or former slaves for their own entertainment). A related Wolof term is *jaambuur,* freeman, freed man.

jamboree[70]

Celebration by emancipated slaves. See *Juneteenth* in section on Celebrations.

jamboree[71]

See *jam.*

jazz[72]

Bantu *jaja,* to make dance. Obsolete forms *jas, jasy.* The numerous applications of this term center on basic v. sense of "to speed up, excite, exaggerate, act in an unrestricted or extreme way." Note corresponding use as n. and as adj., "jazzy." Applied to copulation, frenzied dancing, fast music, exaggerated talk, gaudy patterns and colors, excessive pleasure-seeking. Cf. Mandingo *jasi,* to become abnormal or out of character, either diminished or excessive. Cf. similar Wolof *yees* and Temne *yas,* to be lively or energetic to an extreme degree, applied to exaggerated styles of dancing or music, excessive love-making, etc.

jelly, jelly-roll[73]	Mandingo *jeli,* minstrel, who often gained popularity with women through his skill in the use of words and music. A virile man who curries sexual favors of women. Epithet applied in U.S. to several black musicians, including "Jelly Roll Morton" (piano), "Jelly" Williams (bass), and "Jelly" Thompson (guitar). Convergence with English items of food, jelly and jelly-roll.
jenk[74]	Bantu *njika,* reserve, reticence, inhibition. "To spread my jenk": relax, have a good time.
jiffy[75]	Bantu *tshipi,* short. In a second, in a moment.
jigger[76]	Bantu *njiga,* sand flea, insect.
jiggaboo[77]	Bantu *tshikabo,* they bow the head docilely. Derogatory term for black person. In Black English a jiggaboo is someone who is extremely dark, with strong African features, as opposed to high yellow, or light-skinned.
jitter-(bug)[78]	Mandingo *ji-to,* frightened, cowardly, from *ji,* to be afraid. *Jito-baga,* a frightened, cowardly person. To tremble and shake, have "the jitters"; nervousness, fear, cowardice. *Jitter bug:* an excited swing addict, who shakes and trembles in dancing.
jive[79]	Wolof *jev, jew,* to talk about someone in his absence, esp. in a disparaging way. Misleading talk; to talk in a misleading or insincere way. Applied to sexual and musical activity. Cf. semantic range of *jazz.* Convergence with English *jive, jibe,* to sneer at, disparage.
john[80]	Mandingo *jon,* slave, a person owned by someone else. An average man, esp. one who can be exploited or easily taken in; a male lover, a prostitute's client. Also used in black American folklore, as in John Henry, name of hero-slave frequently in conflict with "massa." The term *massa* provides a convenient convergence of English *master* and Mandingo *massa,* chief. That Mandingo speakers in U.S. were conscious of this convergence is suggested by the cycle of black American tales involving John-versus-Massa, which corresponds to a similar genre of Mandingo tales in West Africa involving *jon,* the slave, versus *massa,* the chief.
juba (1)[81]	A group dance with complex rhythmic clapping and slapping of knees and thighs, as done by plantation slaves (1834). Both dance and word are of African origin.
juba (2)[82]	One of the earliest records of the term *juba* dates to American minstrelsy days. Both Juba and Jube consistently appeared as names of enslaved Africans who were skilled musicians and dancers.
juba (3)[83]	Bantu *juba, jiouba,* or *diubu,* to beat time rhythmically. Used to describe an African dance step, the Charleston; recorded particularly in South Carolina and West Indies. Juba is also the Akan female day name for a child born on Monday.
juba (4)[84]	Traditional slave food. Refers to the food that enslaved Africans working in the plantation house collected from the massa's leftovers. Such leftovers were called juba, jibba, or jiba. On

Saturday or Sunday the leftovers were thrown together; no one could distinguish the meat from the bread and vegetables. This juba was placed in a huge pot and those working in the Big House shared it with those working in the fields.

juba (5)[85]

Bantu *nguba, kingooba,* peanut, groundnut, "goober," from which an old African melody is derived. The Juba dance was originally performed on plantations but became so popular that whites gave it the name Charleston, after the southern city and major slave port. The dance was introduced in 1926 to the American stage in an all-black production by E. F. Miller and Aubrey Lyles entitled *Runnin' Wild,* and as the "Charleston" it became the dance craze of the 1920s.

juke[86]

Wolof *dzug,* to misbehave, lead a disorderly life; Bambara *dzugu,* wicked. Brothel, cheap tavern, low dive. Mainly Gullah and black use in South. *To juke* (1939), to make the rounds of taverns and low dives, go drinking; used mainly by southerners. By early 1940s *to juke* came to mean "to make the rounds drinking and dancing to jukeboxes" (1939). *Juke joints,* taverns or roadhouses that featured jukeboxes. *Juke Juke-joint,* a hand-out bar. Cf. also Bantu *juka,* rise up, do your thing.

ju ju[87]

Bantu *njiu,* danger, harm, accident. A charm or fetish against such.

K

kakatulu vai[88]

Bantu *kukatulu,* to take off, remove; v.i., to be still, immobile. Name of a large bird, mockingbird.

kelt, ketch[89]

Bantu *kelekeja,* filter, strain; catch the drippings, pale stuff. A light-skinned black person.

kickeraboo[90]

The Americanism "to kick the bucket" evolved from *kickeraboo* and *kickatavoo,* killed or dead. Term has two African sources: Krio (the English-based Creole of Sierra Leone) *kekrebu, kekerabu,* dead, to wither (as leaves or fruit); and Ga (West Africa) *kekre,* dry, stiff, and *bo,* to befall, end. "Kicking the bucket" was used in American blackface minstrel songs, regarding the death of a black person, until about mid-nineteenth century, when it moved into Standard American English.

kill[91]

To affect strongly, as in "you kill me!" Similar usage in a number of West African languages, including Wolof and Mandingo, of verbs meaning lit. "to kill."

kook, kooky[92]

Bantu *kuku,* dolt, blockhead. A strange, peculiar person.

kong[93]

Bantu *nkongo,* mixture, conglomeration. Bootleg whiskey.

L

lam[94]

Igbo *lam,* I go, depart, from *la,* to go. I go (or come); depart quickly, run away, escape. Convergence with English *lam,* to beat, thrash, make a quick escape, flight.

lubo[95] First used in America in 1732 to identify slaves from Niger Delta. Use of African name indicated a first-generation African or a newly arrived "saltwater" African.

M

mahoolu, mahoola[96] Bantu *mahula*, secrets, divulged matters, indiscretions. Silly talk.

man[97] Mandingo *ce*, man, the man; power, authority. Term of address.

massa[98] Mande (Mandingo) *masa*, chief.

mat[99] Hausa *mata* or *mace*, woman, wife. Note also *bree, chick, mouse, pharaoh*. See discussion under *mouse*.

mean[100] Similar to *bad*.

mhm, m-m[101] See *uh-huh*.

mojo[102] Fula *moca*, to cast a magic spell by spitting. Hence *mocore*, magic spell, incantation uttered while spitting. Originally, magic spell, charm, amulet, spell cast by spitting. Mainly used today in sense of something working in one's favor: "I got my mojo working!" Also, narcotics. Cf. Gullah *moco*, witchcraft, magic. Black Jamaican English *majoe, mojo*, plant with renowned medicinal powers.

moola, mula[103] Bantu *mulambo*, receipts, tax money. Money, wealth. Cf. Black English "give me some moola!"

mother yo'mama[104] West African, esp. Wolof; used as term of severe abuse or of jocular abuse between friends. Includes use of explicit insults, such as "motherfucker." Note similar but less frequent use of *father*.

mouse[105] Mandingo *muso* and Vai *musu*, woman, wife. Attractive girl, young woman, girlfriend, wife. Convergence with English *mouse*. Of several terms for "woman" taken over into Black English from major West African languages (see also *bree, chick, mat, pharaoh*), no less than three are listed together by Mencken (1936) as jazz terms for "girl," although he had no realization of their African origin.

O

ofay, oofay, fay[106] White man. Extended form: *ofaginzy*. O- occurs as a nominal/adjectival prefix in many West African languages. Term for "white," beginning with "f," also occurs widely: *Bama fe, Gola fua, Ndob fowe*, etc. It has been suggested that *ofay* represents a rearrangement of the letters of the English word *foe* into pig Latin, but from its form, the word is more likely to have an African origin.

okay (1)[107] Mandingo *o-ke*; Dogon *o-kay*; Djabo *o-ke*; Western Fula *eeyi kay*; Wolof *waw kayk, waw ke*, all meaning "yes, indeed!" "that's it, all right." Note widespread use in languages of West Africa of *kay* and similar forms as confirmatory markers, esp. after words meaning "yes." Recorded use of *oh ki*, indicating surprised affirmation, in black Jamaican English 1816; predates by over twenty years the popularization of *OK* in white speech of New England. Affirmative use of *kay-ki* in black speech in U.S. is recorded from as early as 1776. Early attempts were made to explain *OK* as initial letters of misspelling of English words "all correct" or as French words *au quai,* on the quayside. Subsequent attempts have been made to derive term from German, Greek, Scots, English, Finnish, and Choctaw, but little consideration has been given to possibility of origin in black speech.

okay (2)[108] Mandingo *o-ke-len,* after that (lit. "that being done"). Use of this syntactic construction is widespread in West African languages. "After that" serves as link between sentences in running narrative or discourse, serving to confirm the preceding and anticipate the following sentence.

okra[109] Bantu *kingombo,* okra. Main ingredient of gumbo. Food plant indigenous to Central Africa and brought to New World by slaves. Known to most southerners by 1780s.

ol'Hannah[110] Hausa *raanaa, laanaa,* the sun.

ona[111] Igbo *unu,* idea.

oobladee[112] Mandingo *abada,* Hausa *abadaa, abadaa-aabaadi,* forever. From Arabic *abadan, abada 1-abadin,* forever. Excl. of resignation to eternity of life. Cf. similar use of black West African English (Sierra Leone) *abadi-abada,* derived from West African languages.

P

palooka[113] Bantu *paluka* (tshiseki), to have a fit, spasm, convulsion. A stupid person; an inferior prizefighter.

pamper[114] Bantu *pamba,* be worried, upset, afraid, disquieted. To scold or "bless out" someone.

peola[115] Bantu *peula,* peel off outer skin. A light-complexioned black girl.

pharaoh[116] Kanuri *fero,* girl. Girl, girlfriend, blues term.

phoney, foney[117] Mandingo *fani, foni,* (to be) false, valueless; to tell a lie. Counterfeit, sham, something false or valueless. Note also *bogue, bogus.*

pin[118] Temne *pind,* to stare at, see. Black West African English (Sierra Leone) *pin,* staring, as an intensifying adv. after v. denoting "to see." Convergence with English *pin.*

pinto[119] Temne *(a-) bentho,* bier for carrying corpse. In South Carolina and Georgia, means "coffin."

plat-eye[120] Bantu *palatayi,* scratch like a dog at the door. Malevolent, supernatural being thought to haunt Georgetown area of South Carolina. Female, animal-like ghost, feared in South.

poke[121] Bantu *-poko,* deep bag, socket, cavity. A sack, bag, wallet. Cf. "a pig in a poke."

poon tang,
puntang[122]

Bantu *mu ntanga,* under the bed. Sexual intercourse with a black person. Sexually attractive (black) woman, vagina. Cf. Lima *puntuy,* vagina. Convergence with French *putain,* prostitute.

poop[123]

Wolof *pup,* to defecate, of a child. Convergence with similar forms in European languages, including Dutch. Cf. Black English *pup pup.*

poor jo, poor Job[124]

Vai dialect word of Liberia and Sierra Leone (1736), heard mainly in Georgia. Colloquial name for great blue heron.

R

rap[125]

West African English (Sierra Leone) *rap,* to con, fool, get the better of someone in verbal play. Descriptive of a variety of verbal techniques: to speak to, greet; flirt with, make a pass (at a girl); speak in a color way; tease, taunt; con, fool. Used also as n. Recently popularized black American usage of *rap* is, in fact, old. Note *to rap,* meaning "to speak or talk."

rooty-toot[126]

Wolof *rutu-tuti,* rapid drumming sound. Old-fashioned music. Also *rootin-tootin,* noisy, boisterous.

ruckus[127]

Bantu *lukashi,* sound of cheering and applause. Informal, noisy commotion, rumpus.

S

sambo[128]

Bantu *-samba,* to comfort, cheer, console. Cf. also widespread West African personal name: Wolof *Samb, Samba;* Mandingo *Sambu;* Hausa *sambo;* similar names among Bantu. Black man, male child, popular southern use of the name. "Little Black Sambo" story appears to be a corruption of a West African folk tale.

say, says[129]

Mandingo *ko . . . ,* say. Similar use of items meaning lit. "say" found in numerous West African languages, black West African, and Caribbean English. Term used to introduce reported speech, "that . . . ," "he tell him, say . . ." Cf. black speech "say, man . . . ," "he says this . . . "

shucking[130]

Bantu *shikuka,* hold the head high, be willful, be obstinate. Lying, bluffing, faking.

skin[131]

Temne *botme-der,* put skin; Mandingo *i golo don m bolo,* put your skin in my hand. Cf. black speech "give me some skin, man!" (shake hands with me!). Used in 1960s by African Americans before it moved into white speech.

T

tabby[132]

Bantu *ntaba,* muddy place from which mud for building walls is taken. Building material composed of oyster shells, lime, sand, and saltwater, commonly used in building slave houses in Georgia and South Carolina.

too-la-loo[133]   Bantu *tulualua*, we're coming! Words of a song.

tote[134]   Kikongo *tota*, to pick up; Kimbundu *tuta*, to carry, load. Black West African English (Sierra Leone) *tot*, Cameroon *tut*, to carry. Similar forms meaning "carry" found in a number of western Bantu languages.

U

uh-huh, mhm[135]   *Uh-huh*, yes; *mhm*, no. Cf. widespread use throughout Africa of similar responses for "yes" and "no." Scattered use of such forms occurs elsewhere in the world, esp. for "yes," but nowhere as regularly as in Africa, where, in many languages, they constitute regular words for "yes" and "no." Note also occurrence of intonational variants of these forms to indicate differing intensities and situations of response, both in African languages and black American English, as well as in black African and Caribbean English. African origin of these items is confirmed by their much wider use in American than in British English.

uuh-uh[136]   No. See *uh-huh*.

V

voodoo[137]   Fon (Dahomey) *vodu, vodun*, fetish, witchcraft; to bewitch. Entered English via black French of New Orleans. See *hoodoo*.

W

wyacoo[138]   Mandingo epithet for a bad but powerful chief. Arabic *Yaqub*, Jacob. Also Yacub, described by Malcolm X as creator of white race. A white racist.

Y

yah[139]   Crebo *ya*, used after commands; Temne *yo*, used after statements or commands. An emphatic concluding particle: "Indeed!" Often said in endearing tone, thus softening a statement or command. Also black West African and Caribbean English *ya*, said after statements or commands.

yam[140]   Wolof *nyam*, taste; Serer *nyam*, eat; Fula *nyama*, eat; black West African and Caribbean English *nyam*, eat. Also Bantu *nyambi*, sweet potato. To eat.

yackety-yak[141]   Bantu *yakula-yakula*, gabbing, chattering, talking. Voluble chatter.

yatata   Bantu *ya ntata ya ntata*, of the passing moment,

yatata[142]

only temporary. Idle chatter, monotonous talk.

you-all

See *you-uns.*

you-uns[143]

You pl.; similar use of *you-all.* Regular differentiation between second-person sing. and pl. pron. in African languages undoubtedly played a part in introduction of comparable differentiation in American English, esp. in South. Reinforced perhaps by differentiated pron. of French and Spanish. Cf. esp. Wolof *yow,* you sing., versus *yeen, yena,* you pl. Hence convergence with *you* in sing. and *you* + *one* as new second-person pl. form. Note first-person *we-uns* by analogy. Cf. black West African and Caribbean English *yu,* you sing., versus *una, unu,* you pl. used in Sierra Leone, Cameroon, Jamaica, and elsewhere. In Gullah, *yu* versus *une,* and in black Guyana English, *you* versus *you-all.*

Z

zero copula[144]

Temne *o bana,* he is big (lit. "he big"). Similar omission of v. *is* in many West African languages.

ziggaboo

Someone extremely dark. See *jiggaboo.*

zombie[145]

Tshiluba *Nzambi,* God, and *mujangi,* spirit of the dead; Kimbundu *nzumbi,* ghost, phantom. Supernatural force that brings a corpse back to life. Cf. black Haitian French *zombi,* black West African and Caribbean English *jombi,* Sierra Leone and Cameroon *jumbi,* Guyana and Jamaica *zombie.*

FOODS

B

benne

See *sesame* in this section.

C

cala[146]

Sweetened rice cake, African in origin, served with morning *café au lait,* formerly sold by black women in French Quarter of New Orleans. In Duala (Bantu) dialect of Cameroon, rice is called *wond' a bakala,* beans of Europeans. In Georgia this sweetened rice cake was called *saraka:* "Yes'um. I membuh how she made it. She wash rice, ann po off all duh watah. She let wet rice sit all night, and put in mawtuhm an beat it tuh paste wid wooden pastle. She add honey, sometime shuguh, add it in floot cake wid uh kams. *Saraka,* she call um." Still a popular dish among southern blacks.

calalou[147]

Thick soup or stew similar to gumbo. Ferdinand Ortiz traced *calalu* to African *colilu,* Mandingo name for plant resembling spinach. In Pointe Coupee, Louisiana, it is a rich soup or stew in which one or more kinds of calalu leaves are the chief ingredients. Name given to several plants having edible leaves, eaten as greens, in soup, or used medicinally. In Suriname, also called *calalu.*

coffee[148]

Word Derived from Kaffa, region in Ethiopia.

cowpeas[149]

Vigna unguiculata, black-eyed peas. Used in southern U.S. by both blacks and whites. Traveled from Africa to North America in holds of slave ships as food for the cargoes.

cush, cushie[150]

Sweet, fried cornmeal cake, first appeared in American English 1770. Gullah *kush* or *kushkush.* Related to Hausa via Arabic *kusha.*

F

fufu (1)[151]

Called "turn meal and flour" in South Carolina. A mixture of cornmeal and flour is poured into a pot of boiling water. From this *fufu* mixture slaves made "hot cake" in fields. This later evolved into "pancakes" and "hotwater cornbread."

fufu (2)[152]

Fufu twi, a little white thing. Common food throughout Africa and New World, consisting of yams, plantains, and cassava root (manioc, tapioca) cut into pieces and boiled together; maize or Indian corn beaten into one mass and eaten with pepper, boiled in a pot with okra. A substantial dish of *fufu* is composed of *eddoes, ochas,* and mashed plantains made savory with rich crabs and pungent with cayenne pepper.

fungi[153]

Kimbundu *fonji, funji,* and *funja; awyola funzi,* cassava mush, made from cornmeal and cassava flour boiled down until it is hard. Often called "corn meal pone" or "musa." Other ingredients, such as okra, may be added. In West Indies *fungu* is a mixture of bananas and coconut milk, to which cornmeal and cassava flour are added.

G

goober[154]

Bantu *nguba,* peanut (recorded 1834). Another word for peanut is *pinder,* from Congo *mpinda.* First recorded in Jamaica 1707, South Carolina 1848. Used as food for cargoes on slave ships. Pinder Town, a place name in South Carolina.

grits[155]

Catesby noted that slaves took hominy (Indian corn) and made grits similar to *eba* eaten in Africa.

guinea corn[156]

Guinea corn (*Sorghum vulgave*), indigenous African crop transported to U.S. by Africans. Catesby noted in 1743 how blacks used it to make bread: "This grain is propagated and that chiefly by Negroes, who make bread of it, and boil it. Its chief use is for feeding fowls. First introduced from Africa by the Negroes."

gumbo[157]	Tshiluba *kingombo,* Umbundu *ochingombo,* okra. By 1805, a soup made of okra pods, shrimp, and powdered sassafras leaves. *Gumbo file* and *gumbo maile* made of pulverized okra (1823). Known to most southerners by 1780s.
gunger cake[158]	Gingerbread originated in Congo and was a carryover by enslaved Africans on plantations.
hop'n johns[159]	Traditional West African dish of black-eyed peas and rice cooked together. Common in black southern cuisine.

J

jambalaya[160]	Bantu *tshimbolebole,* dish of tender, cooked corn. Africa-influenced dish similar to *gumbo,* particular to New Orleans. Brought to Louisiana by Africans from Congo.
jollof rice[161]	Style of cooking red rice brought to American South in 1700s.

M

maluvu[162]	Tshiluba *maluvu,* palm wine. Produced throughout Africa from sap or juice collected from palm trees. African descendants continued to make it in Savannah, Georgia; in South Carolina the palmetto tree is the source. Material called palm cabbage or palmetto cabbage is taken from center of tree and either cooked or fermented for wine.
millet bread[163]	Mentioned as African food provided for cargoes by slavers.

O

okra[164]	*Abelmoschus esculentus,* also called *guibo* and *guimyombo.* Originated in what geobotanists call the Abyssinian (Ethiopian) center of origin. Cultivated in present-day Ethiopia, plateau portion of Eritrea, and parts of Sudan.

P

peanut oil	Use introduced by slaves in American South. African cooks in the "Big House" introduced deep-fat frying, a cooking style which originated in Africa.
pone bread[165]	Naturalist Catesby noted as early as 1739 that slaves made mush from cornmeal and called it pone bread.

R

rice[166]	*Oryza sativa* and *Oryza glaberrimi,* indigenous varieties of rice imported in 1685 from island of Madagascar to South Carolina. Wood (1974) noted that Africans first showed early Americans how to cultivate rice. By 1740s, rice had become a staple in South Carolina.

S

sesame	Benne (sesame) seed, brought by West Africans to South Carolina. Sesame oil also introduced to U.S. by slaves. (See *benne* in section on Crops.)
soul food	Black cuisine strongly influenced by African style of cooking, stemming from slavery period. Soul food goes back to days when plantation owners gave slaves discarded animal parts, such as hog maw (stomach), hog jowl, pig's feet, ham hocks. To this, blacks added a touch of African cooking, which included collard greens, dandelion greens (first recorded 1887), poke greens, turnip greens, black-eyed peas (first brought to Jamaica from Africa in 1674 and to North America in 1738).
tania[167]	*Colocasia esculenta,* coco yam; *eddo* in West Africa, *tanya* in West Indies. Appears indigenous to Central Africa. Two known varieties: "Old coco yam" (*Colocaccia antiquorum*) probably originated in Congo basin, with earliest citation in reference to Africa made by Portuguese in fifteenth century; "Coco yam tania" (*Xanthosomaa sagitifolium*) was a popular root plant in Sea Islands of Georgia and South Carolina until storm of 1893 destroyed most of the crop. As a coastal resident reported, "They ate funny kine uh food, roas wile locus an mushruhm an *tanyan* root. It lak elephant-eah and taase like Irish potatuh."

Y

yam[168]	Gullah *nyam, njam,* to eat. First recorded in America 1676.

CROPS

benne[169]	*Sesamum indicum,* sesame, also known as "benne seed" in South Carolina, brought there from West Africa. Slaves raised large crops of it, being fond of the seeds to make soups and puddings.
cowpeas[170]	*Vigna unguiculata,* black-eyed peas. Introduced into West Indies from Central Africa and thence into Carolinas before 1700s. See *cowpeas* in section on Foods.
goober[171]	*Arachis hypogaea,* American peanut. Also called groundnut, earthnut, pinder in South. Bantu *nguba,* peanut, recorded 1834. While vine is indigenous to South America as a crop, it was first brought to North America (Virginia) by slaves during transatlantic slave trade. See *goober* in section on Foods.
fluted pumpkin[172]	*Telfairia occidentials,* gourd, bottle gourd, calabash. Cultivated in both Old and New World in pre-Columbian era. Old World gourds were first domesticated in western Sudan.
kola[173]	*Cola acuminata* and *Cola nitida,* tree native to western Sudan. Nuts are source of major ingredient used in making modern

cola drinks. During slave trade, kola nuts were given by crews to passengers to suppress hunger and thirst. A transatlantic slaver wrote: "The seed, brought in a Guinean ship from that country, is called 'bichy' by the Colomanty and is eaten and used for pains in the belly."

guinea melon[174]   Variety of muskmelon with origin in Africa.

watermelon[175]   *Citrullus vulgaris,* spread from Sudan to Egypt during second millennium B.C. Now distributed throughout world. Transatlantic slave trade served as major vehicle of watermelon's transport to New World.

sorghum[176]   *Sorghum vulgare,* formerly *Andropogon sorghum;* also called guinea corn and millet. Introduced to America by Africans during transatlantic slave trade.

guinea yam[177]   *Disoncorem cayenesis* and *Disoncorn rontundata.* Indigenous to Guinea coastal area extending into southern Sudan. Survived in New World via transatlantic slave trade.

akee[178]   *Blighia sapida,* Akee apple. Fruit tree indigenous to West Africa; carried to New World during transatlantic slave trade.

ambary hemp[179]   *Hibiscus cannabinus.* Other names: weed, marijuana. Originated and is widespread in Africa. Found way to New World around time of transatlantic slave trade. Used to make rope.

cotton[180]   *Gossypium herbaceum.* Originated in western Sudan from indigenous *Gossypium anomalum.*

guinea grass[181]   Slave trader Henry Laurens of Charleston acquired seeds for guinea grass, a tall African grass.

ANIMALS AND INSECTS

guinea fowl[182]   Guinea hen was first domesticated in West Africa. This African chicken was introduced into North America during the eighteenth century.

guinea worm[183]   Catesby discovered guinea worm among insects found in Carolinas.

COWBOY CULTURE

bronco[184]   Term, probably of Ibibio origin, used centuries ago to denote Spanish and African slaves who worked with and cared for cattle.

buckaroo[185]   Ibibio *buckra,* poor white man; a white person bucking a bronco.

cowboy[186]   Originated in Colonial period when African labor and skills were closely associated with cattle raising. Africans stationed at cow pens with herding responsibilities were referred to as "cowboys," just as Africans who worked in the "Big House" were known as "houseboys." As late as 1865, following Civil War, Africans whose livestock responsibilities were with cattle were referred to as "cowboys" in plantation records. After 1865, whites associated with cattle industry referred to themselves as "cattlemen" to distinguish themselves from "cowboys."

dogies[187]

On trail drives, cowboys sang to their herds:

Sing hooplio, get along, my little dogies,
For Wyoming shall be your new home.
Its hooping and yelling
And cursing those dogies
To our misfortune
And none of your own.

Dogies originated from Kimbundu *kidogo,* a little something, and *dodo,* small. After Civil War, when great cattle roundups began, black cowboys introduced such Africanisms to cowboy language and songs.

open grazing[188]

Practice used worldwide in cattle culture today; introduced along with longhorn cattle in South Carolina by Fulanis from Senegambia. These expert cattlemen were also responsible for introducing other African husbandry patterns. Harvesting of cattle and cattle drives to centers of distribution were innovations Africans contributed to the developing industry.

MUSICAL INSTRUMENTS

musical bow[189]

One-stringed instrument used in southern U.S. that originated in Africa. Found today throughout that continent, except for East Africa. The *embe* of the Congo has a single string stretched across the "bowl" of a gourd. In U.S., one-stringed instruments evolved into the "bottleneck." Slide-guitar style common to Mississippi Delta blues was derived from techniques of playing African instruments.

washtub bass[190]

Also called tub or gutbucket. A cord is attached to the center of an inverted washtub or appropriate substitute. The other end of the cord is attached to a broomstick. The free end is braced against the lip of the inverted tub so that the string provides a musical tone, with the tub acting as a resounding chamber. Pressure against the stick varies the tautness of the cord and produces different tones. This instrument provides the needed bass tones for a group. The player usually stands with one foot on the edge of the tub to keep it firmly on the ground. African earth-bow is the tub's most likely predecessor.

nookaw[191]

From Tshiluba *nukoka,* you pull. Two jagged sticks, with a row of notches cut into them, rubbed together rhythmically. The player pulls the sticks back and forth. This instrument, found today in southern U.S., has been used for accompaniment by singers in present-day Zaire.

jenkgoving[192]   Folk instrument used in making a rhythmic accompaniment to singing and dancing, by clapping a hand down over the mouth of an open jar or a clay pot. This is called jenkgoving. Cf. Bantu *tshinkomo,* a hand closed into a fist, for the purpose of hitting or striking something.

agogo[193]   Bantu *ngongo,* bell. Also a Yoruba musical instrument made in the shape of a cowbell.

banjo[194]   Kimbundu *mbanzo.* Thomas Jefferson wrote in 1781: "The instrument proper to them [African Americans] is the *Banjar,* brought from Africa, and which is the origin of the guitar, its chords being precisely the four lower chords of the guitar." The banjo was known in America as an African instrument until the 1840s, when minstrel shows took it as a part of their blackface acts. As a result, the banjo became a badge of ridicule and blacks abandoned it, allowing southern whites to claim it as their own invention.

thumb piano[195]   African *mbira,* common in the late nineteenth century in New Orleans. See *funda nkata* in the section on Gestures.

cane fifes[196]   Found in both West and Central Africa. The making and playing of cane fifes survived the middle passage. Africans and African Americans use the same technique to make them.

quills, panpipes[197]   Found throughout Africa and southern U.S. "We plays de quill, made from willow stalk when de sap am up. You takes de stick and pounds de bark loose, an slips it off, den split de wood in one end and down one side, put it back on de stick. De quill plays like de flute."

tambourine[198]   Instrument borrowed by Europeans from Africans.

triangle[199]   A piece of bent iron, beaten by a rod of the same metal as that used in making drums. This musical instrument, which belongs to the percussion family, was borrowed by British from Africans for use in the British army.

xylophone[200]   Called *balafa* and *madimba,* this is a common instrument throughout West and Central Africa. It is composed of pieces of hardwood of different lengths laid across a frame. To the underneath side of the frame are attached a row of gourds, varying in size from small to large, according to the length of the slats. They provide resonance and enhance the volume of the musical tones, made by striking the slats with a mallet covered on one end with a ball of raw rubber. This instrument was known even in northern states and was used by slaves at African festivals, such as the Pinkster Festival.

drums[201]   African-style drums emerged almost as soon as the first Africans landed at Jamestown in 1619. "Talking drums" were well known on both sides of the Atlantic, esp. for their use in slave revolts. The first account of the use of drums in America comes from the official account of the Stono slave rebellion in South

Carolina in 1739: "on the 9th day of September last, being Sunday, which is the day the Planters allow them to work for themselves, some Angola Negroes assembled, to the number of twenty, at a place called Stonehow [Stono]. . . . Several Negroes joined them, they calling out 'Liberty!' marched on with colour displayed and two drums beating, pursuing all white people they met, and killing man, woman and child. . . . They increased every minute by new Negroes coming to them, so that they were above sixty, some say a hundred, on which they halted in a field and set to dancing, singing and beating drums, to draw more Negroes to them, thinking that they were victorious over the whole province, having marched ten miles and burnt all before them without opposition." Afterward, the colony of South Carolina passed laws prohibiting "drums, horns or other loud instruments," in the Slave Act of 1740. In 1811 an uprising took place in St. John the Baptist Parish near New Orleans, where an army of insurgents consisting of 500 men and women divided into companies, commanded by Africans. They marched on New Orleans, beating drums and kettles.

DANCE

buzzard lope[202]

Originated in Africa and survived in the coastal communities of Georgia until the 1940s. One informant described the dance as follows: "We calls it, 'Come Down tuh duh Myuh.' We dance round and shake du han and fiddle duh foot, one u duh succle. Den we call out and rise and shout round, and we all fling duh foot agen."

cakewalk[203]

Of African-American origin, a stylized caricature of whites minueting or waltzing. Eliza Diggs Johnson, a former slave and mother of performer Charles Johnson, told of the cakewalk held on the Missouri plantation where she was born. As *Ebony* reported, she told her son that "in the old days, white folks from the Big House carriaged down to the clearing in back of the piney woods to watch their slaves couple off and do a dance-walk that was as elegant and poised as a Mozart minuet, but yet was flavored with an exaggerated grace that was sometimes comical. Music for the cadenced walking and high stepping was supplied usually by a violin, a drum and horn of some kind. Prize for the winning couple would usually be a towering, extra sweet coconut cake." Johnson, dubbed the "Cakewalk King," with his wife, Dora Dean, and the team of Williams and Walker, took the cakewalk to Broadway as early as 1895. What started as a parody of whites became a financial success for Johnson and Dean. The cakewalk inspired theatrical productions, including *Clorindy,* by Will Marion Cook and Paul Lawrence Dunbar. It was adapted by Debussy in his *Petite Suite* and was used in the works of Sousa and Stravinsky. The phrase

"Doesn't that take the cake!" denoting an element of surprise, or something that is not to be outdone, is uttered today with little knowledge of its origin.

calimbe[204] Dance of African origin with related music and songs. It was performed at wakes, two men holding a couple of poles parallel, while a third man danced on the poles to the strains of the song.

calenda[205] Congo-Angolan dance which became very popular in Santo Domingo, Haiti, and New Orleans. As early as 1704, a police ordinance prohibited night gatherings of Congo-Angolans performing the calenda on plantations. It was a variation of a dance used in voodoo ceremonies, always performed with male and female dancers in couples. They move to the middle of the circle and start dancing. The male dancer turns circles around his partner, who turns to change her position, waving the ends of a handkerchief she holds. Her partner raises his hands up and down alternately, with his elbows close to his body, his fists almost clenched. Bastide describes the calenda as a navel-to-navel dance performed by male-female partners.

Charleston[206] Brought to South Carolina and Louisiana by enslaved Africans from the Congo. This slave dance, called Juba, evolved into the Charleston. It is a dance with undulations, kicking patterns, and timing similar to the one-legged *sembuka* style of kicking and handclapping, common in parts of northern Congo. Cf. Bantu *-sambuka*, step over or across.

chica[207] Popular dance during the slavery era. "The talent of the female dancer resides in the perfection of her ability to move her hips, the bottom parts of her waist, with the rest of the whole remaining in a sort of stillness which does not disturb the weak swaying of her hands, waving the ends of a handkerchief or her waist petticoat. A male gets closer to her, leaping up suddenly, and falls back rhythmically, almost touching her. He pulls back, leaps up again and challenges her to the most seductive duel. The dance gets animated and soon becomes lustful." Cf. Bantu *tshika*, move, be excited.

Congo Square[208] La Place du Congo, Congo Square, is in old New Orleans. An ordinance of the Municipal Council, adopted on October 15, 1817, made the name of this traditional place law. It was considered one of the unique attractions of old New Orleans, ranking second only to the Quadroon Ball. At the square, women wore dotted calico dresses with brightly colored Madras kerchiefs tied about their hair, to form the popular headdress called the tignon. Children wore garments with bright feathers and bits of ribbon. The favorite dances of the slaves in Congo Square were the bamboula and the calinda, two Congo dances, the latter being a variation of the former that was also danced in voodoo ceremonies.

Cuttin' the Pigeon Wings[209] A slave dance with African characteristics. The dancers mimicked the pigeon by holding their necks stiff while flapping their arms, going to the east and then to the west. It was a courting dance that allowed the dancers to kiss without embracing.

ombliguide[210]   A dance criticized in 1766 by the New Orleans City Council. Performed by four men and four women, it involved objectionable movements with navel-to-navel contact, a common trait of Angolan traditional dancing. Slaves came regularly to Congo Square to perform the ombliguide and other Congo dances, such as the calenda, bamboula, and chica, all transplanted directly from Central Africa. The partial Europeanization of some of these African movements eventually created the native dances of Latin American countries such as the marcumbi, a dance learned by the Spanish and later brought to the New World via Spain. The fandango, the national dance of Spain, originated in Cuba, from African dances. Other dances derived from the ombliguide are the chacharara, cadomba, melongo, malamba, gati, semba, rhumba, mamba, conga, and tango.

CELEBRATIONS

Pinkster Day[211]   A religious festivity, partly pagan and partly Christian. "Many of the old colored people, then [1815] in Albany, were born in Africa and would have wild dances and sing in the native language. Pinkster festivities took place usually in May and lasted an entire week. They began the Monday following Whitsunday, being the carnival-time of the African race. The major and leading spirit was Charley of the Pinkster Day, who was brought from Angola, in the Guinea Gulf, in his infant days."

John Canoe[212]   An African celebration observed by slaves in eastern North Carolina. A leader, accompanied by a group of singers, would march, wearing costumes and headdresses and playing percussion instruments. Celebrants danced a "type of dance which is danced backward, with the hands behind the back."

Juneteenth[213]   Emancipation Day celebration observed by African Americans in Texas, Arkansas, Louisiana, Kentucky, Tennessee, Georgia, Alabama, and Florida. It is characterized by remnants of African drum dancing, music, and parading. In 1972, Texans honored their African-American citizens by passing House Resolution 23 and House Bill 1016, officially recognizing Juneteenth as an annual state holiday.

GESTURES

funda nkata[214]   Cross-legged position. Appeared early in the nineteenth century in New Orleans' Congo Square, where a performer, sitting cross-legged, held a *mbira* (thumb piano) in both hands and played it by plucking the ends of the reeds with the thumb-nails. Cf. Tshiluba *-funda,* design, draw, and *nkata,* coil or wheel. To form a "wheel" with the body, the performer took a coiled-up sitting position while playing the *tshisanji,* finger-piano.

tuluwa twa lumbu[215]   Arms crossed on the chest, symbolizing wordlessness, self-encirclement in silence. Still observed in some African-American communities, the gesture, with contrasting Yoruba and Congo meanings, appears in a strongly Congo-flavored folk dance, the rhumba yambu. Cf. Tshiluba *tulu tua lumbu,* enclosed sleep, sleep with a wall around it.

nunsa[216]   Standing or seated pose with head averted, turned. The nunsa position is common in the Congo and is also present in African-American culture. Cf. Tshiluba *mununsa,* turn.

kebuka[217]   Related to the position taken when playing the congas or drums by African Americans. Cf. Tshiluba *kubuka,* to take flight, take off. Stance of drummer about to "do his own thing," "blow it free," play extemporaneously.

pakalala[218]   To stand with arms akimbo, both hands on the hips. This position among the Bakongo proclaims the person ready to accept the challenges of a situation. Cf. Tshiluba *kalala,* deputy, officer; position of authority.

SOCIAL CULTURE

ring shout[219]   Counterclockwise dance involving people moving around in a circle, rhythmically shuffling their feet and shaking their hands while those outside the ring clap, sing, and gesticulate. "Movement in a ring during ceremonies honoring ancestors was an integral part of life in Central Africa." Believed to have been transported to South Carolina during the transatlantic slave trade.

fish sconching[220]   Ritual preparation of a fish by making three incisions on it, still practiced on St. Helena Island, S.C. "In northern Congo, specialized ritual experts called . . . *nganga nsibi* cut designs in the bodies of living fish, or turtles, and then release these creatures in their element." Also called *banganga nkodi,* these specialists in sending messages to the ancestors "cut their signs *(bidimbu)* into the shell of a tortoise" to carry these messages "across the *Kalunga* line" to the sacred world. "There the ancestors will receive the encoded messages and act upon them on behalf of their descendants."

grave decoration[221]   Custom of placing objects on top of graves, traced directly back to the Bantu. The Ovimbundu place baskets, gourds, etc., on top of the grave sites. Final resting places are marked with crockery, empty bottles, old cooking pots. Other objects placed on graves include medicine bottles, tobacco, and shells. "Negro graves [near Savannah] were always decorated with the last article used by the departed. Broken pitchers and broken bits of colored glass were considered even more appropriate as decoration than white shells from the beach nearby. "Sometimes they carved rude wooden figure-like images of idols, and sometimes a patchwork quilt was laid upon the grave."

burial ritual[222]

Second burials are common throughout Central and West Africa, and this practice carried over to the southern U.S. "We alluz hab two fewnal fuh duh pusson. We have duh regluh fewnal wen yuh die. Den once a yeah we hab one big preaching fuh ebrybody wat die dat year."

burial at home[223]

In traditional African society the dead are always brought home for burial. The belief is that unless you are buried at home your spirit will not be able to join the spirits of your ancestors. In the Sea Islands this tradition is also practiced. "Wen he die fah off, we bring um home tuh bury um, dohn leh no strainjuh be bury wid um. Yuh gib people wut aim belong tuh yuh annuddah piece uh groun tuh be bury in to bring the dead by home." "Fus the spirit tuh rest in the grave folks have tuh be buried at home. They nevuh feel right ef they buried from home the spirit just wanduh around."

the gift of eggs[224]

In the Sea Islands, as the inhabitants visited they would bring gifts of eggs. The courteous practice of presenting eggs as gifts is still most true of the Luba, Lulua, and Kuba peoples. Rossa B. Cooley, principal of Penn School, tells of Aunt Tina who stopped at her house to see how she was doing. Upon leaving she gave her two eggs as her gift. This is another hand-down from old Africa days; for there friends bring eggs as a gift after a visit.

Iron smithing[225]

The early use of iron by African metal workers proved a major landmark in developing the forging and smithing trade. The high level of craftsmanship demonstrated by Africans was the evolutionary product of centuries of tradition which later came to be called the ancestral arts. The wrought-iron balconies of the French Quarter of New Orleans and certain houses in Mobile, Alabama, and Charleston, South Carolina, have been shown to be proofs of the survival of skills in metallurgy brought directly from Africa. In Charleston and Louisiana there exists a type of plantation design produced by slave craftsmen that bore the unmistakable marks of African influences in the distinguishing peculiarities of surface design.

Wearing of earrings by males[226]

The Americanism of wearing earrings by males in either the left or right ear was once an Africanism. Africans on American plantations wore earrings to indicate their national origin. "Doze Africans alluz call one anudduh 'countryman.' Dey know ef dey come frum duh same tribe by duh mahk dey hab. Some hab a long mahk an some hab a roun un. Udduhs weah eahring in duh eah. Some weahs it in duh lef eah an doze from anudduh tribe weahs it in duh right eah."

Notes

LORENZO DOW TURNER

1. When Joseph E. Holloway visited St. Helena in 1983, some of Turner's informants still had vivid memories of his visits.

2. Some studies have documented Africanisms in Native American speech; see, for example, Daniel G. Dinton, "On Certain Supposed Nanticoke Words, Shown to Be of African Origin," *American Antiquarian* 9, no. 6 (1887), 350–54.

3. Information on Turner comes in part from Howard Cohen, "Lorenzo Turner: Professor, Linguist, Author," *R.V. Torch* (Dec. 10, 1962), and David Anderson, "He Worked His Way through College," *Chicago Sun Times* (May 19, 1969).

4. Melville J. Herskovits, "The Present Status and Needs of Afro-American Research," *Journal of Negro History* 36 (1951), 125.

5. Ibid., 125–26.

6. Lorenzo Dow Turner, "Problems Confronting the Investigator of Gullah."

INTRODUCTION

1. Examples from W. M. Morrison, *Grammar of the Buluba-Lulua Language as Spoken in the Upper Kasai and Congo Basin.*

2. Francis Grose, *A Classical Dictionary of Vulgar Tongue.*

3. John Atkins, *A Voyage to Guinea, Brazil and the West Indies,* in a list of "Some Negrish Words," 60.

4. John G. Jackson, *Introduction to African Civilizations,* 200.

5. Joseph E. Holloway, ed., *Africanisms in American Culture,* 5.

6. Interview by Joseph E. Holloway with David P. Gamble, Dec. 5, 1985; D. J. Muffett, "Uncle Remus Was a Hausaman?" Also in Holloway, ed., *Africanisms.*

7. Ulrich Bonnell Phillips, *American Negro Slavery: A Survey of the Supply, Employment and Control of Negro Labor as Determined by the Plantation Regime* (New York: D. Appleton, 1940), 16.

8. Elizabeth Donnan, *Documents Illustrative of the History of the Slave Trade,* vol. 2; see "Memoirs of the Life of Job Ben Solomon," 420–27.

9. Terry Alford, *Prince among Slaves: The True Story of an African Prince Sold into Slavery in the American South.*

10. Malcolm Guthrie, "Some Developments in the Prehistory of the Bantu Languages."

11. A. Michiels and N. Laude, *Notre colonie,* 290, 296.

12. Philip D. Curtin, *The Atlantic Slave Trade: A Census,* 251–62.

13. Peter H. Wood, "More Like a Negro Country: Demographic Patterns in Colonial South Carolina, 1700–1740," 132.

14. Winifred K. Vass, *The Bantu Speaking Heritage of the United States,* 41–122.

15. Melville J. Herskovits, *The Myth of the Negro Past.*

16. Roger Bastide, *African Civilizations in the New World.*

17. Joseph E. Holloway, "The Origins of African-American Culture," in Holloway, ed., *Africanisms,* 1.

18. Curtin, *Atlantic Slave Trade,* 87.

19. James A. Rawley, *The Transatlantic Slave Trade* (New York: Norton, 1981).

20. J. K. Abe Ajayi and J. E. Inikori, "Slavery and the Slave Trade in the Context of West African History," in *Forest Migration* (New York: Africana, 1979), 154–66.

21. Donnan, *Documents,* vol. 4; Holloway, ed., *Africanisms,* 3.

22. Peter H. Wood, *Black Majority: Negroes in Colonial South Carolina from 1670 through the Stono Rebellion,* 132; Samuel Dyssli, Dec. 3, 1737 (SCHGM), 90, quoted in Holloway, ed., *Africanisms,* 4.

23. Donnan, *Documents,* vol. 4.

24. Margaret Washington Creel, *"A Peculiar People": Slave Religion and Community-Culture among the Gullahs.*

25. Wood, *Black Majority.*

26. Creel, *"A Peculiar People."*

1. THE BANTU VOCABULARY CONTENT OF GULLAH

1. John F. Szwed, "Africa Lies Just off the Coast of Georgia," 31.

2. Mason Crum, *Gullah: Negro Life in the Carolina Sea Islands,* 99.

3. Ibid., 129.

4. Ibid., 99.

5. *Gainesville* (Florida) *Sun,* Apr. 8, 1977.

6. Crum, *Gullah,* 127.

7. F. W. Bradley, "A Word-List from South Carolina," 39.

8. John Bennett, *Doctor to the Dead: Grotesque Legends and Folk Tales of Old Charleston,* 256.

9. Ibid., 99.

10. Ibid., 122.

11. Ibid., 122–23.

12. Ibid., 123.

13. Betsy Fancher, *Lost Legacy of Georgia's Golden Isles,* 45.

14. Bradley, "Word-List," 25.

15. Crum, *Gullah,* 105.

16. Bradley, "Word-List," 25.

17. Carl Lamson Carmer, *Stars Fell on Alabama,* 177–78.

18. Crum, *Gullah,* 105.

19. Ibid.

20. Ibid.

21. Ibid., 129; Bradley, "Word-List," 11.

22. Crum, *Gullah,* 105.

23. Ibid.

24. Ibid., 125.

2. BLACK NAMES IN THE UNITED STATES

1. Francis Le Lau to Sec. S.P.G., Aug. 30, 1712, S.P.G. MS.A, no. 27 (Propagation of Gospel).

2. "An Account of the Negro Insurrection in South Carolina," *CRSG* 2, part 2, 233.

3. *South Carolina Gazette,* Sept. 17, 1737.

4. Ibid., June 14, 1740; Sept. 22, 1746.

5. Ibid., Feb. 8, 1748; Feb. 25, 1749; May 28, 1750; Feb. 18, 1751.

6. Phillips, *American Negro Slavery,* 20; also in Mechal Sobel, *Trabelin' on the Slave Journey to an Afro-Baptist Faith* (Princeton, N.J.: Princeton University Press, 1988), 37.

7. *South Carolina Gazette,* July 8, 1732.

8. Ibid., Dec. 21, 1738.

9. Ibid., Oct. 3, 1743.

10. Ibid., Feb. 1, 1746.

11. Ibid., Nov. 8, 1751; June 14, 1742; Jan. 17, 1743.

12. Ibid., Jan. 17, 1743.

13. Ibid., Oct. 26, 1734.

14. Ibid., Feb. 9, 1738.

15. Ibid., Mar. 16, 1738.

16. Ibid., Mar. 30, 1734.

17. Ibid., Jan. 22, 1734.

18. Quoted in "The Speech of Negroes in Colonial America."

19. Edward Long, *The History of Jamaica,* 427; Hennig C. Cohen, "Slave Names in Colonial South Carolina," 105.

20. Cohen, "Slave Names," 105.

21. Whittington Bernard Johnson, "Negro Laboring Classes in Early America, 1750–1820."

22. J. L. Dillard, *Black Names.*

23. *Drums and Shadows: Survival Studies among the Georgia Coastal Negroes.*

24. Norman R. Yetman, ed., *Life under the "Peculiar Institution,"* 13.

25. Inventories 1732–1736 of Charleston, S.C., Probate Court.

26. Cohen, "Slave Names," 104.

27. H. L. Mencken, *The American Language,* 524.

28. Cohen, "Slave Names."

29. Land Patent Book No. 4, 23.

30. Dillard, *Black Names.*

31. Frederick Douglass, *Narrative of the Life of Frederick Douglass,* 147–48.

32. Alex Haley, *The Autobiography of Malcolm X.*

33. Dillard, *Black Names,* 25.

34. Lorenzo Dow Turner, *Africanisms in the Gullah Dialect.*

35. Carmer, *Stars Fell on Alabama,* 96.

36. Winifred K. Vass, unpublished material.

37. Joseph E. Holloway, personal interview with the Rev. Ervin L. Greene, Jr., in Beaufort, S.C., Jan. 16, 1984.

38. *USA Today,* "A Mutombo by Any Other Name."

39. Joseph E. Holloway, interview with Mrs. Etta Williams (age 86), St. Helena Island, Jan. 18, 1984.

40. Joseph E. Holloway, field notebook.

41. J. T. Munday, "Spirit Names among the Central Bantu," 39–40.

42. Ibid., 44.

43. Malcolm Guthrie, *Comparative Bantu,* vol. 1, 25–54, "The Compilation of Common Bantu" and "The Construction of Starred Forms."

3. AFRICANISMS OF BANTU ORIGIN IN BLACK ENGLISH

1. *Drums and Shadows,* 251.

2. Henry Edward Krehbiel, *Afro-American Folksongs,* 66.

3. Harold Wentworth and Stuart Berg Flexner, *The Dictionary of American Slang,* 18.

4. Harold Courlander, *Negro Folk Music, U.S.A.,* 191.

5. Guy Johnson, *Folk Culture on St. Helena Island, South Carolina,* 59.

6. Reed Smith, *Gullah,* 28.

7. Frank A. Collymore, *Barbadian Dialect,* 12. This reference is useful because of the close relationship between Charleston, S.C., and Barbados. Most of the words listed by Collymore are also listed in South Carolina vocabulary lists and references.

8. Wentworth and Flexner, *Dictionary of American Slang,* 17.

9. *Random House Dictionary of the English Language.*

10. Newbell Niles Puckett, *Folk Beliefs of the Southern Negro*, 18–19.

11. Orin Sage Wightman and Marguerite Davis Cate, *Early Days of Coastal Georgia*, St. Simons, 219.

12. Lydia Parrish, *Slave Songs of the Georgia Sea Islands*, 41–42.

13. *Random House Dictionary*.

14. M. M. Mathews, *Some Sources of Southernisms*, 101–5, 142.

15. *Ibid.*, 100–101.

16. Stetson Kennedy, *Palmetto Country*, 67.

17. Bradley, "Word-List," 13.

18. *Random House Dictionary*.

19. *Ibid.*

20. *Drums and Shadows*, 251.

21. Krehbiel, *Afro-American Folksongs*, 66.

22. Kennedy, *Palmetto Country*, 155.

23. Zora Neale Hurston, *Mules and Men*, 190.

24. Fancher, *Lost Legacy*, 45.

25. *Random House Dictionary*, 145.

26. Hurston, *Mules and Men*, 64, 132.

27. Correspondence with Madge B. Maclachlan, Jacksonville, Fla.

28. Puckett, *Folk Beliefs*, 20.

29. *Random House Dictionary*, 169.

30. *Drums and Shadows*, 251.

31. Hurston, *Mules and Men*, 192.

32. Wentworth and Flexner, *Dictionary of American Slang*, 69.

33. Bradley, "Word-List," 12.

34. *Random House Dictionary*, 169.

35. Samuel G. Stoney and Gertrude M. Shelby, *Black Genesis*, 177.

36. *Random House Dictionary*, 177.

37. *Drums and Shadows*, 81.

38. Bradley, "Word-List," 18.

39. Johnson, *Folk Culture*, 43.

40. Collymore, *Barbadian Dialect*, 20.

41. Bradley, "Word-List," 18.

42. Mathews, *Some Sources*, 117.

43. *Ibid.*, 99.

44. Harold Wentworth, *American Dialect Dictionary* (New York: Crowell, 1944, 1960).

45. Collymore, *Barbadian Dialect*, 22.

46. C. M. Woodward, "A Word List from Virginia and North Carolina," 9.

47. Johnson, *Folk Culture*, 44.

48. Bradley, "Word-List," 19.

49. Hurston, *Mules and Men*, 78, 179.

50. *Journal of American Folklore*, 32, no. 125 (1919), 376.

51. Thomas W. Talley, *Negro Folk Rhymes*, 74.

52. *Random House Dictionary*, 257.

53. *Ibid.*

54. Puckett, *Folk Beliefs*, 20.

55. *Random House Dictionary*, 309.

56. Wentworth and Flexner, *Dictionary of American Slang*, 119.

57. Collymore, *Barbadian Dialect*, 26.

58. Bradley, "Word-List," 22.

59. Wentworth and Flexner, *Dictionary of American Slang*, 115.

60. Puckett, *Folk Beliefs*, 16, 20.

61. Courlander, *Negro Folk Music*, 191.

62. *Ibid.*
63. Krehbiel, *Afro-American Folksongs,* 128.
64. Wentworth and Flexner, *Dictionary of American Slang,* 125.
65. Bradley, "Word-List," 24.
66. Ibid.
67. *Drums and Shadows,* 194.
68. Smith, *Gullah,* 28.
69. Bradley, "Word-List," 25.
70. Charles C. Jones, *Negro Myths from the Georgia Coast,* 167.
71. Johnson, *Folk Culture,* 59.
72. Stoney and Shelby, *Black Genesis,* xvi.
73. Wentworth and Flexner, *Dictionary of American Slang,* 146.
74. Kennedy, *Palmetto Country,* 154–55.
75. *Drums and Shadows,* 251.
76. Wentworth and Flexner, *Dictionary of American Slang,* 148.
77. Wentworth, *American Dialect Dictionary.*
78. Woodward, "Word-List," 12.
79. *Journal of American Folklore* 32, no. 125 (1919), 398.
80. Collymore, *Barbadian Dialect,* 33.
81. W. A. B. Musgrave, "Ananci Stories," 53–55.
82. Collymore, *Barbadian Dialect,* 33.
83. Krehbiel, *Afro-American Folksongs,* 128.
84. *Random House Dictionary,* 540.
85. Collymore, *Barbadian Dialect,* 39.
86. *Random House Dictionary,* 552.
87. Wentworth and Flexner, *Dictionary of American Slang,* 196.
88. Hurston, *Mules and Men,* 302.
89. Smith, *Gullah,* 26.
90. A. M. H. Christensen, *Afro-American Folk-Lore,* 38.
91. *Random House Dictionary,* 582.
92. *Ibid.,* 588.
93. Bradley, "Word-List," 31–32.
94. Parrish, *Slave Songs,* 41.
95. Bradley, "Word-List," 32.
96. Wentworth and Flexner, *Dictionary of American Slang,* 214.
97. Kennedy, *Palmetto Country,* 154–55.
98. Hurston, *Mules and Men,* 190.
99. *Drums and Shadows,* 66.
100. Puckett, *Folk Beliefs,* 19.
101. *Random House Dictionary,* 609.
102. Hurston, *Mules and Men,* 244, 281.
103. Wentworth and Flexner, *Dictionary of American Slang,* 223.
104. *Ibid.*
105. Jones, *Negro Myths,* 168.
106. Ambrose Gonzales, *The Black Border,* 304.
107. Smith, *Gullah,* 27.
108. Jones, *Negro Myths,* 168.
109. *Random House Dictionary,* 628.
110. Kennedy, *Palmetto Country,* 173.
111. *Random House Dictionary,* 630.
112. Mathews, *Some Sources,* 119–20.
113. Bradley, "Word-List," 34.
114. Puckett *Folk Beliefs,* 20.

115. *Drums and Shadows,* 251.
116. Bradley, "Word-List," 36.
117. Wentworth and Flexner, *Dictionary of American Slang,* 258.
118. Gates Thomas, "South Texas Negro Folk Songs," 172.
119. *Ibid.*
120. Correspondence with Madge B. Maclachlan, Jacksonville, Fla., regarding terms used by her childhood playmates on the turpentine "flats."
121. Puckett, *Folk Beliefs,* 20.
122. Gonzales, *Black Border,* 307.
123. Christensen, *Afro-American Folk-Lore,* 116.
124. Bradley, "Word-List," 39.
125. Jones, *Negro Myths,* 168.
126. *Random House Dictionary,* 762.
127. *Ibid.,* 764.
128. Wentworth and Flexner, *Dictionary of American Slang,* 288.
129. Hurston, *Mules and Men,* 233, 277.
130. *Random House Dictionary,* 767.
131. *Ibid.,* 768.
132. *Ibid.*
133. Wentworth and Flexner, *Dictionary of American Slang,* 292.
134. *Random House Dictionary.*
135. Wentworth and Flexner, *Dictionary of American Slang,* 292, 295.
136. Hurston, *Mules and Men,* 233, 277.
137. Bennett, *Doctor to the Dead,* 251.
138. Mathews, *Some Sources,* 145.
139. *Drums and Shadows,* 251.
140. Hurston, *Mules and Men,* 55, 95, 141.
141. Mathews, *Some Sources* 99.
142. Collymore, *Barbadian Dialect,* 150.
143. C. M. N. White, "The Supreme Being in the Beliefs of the Balovale Tribes," 30.
144. Hurston, *Mules and Men,* 258.
145. Frank Durham, *The Collected Short Stories of Julia Peterkin,* 250, 264.
146. Bennett, *Doctor to the Dead,* 257.
147. *Random House Dictionary,* 794.
148. Puckett, *Folk Beliefs,* 17.
149. Smith, *Gullah,* 30.
150. *Random House Dictionary,* 803.
151. Gonzales, *Black Border,* 311.
152. *Ibid.*
153. *Random House Dictionary,* 840.
154. *Ibid.,* 843.
155. Puckett, *Folk Beliefs,* 18.
156. Gates Thomas, "South Texas Negro Work Songs," 164.
157. Correspondence with Madge B. MacLachlan, Jacksonville, Fla., about backwoods Florida vocabulary.
158. Kennedy, *Palmetto Country,* 173–75.
159. *Drums and Shadows,* 251.
160. *Ibid.*
161. *Ibid.*
162. Wentworth and Flexner, *Dictionary of American Slang,* 331.
163. *Drums and Shadows,* 66.
164. Johnson, *Folk Culture,* 55, 57.
165. Bradley, "Word-List," 47.

166. *Random House Dictionary,* 869.
167. Kennedy, *Palmetto Country,* 131–33.
168. *Journal of American Folklore* 32, no. 125 (1919), 363–65, 383.
169. *Random House Dictionary,* 877.
170. *Drums and Shadows,* 251.
171. Durham, *Collected Short Stories of Julia Peterkin,* 273.
172. Bradley, "Word-List," 46.
173. Durham, *Collected Short Stories of Julia Peterkin,* 76.
174. Puckett, *Folk Beliefs,* 19.
175. Wentworth and Flexner, *Dictionary of American Slang,* 341.
176. *Random House Dictionary,* 929.
177. *Ibid.*
178. *Ibid.*
179. *Drums and Shadows,* 252.
180. *Ibid.,* 66.
181. Wentworth and Flexner, *Dictionary of American Slang,* 350.
182. Kennedy, *Palmetto Country,* 175–79.
183. Wentworth and Flexner, *Dictionary of American Slang,* 350.
184. *Journal of American Folklore* 32, no. 125 (1919), 442.
185. Parrish, *Slave Songs,* 35.
186. Musgrave, "Ananci Stories," 54.
187. Puckett, *Folk Beliefs,* 19.
188. Wentworth and Flexner, *Dictionary of American Slang,* 367.
189. Bennett, *Doctor to the Dead,* 244.
190. Crum, *Gullah,* 118.
191. Gonzales, *Black Border,* 317.
192. *Random House Dictionary,* 1040.
193. Collymore, *Barbadian Dialect,* 63.
194. Bradley, "Word-List," 51.
195. Wentworth and Flexner, *Dictionary of American Slang,* 382.
196. Crum, *Gullah,* 125.
197. *Random House Dictionary,* 1091.
198. Mathews, *Some Sources,* 111, 144.
199. Smith, *Gullah,* 29.
200. Wentworth and Flexner, *Dictionary of American Slang,* 397.
201. *Random House Dictionary,* 1112.
202. Collymore, *Barbadian Dialect,* 67.
203. Wentworth and Flexner, *Dictionary of American Slang,* 401.
204. Hurston, *Mules and Men,* 176.
205. *Ibid.,* 228.
206. Bradley, "Word-List," 54.
207. *Ibid.,* 53, 55.
208. Guion G. Johnson, *A Social History of the Sea Islands,* 36.
209. *Random House Dictionary,* 1250.
210. Wentworth and Flexner, *Dictionary of American Slang,* 440.
211. *Ibid.,* 457.
212. Hurston, *Mules and Men,* 215, 322.
213. Bradley, "Word-List," 54.
214. Julia Peterkin, *Scarlet Sister Mary,* 124.
215. *Drums and Shadows,* 66.
216. Gonzales, *Black Border,* 273, 285.
217. Parrish, *Slave Songs,* 42.
218. Wentworth and Flexner, *Dictionary of American Slang,* 534.

219. *Random House Dictionary,* 1445.
220. Correspondence with Madge MacLachlan, Jacksonville, Fla.
221. *Random House Dictionary.*
222. Puckett, *Folk Beliefs,* 17.
223. *Ibid.,* 19.
224. Bradley, "Word-List," 67.
225. *Ibid.,* 60.
226. *Ibid.*
227. *Random House Dictionary,* 1497.
228. Hurston, *Mules and Men,* 302.
229. Wentworth and Flexner, *Dictionary of American Slang,* 557.
230. Bennett, *Doctor to the Dead,* 256.
231. Collymore, *Barbadian Dialect,* 60.
232. Hurston, *Mules and Men,* 225.
233. Collymore, *Barbadian Dialect,* 93.
234. Bradley, "Word-List," 70–71.
235. Puckett, *Folk Beliefs,* 19.
236. Bradley, "Word-List," 12.
237. *Random House Dictionary,* 1652.
238. *Ibid.*
239. *Ibid.,* 1653.
240. Bradley, "Word-List," 73.
241. Jones, *Negro Myths,* 170.
242. Durham, *Collected Short Stories of Julia Peterkin,* 186, 197, 255, passim.
243. Krehbiel, *Afro-American Folksongs,* 68.
244. *Random House Dictionary,* 767.
245. Wentworth and Flexner, *Dictionary of American Slang,* 594.

4. BANTU PLACE NAMES IN NINE SOUTHERN STATES

1. George R. Stewart, *Names on the Land,* 329.
2. Claude Henry Neuffer, "Some Edisto Island Names," 14.
3. William A. Read, *Indian Place Names in Alabama,* xiii.
4. Ibid.
5. H. B. Cushman, *History of the Choctaw, Chickasaw and Natchez Indians,* 600.
6. *Hammond's New World Atlas.*
7. *Alabama: A Guide to the Deep South,* 359.
8. Personal interview with Henry C. Williams, Africatown
9. Wightman and Cate, *Early Days,* 67.
10. Curtin, *Atlantic Slave Trade,* 143, 158.
11. Wightman and Cate, *Early Days,* 67.
12. Daniel D. Mannix, *Black Cargoes,* 278.
13. Bantu place names not located on the map for Georgia: Fulemmy Town, Occola, Picola, Talloka.
14. Russell Garvin, "The Free Negroes in Florida before the Civil War," 1–3.
15. Vernon Lane Wharton, *The Negro in Mississippi, 1867–1890,* 10–11.
16. *Mississippi: A Guide to the Magnolia State,* 31.
17. Dawson A. Phelps and Edward Hunter Ross, "Names Please: Place-Names along the Natchez Trace," 248.
18. Hurston, *Mules and Men,* 215.
19. Winifred K. Vass, correspondence with Lucille Gregory, Kosciusko, Miss., regarding place name Zama, October 1970.
20. Place name not located on map of Mississippi: Shakerag.

21. N. S. Bassett, *Slavery and Servitude in the Colony of North Carolina,* 175.

22. Donnan, *Documents,* vol. 4, 235.

23. Winifred K. Vass, correspondence with John B. Gray, Garner, N.C., regarding place name Makatoka, December 1970.

24. Place names not located on map of North Carolina: Gela, Chetola, Chiska, Oine, Quaqua, Solola.

25. Mannix, *Black Cargoes,* 167–69.

26. Place names not located on map of South Carolina: Ampezam, Attakullaq, Becca, Beetaw, Boo-boo, Boyano, Caneache, Canehoy, Cashua Neck, Chachan, Chebash, Chepasbe, Chichessa, Chinch Row, Chiquola, Chota, Chukky, Cofitachequi, Coosabo, Cooter borough, Cuakles, Dibidue, Elasie, Flouricane, Gippy or Jippy, Hoot Gap, Kecklico, Kissah, Loblolly Bay, Malpus Island, Mazych, Muckawee, Mump Fuss, Oniseca, Opopome, Oshila, Palachocolas, Palawana, Parachula, Pindar Town, Pooshee, Quocaratchie, Sauta, Shiminally, Teckle-gizzard, Toogoodoo, Untsaiyi, Wantoot, Watacoo, We Creek, Weetaw, Wosa, Yoa, Yuka.

27. Donnan, *Documents,* vol. 4, 2–7.

28. Place names not found on Virginia map: Arcola, Dongola.

29. Source: Winifred K. Vass.

30. *Hammond's New World Atlas,* 189.

31. William S. Powell, *The North Carolina Gazetteer,* 5.

32. William A. Read, *Florida Place Names of Indian Origin,* 42.

33. *Hammond's New World Atlas,* 198.

34. Ibid., 207.

35. *Names in South Carolina* 13 (November 1966), 5.

36. Source: Vass.

37. Ibid.

38. Powell, *North Carolina Gazetteer.*

39. Source: Vass.

40. Powell, *North Carolina Gazetteer,* 12.

41. Raus McDill Hanson, *Virginia Place Names,* 124.

42. *Hammond's New World Atlas,* 198.

43. *Names in South Carolina* 13 (November 1966), 15.

44. Read, *Florida Place Names,* 45.

45. Ibid.

46. Source: Vass.

47. *Names in South Carolina* 10 (Winter 1963), 32.

48. Ibid.

49. Hanson, *Virginia Place Names,* 92.

50. *Names in South Carolina* 10 (Winter 1963), 39.

51. *Mississippi: A Guide to the Magnolia State,* 319.

52. Source: Vass.

53. *Hammond's New World Atlas,* 209.

54. *Names in South Carolina* 14 (Winter 1967), 13.

55. Ibid. 4 (Winter 1957), 38.

56. Ibid. 8 (Winter 1961), 85.

57. Ibid. 7 (Winter 1960), 78.

58. Source: Vass.

59. *Hammond's New World Atlas,* 189.

60. Ibid., 194.

61. Phelps and Ross, "Names Please," 219, 226.

62. *Names in South Carolina* 8 (Winter 1961), 85.

63. Ibid.

64. Ibid.

65. Hanson, *Virginia Place Names,* 92.

66. Powell, *North Carolina Gazetteer,* 117.
67. *Names in South Carolina* 15 (Winter 1969), 14.
68. Willard E. Wight, "Georgia Post Offices, 1859," 4.
69. Bertha Ernestine Bloodworth, "Florida Place Names," 51.
70. *Names in South Carolina* 12 (Winter 1965), 208.
71. *Alabama: A Guide to the Deep South,* 334.
72. *Names in South Carolina* 17 (Winter 1970), 15.
73. Ibid. 14 (Winter 1967), 28.
74. Wight, "Georgia Post Offices," 4.
75. *Hammond's New World Atlas,* 194.
76. *Names in South Carolina* 9 (Winter 1962), 113.
77. Powell, *North Carolina Gazetteer,* 104.
78. Read, *Indian Place Names,* 17.
79. *Alabama: A Guide to the Deep South,* 374.
80. *Names in South Carolina* 4 (Winter 1957), 38.
81. Ibid. 10 (Winter 1963), 34.
82. Ibid., 28.
83. Powell, *North Carolina Gazetteer,* 104.
84. Source: Vass.
85. Ibid.
86. *Names in South Carolina* 4 (Winter 1957), 38.
87. Read, *Indian Place Names,* 12.
88. Read, *Florida Place Names,* 46.
89. Source: Vass.
90. *Names in South Carolina* 8 (Winter 1961), 4.
91. Powell, *North Carolina Gazetteer,* 105.
92. Read, *Florida Place Names,* 46.
93. Read, *Indian Place Names,* xv.
94. Phelps and Ross, "Names Please," 219–26.
95. *Names in South Carolina* 8 (Winter 1961), 44.
96. Ibid., 86.
97. Hanson, *Virginia Place Names,* 92.
98. *Hammond's New World Atlas,* 199.
99. Bloodworth, "Florida Place Names," 145.
100. Read, *Florida Place Names,* 48.
101. Read, *Indian Place Names,* 20.
102. *Alabama: A Guide to the Deep South,* 374.
103. *Names in South Carolina* 8 (Winter 1961), 14.
104. Read, *Florida Place Names,* 47.
105. *Names in South Carolina* 13 (November 1966), 11.
106. Read, *Indian Place Names,* 23.
107. *Hammond's New World Atlas,* 207.
108. Powell, *North Carolina Gazetteer,* 107.
109. Ibid., 117.
110. *Names in South Carolina* 10 (Winter 1963), 34.
111. Ibid. 8 (Winter 1961), 86.
112. Ibid. 12 (Winter 1965), 11, 190; 1 (Spring 1954), 19; 8 (Winter 1961), 4.
113. Read, *Indian Place Names,* 25.
114. Ibid., 26.
115. *Names in South Carolina* 14 (Winter 1967), 84.
116. Bloodworth, *Florida Place Names,* 145.
117. *Names in South Carolina* 7 (Winter 1960), 8.
118. Ibid.

119. Ibid. 13 (November 1966), 11.
120. Ibid. 16 (Winter 1969), 24.
121. *Hammond's New World Atlas,* 189.
122. *Names in South Carolina* 15 (Winter 1968), 62.
123. Ibid. 13 (November 1966), 41.
124. *Hammond's New World Atlas,* 199.
125. Ibid., 198.
126. Ibid., 194.
127. *Names in South Carolina* 8 (Winter 1961), 86.
128. Source: Vass.
129. Read, *Florida Place Names,* 48.
130. Read, *Indian Place Names,* 32; *Alabama: A Guide to the Deep South,* 340–41; J. Norman Heard, *The Black Frontiersmen* (New York: John Day, 1969), 14.
131. Powell, *North Carolina Gazetteer,* 165.
132. Source: Vass.
133. *Names in South Carolina* 8 (Winter 1961), 86.
134. George Raffalovich, *Dead Towns of Georgia,* 84.
135. *Names in South Carolina* 16 (Winter 1969), 21.
136. Powell, *North Carolina Gazetter,* 188.
137. *Names in South Carolina* 7 (Winter 1960), 78.
138. *Hammond's New World Atlas,* 207.
139. Wight, "Georgia Post Offices," 10.
140. *Names in South Carolina* 7 (Winter 1960), 71.
141. *Hammond's New World Atlas,* 207.
142. *Mississippi: A Guide to the Magnolia State,* 319.
143. *Hammond's New World Atlas,* 202.
144. Hanson, *Virginia Place Names,* 115.
145. Source: Vass.
146. Ibid.
147. Bloodworth, "Florida Place Names," 115.
148. *Names in South Carolina* 8 (Winter 1961), 87.
149. *Hammond's New World Atlas,* 190.
150. Source: Vass.
151. Read, *Florida Place Names,* 49.
152. Read, *Indian Place Names,* 37–38.
153. *Names in South Carolina* 12 (Winter 1965), 215.
154. Source: Vass.
155. *Hammond's New World Atlas,* 207.
156. *Names in South Carolina* 9 (Winter 1962), 13.
157. Bloodworth, "Florida Place Names," 203.
158. *Hammond's New World Atlas,* 209.
159. Powell, *North Carolina Gazetteer,* 257.
160. *Hammond's New World Atlas,* 207.
161. Read, *Indian Place Names,* 39.
162. Ibid., 40.
163. Hanson, *Virginia Place Names,* 145.
164. *Names in South Carolina* 8 (Winter 1961), 96.
165. *Hammond's New World Atlas,* 190.
166. Ibid., 207.
167. *Names in South Carolina* 5 (Winter 1958), 19.
168. Ibid. 14 (Winter 1967), 28.
169. Ibid. 7 (Winter 1960), 10.
170. *Mississippi: A Guide to the Magnolia State,* 317.

171. Powell, *North Carolina Gazetteer,* 310.
172. *Names in South Carolina* 9 (Winter 1962), 157.
173. Source: Vass.
174. Ibid.
175. *Names in South Carolina* 13 (November 1966), 43.
176. Ibid. 12 (Winter 1965), 208.
177. Hanson, *Virginia Place Names,* 133.
178. Source: Vass.
179. *Names in South Carolina* 8 (Winter 1961), 88.
180. Ibid. 4 (Winter 1957), 38.
181. Powell, *North Carolina Gazetteer,* 334.
182. *Hammond's New World Atlas,* 190.
183. Hanson, *Virginia Place Names,* 33.
184. *Hammond's New World Atlas,* 207.
185. Ibid.
186. Read, *Indian Place Names,* 65.
187. Read, *Florida Place Names,* 51.
188. Wight, "Georgia Post Offices," 16.
189. Powell, *North Carolina Gazetteer,* 361.
190. Hanson, *Virginia Place Names,* 133.
191. *Names in South Carolina* 9 (Winter 1962), 20.
192. Ibid., 113.
193. Ibid. 10 (Winter 1963), 134.
194. *Mississippi: A Guide to the Magnolia State,* 386.
195. *Names in South Carolina* 8 (Winter 1961), 97.
196. Ibid. 9 (Winter 1962), 113.
197. Ibid., 22.
198. Ibid., 20.
199. Edward S. Sell, *Geography of Georgia,* 46.
200. *Names in South Carolina* 16 (Winter 1969), 48.
201. Ibid. 17 (Winter 1970), 14.
202. Source: Vass.
203. *Names in South Carolina* 8 (Winter 1961), 97.
204. Powell, *North Carolina Gazetteer,* 400.
205. *Names in South Carolina* 9 (Winter 1962), 111.
206. Ibid. 7 (Winter 1960), 10.
207. Bloodworth, "Florida Place Names," 201.
208. *Hammond's New World Atlas,* 202.
209. *Names in South Carolina* 9 (Winter 1962), 111.
210. Phelps and Ross, "Names Please," 248.
211. *Names in South Carolina* 1 (Spring 1954), 19.
212. *Mississippi: A Guide to the Magnolia State,* 386.
213. Powell, *North Carolina Gazetteer,* 463.
214. Read, *Florida Place Names,* 52–53.
215. Wight, "Georgia Post Offices," 21.
216. Identified by Vass.
217. Wight, "Georgia Post Offices," 22.
218. *Hammond's New World Atlas,* 207.
219. Identified by Vass.
220. Ibid.
221. *Hammond's New World Atlas,* 209.
222. *Names in South Carolina* 16 (Winter 1969), 22.
223. Identified by Vass.

224. Ibid.
225. *Hammond's New World Atlas,* 190.
226. Bloodworth, "Florida Place Names," 50.
227. *Names in South Carolina* 9 (Winter 1962), 12.
228. Ibid. 13 (November 1966), 13.
229. Ibid.
230. Source: Vass.
231. *Names in South Carolina* 15 (Winter 1968), 63.
232. *Hammond's New World Atlas,* 209.
233. *Names in South Carolina* 9 (Winter 1962), 99.
234. Powell, *North Carolina Gazetteer,* 502.
235. Bloodworth, "Florida Place Names," 50.
236. Read, *Florida Place Names,* 50.
237. Powell, *North Carolina Gazetteer,* 506.
238. *Hammond's New World Atlas,* 198.
239. *Names in South Carolina* 9 (Winter 1962), 112.
240. Wight, "Georgia Post Offices," 21.
241. Read, *Florida Place Names,* 54.
242. *Names in South Carolina* 15 (Winter 1968), 214.
243. *Hammond's New World Atlas,* 190.
244. Ibid.
245. Read, *Florida Place Names,* 37.
246. Ibid.
247. Powell, *North Carolina Gazetteer,* 514.
248. *Names in South Carolina* 9 (Winter 1962), 113.
249. Ibid., 98.
250. Ibid., 112.
251. Ibid.
252. Ibid.
253. Ibid.
254. Read, *Florida Place Names,* 54–55.
255. *Hammond's New World Atlas,* 206.
256. *Names in South Carolina* 11 (Winter 1964), 146.
257. Read, *Indian Place Names,* 76.
258. *Names in South Carolina* 9 (Winter 1962), 113.
259. Ibid.
260. Read, *Indian Place Names,* 77.
261. *Hammond's New World Atlas,* 207.
262. *Names in South Carolina* 9 (Winter 1962), 113.
263. Ibid. 15 (Winter 1968), 49.
264. Source: Vass.
265. *Names in South Carolina* 16 (Winter 1969), 24.
266. Ibid. 9 (Winter 1962), 24.
267. Ibid.
268. Phelps and Ross, "Names Please," 226–27.
269. *Hammond's New World Atlas,* 190.
270. Ibid.
271. Ibid., 209.
272. Hanson, *Virginia Place Names,* 211.
273. *Hammond's New World Atlas,* 198.
274. Ibid., 202.
275. Hanson, *Virginia Place Names,* 211.
276. Turner, *Africanisms in the Gullah Dialect,* 190.

5. AFRICANISMS IN CONTEMPORARY AMERICAN ENGLISH

1. Turner, *Africanisms in the Gullah Dialect.*
2. Ibid.
3. David Dalby, "The African Element in Black English," 171.
4. Ibid.
5. Ibid.
6. Wentworth and Flexner, *Dictionary of American Slang,* 18; Dalby, "African Element."
7. *Webster's Ninth New Collegiate Dictionary,* 127.
8. Dena J. Epstein, "The Folk Banjo: A Documentary History," *Ethnomusicology* (September 1975); Dena J. Epstein, *Sinful Tunes and Spirituals: Black Folk Music to the Civil War* (Urbana: University of Illinois Press, 1977), 120–22, 147; John A. Holm and Allison Watt Shilling, *The Dictionary of Bahamian English;* Dalby, "African Element."
9. Dalby, "African Element," 177.
10. Holm and Shilling, *Dictionary;* Dalby, "African Element."
11. Dalby, "African Element," 177.
12. Ibid.
13. *Random House Dictionary,* 169.
14. Hurston, *Mules and Men,* 192.
15. Wentworth and Flexner, *Dictionary,* 69.
16. Bradley, "Word-List," 12.
17. *Random House Dictionary,* 169; Dalby, "African Element," 178.
18. Stoney and Shelby, *Black Genesis,* 177.
19. *Random House Dictionary.*
20. Dalby, "African Element," 77.
21. Ibid.
22. Julian Mason in *American Speech* 35 (1960), 51–55, gives a detailed discussion of the etymology of *buckaroo.*
23. Holm and Shilling, *Bahamian Dictionary.*
24. Dalby, "African Element."
25. Ibid.
26. Ibid.
27. Ibid.
28. Bastide, *African Civilizations.*
29. Wolof in origin: cf. *hip-kat.*
30. C. M. Woodward, "Word List," 9; Johnson, *Folk Culture,* 44.
31. Hurston, *Mules and Men* 78, 79; *Journal of American Folklore* 32, no. 125 (1919), 376; Thomas W. Talley, *Negro Folk Rhymes,* 74.
32. Dalby, "African Element," 179.
33. Holm and Shilling, *Dictionary.*
34. *Random House Dictionary,* 257.
35. Ibid.
36. Harry Hamilton Johnston, *George Grenfell and the Congo: A History and Description of the Congo* (London: Hutchinson, 1908; New York: Kraus, 1969).
37. Collymore, *Barbadian Dialect,* 26.
38. Dalby, "African Element," 179.
39. Courlander, *Negro Folk Music,* 191.
40. *Webster's Ninth New Collegiate Dictionary.*
41. Holm and Shilling, *Dictionary;* Dalby, "African Element," 179; Joseph E. Holloway, "Africanisms in Gullah Oral Tradition," *Western Journal of Black Studies* 13, no. 3 (1989), 119.
42. Dalby, "African Element."
43. Ibid.
44. Ibid.
45. Holm and Shilling, *Dictionary.*

46. Ibid., 180.
47. Ibid.
48. Ibid.
49. Ibid.
50. Ibid.
51. Ibid., *Random House Dictionary,* 582.
52. Turner, *Africanisms in the Gullah Dialect,* 194.
53. *Random House Dictionary,* 609.
54. Hurston, *Mules and Men,* 244, 281.
55. Robert Farris Thompson, "Kongo Influences on African-American Artistic Culture," in Holloway, ed., *Africanisms,* 148–84.
56. Dalby, "African Element," 180.
57. Jessie Gaston Mulira, "The Case of Voodoo in New Orleans," in Holloway, ed., *Africanisms,* 56; N. W. Newell, in *Journal of American Folklore* 2 (1889), 44.
58. Turner, *Africanisms in the Gullah Dialect.*
59. *Random House Dictionary,* 180.
60. Dalby, "African Element."
61. Ibid.
62. Ibid.
63. Ibid.
64. Ibid.
65. Ibid.
66. Mulira, "Case of Voodoo," 56.
67. Thomas, "South Texas Negro Folk Songs"; Vass, correspondence with Madge B. MacLachlan, Jacksonville, Fla., regarding terms used by her childhood playmate on the turpentine "flats."
68. Puckett, *Folk Beliefs,* 18–19.
69. Dalby, "African Element," 178.
70. Ibid.
71. Ibid., 181.
72. Ibid.; *Random House Dictionary,* 762; Vass, *Bantu Speaking Heritage.*
73. Dalby, "African Element," 181.
74. Source: Vass.
75. *Random House Dictionary,* 767.
76. Ibid., 768.
77. Ibid.
78. Dalby, "African Element," 182.
79. Ibid.
80. Ibid.
81. Beverly J. Robinson, "Africanisms and the Study of Folklore" in Holloway, ed., *Africanisms,* 215; Mathews, *Some Sources,* 145; Vass, *Bantu Speaking Heritage.*
82. Robinson, "Africanisms and the Study of Folklore."
83. Ibid.
84. Ibid.
85. Ibid.
86. Dalby, "African Element."
87. Material from Vass.
88. Source: Vass.
89. Ibid.
90. J. L. Dillard, *All-American English.*
91. Dalby, "African Element," 182.
92. *Random House Dictionary,* 794.
93. Vass, *Bantu Speaking Heritage.*

94. Dalby, "African Element," 182.

95. *Common Trail Songs and Traditional Cowboy Folklore.*

96. Wentworth and Flexner, *Dictionary of American Slang,* 331.

97. Dalby, "African Element," 182.

98. Ibid.

99. Ibid.

100. Ibid.

101. Ibid.

102. Ibid., 182–83.

103. *Random House Dictionary,* 929.

104. Dalby, "African Element," 182.

105. Ibid.

106. Ibid., 183.

107. Ibid.

108. Ibid.

109. George Peter Murdock, *Africa: Its Peoples and Their Culture History* (New York: McGraw-Hill, 1956), 69.

110. Dalby, "African Element," 184.

111. Turner, *Africanisms in the Gullah Dialect,* 203.

112. Dalby, "African Element," 184.

113. *Random House Dictionary,* 1040.

114. Collymore, *Barbadian Dialect,* 63.

115. Wentworth and Flexner, *Dictionary of American Slang,* 382.

116. Dalby, "African Element," 184.

117. Ibid.

118. Ibid.

119. Ibid.

120. Smith, *Gullah,* 28.

121. *Random House Dictionary,* 112.

122. Wentworth and Flexner, *Dictionary of American Slang,* 401; Vass, *Bantu Speaking Heritage,* 113; Dalby, "African Element," 184.

123. Dalby, "African Element," 184.

124. Ibid.

125. Ibid.

126. Ibid.

127. *Random House Dictionary,* 1250.

128. Turner, *Africanisms in the Gullah Dialect;* Dalby, "African Element," 184.

129. Dalby, "African Element," 184.

130. Ibid.

131. Ibid.

132. *Random House Dictionary;* Vass, *Bantu Speaking Heritage,* 114.

133. *Random House Dictionary;* Vass, *Bantu Speaking Heritage,* 114; Dalby, "African Element," 185.

134. Bradley, "Word-List," 67.

135. Dalby, "African Element," 185.

136. Ibid.

137. William A. Read, *Louisiana-French,* rev. ed. (Baton Rouge: Louisiana State University Press, 1963).

138. Dalby, "African Element," 185.

139. Ibid.

140. Ibid.

141. *Random House Dictionary,* 1652.

142. Ibid.

143. Dalby, "African Element."

144. Ibid.

145. *Random House Dictionary,* 767; Read, *Louisiana-French,* 128; Dalby, "African Element," 186.

146. Read, *Louisiana-French,* 118; Carl Meihoff, *Die Sprache der Duala in Kamerun,* 63, 411; Johnson, *Drums and Shadows,* 162.

147. *Drums and Shadows,* 119.

148. Murdock, *Africa,* 23.

149. Victor Boswell, "Our Vegetable Travelers," *National Geographic* (August 1949), 193–211.

150. F. G. Cassidy and R. B. LePage, *Dictionary of Jamaican English.*

151. Joseph E. Holloway, field interview, St. Helena, 1983.

152. Turner, *Africanisms in the Gullah Dialect.*

153. Cassidy and LePage, *Dictionary;* Holm and Shilling, *Dictionary.*

154. Read, *Louisiana-French,* 121; *Random House Dictionary,* 69.

155. Mark Catesby, *The Natural History of Carolina, Florida, and the Bahama Islands* (London: C. Marsh, 1743), appendix, xviii.

156. Ibid.

157. Read, *Louisiana-French,* 122; *Random House Dictionary,* 630; *L'Observateur Reserve,* Louisiana Parish, Mar. 17, 1922.

158. *Drums and Shadows.*

159. *Penn School and Sea Islands Heritage Cookbook* (St. Helena: Fundcraft, 1978).

160. *Random House Dictionary,* 762.

161. Helen Mendes, *The African Heritage Cookbook* (New York: Macmillan, 1971); *The African News Cookbook: African Cooking for Western Kitchens* (North Carolina, 1985), 71.

162. *Drums and Shadows.*

163. Catesby, *Natural History,* appendix, xviii.

164. Romeo B. Garrett, "African Survivals in American Culture," 239.

165. Catesby, *Natural History,* appendix, xviii.

166. Wood, *Black Majority.*

167. *Drums and Shadows.*

168. Dalby, "African Element," 186.

169. C. Bryant, *Flora Diaetetica, or History of Esculent Plants* (London, 1783), 345.

170. William Grimé, *Ethno-botany of the Black Americans* (Algonac, Mich.: Reference Publication, 1979), 27.

171. Ibid., 20.

172. Murdock, *Africa,* 69.

173. Ibid.; H. Sloana, *The Natural History of Jamaica,* 2 vols. (London, 1707–25).

174. John Lawson, *A New Voyage to Carolina* (London, 1799); Murdock, *Africa,* 69.

175. Murdock, *Africa,* 69.

176. Catesby, *Natural History,* appendix, xviii.

177. Murdock, *Africa,* 69.

178. Ibid.

179. Ibid.

180. Ibid.

181. Ibid.

182. Catesby, *Natural History,* appendix, xviii.

183. Lawson, *New Voyage,* 81–82.

184. Texas newspaper article.

185. Holm and Shilling, *Dictionary.*

186. Wood, *Black Majority,* 32.

187. Texas newspaper article.

188. Wood, *Black Majority,* 30.

189. Evans, p. 233.

190. Courlander, *Negro Folk Music,* 206.

191. Mathews, *Some Sources,* 103.

192. Personal communication, Holloway with Vass, Feb. 21, 1984.

193. Turner, *Africanisms in the Gullah Dialect,* 190.

194. Koch and Peder (ed.), *The Life and Selected Writings of Thomas Jefferson* (New York: Modern Library, 1944), 258.

195. John Michael Vlach, *The Afro-American Tradition in Decorative Arts* (Cleveland: Cleveland Museum of Art, 1978), 26.

196. Yetman, *Life under the "Peculiar Institution,"* 170.

197. Ibid.

198. Epstein, *Sinful Tunes,* 1.

199. Thomas Masterson Winterbottom, *An Account of the Native Africans in the Neighborhood of Sierra Leone* (London: Cass, 1969), 111–44.

200. Younnf, "Tour," in *Edwards History III,* 276.

201. General Oglethope to the Accontant, Mr. Harman Verselet, Oct. 9, 1739, in Chandler Company Colonial Records, XXIII, XXII, 235.

202. *Drums and Shadows,* 141.

203. Robinson, "Africanisms in the Study of Folklore."

204. Bastide, *African Civilizations.*

205. Ibid.

206. Thompson, "Kongo Influences," 151.

207. Moreau de St. Mery, Description topographique, physique, civile, politique et historique de la patrie française de l'île de Saint Domingue, vol. 4 (1875), 52–56.

208. Herbert Asbury, *The French Quarter: An Informal History of the New Orleans Underworld* (New York: Knopf, 1937), 242–43.

209. Eugene D. Genovese, *Roll, Jordon, Roll: The World the Slaves Made* (New York: Vintage, 1976), 566–67.

210. Asbury, *French Quarter,* 242–43.

211. See Epstein, *Sinful Tunes.*

212. Ira De A. Reid, "The John Canoe Festival," *Phylon* 3 (1942), 361.

213. William H. Wiggins, Jr., *O Freedom! Afro-American Emancipation Celebration* (Knoxville: University of Tennessee Press, 1987).

214. Thompson, "Kongo Influences," 158–59.

215. Ibid.

216. Ibid.

217. Ibid.

218. Ibid.

219. *Southern Christian Advocate,* Oct. 30, 1846, "Town Diary," 52; Stuckey, *Slave Culture,* 85–90.

220. Thompson, "Kongo Influences," 152; Holloway field notebook, South Carolina, 1983.

221. Thompson, "Kongo Influences."

222. *Drums and Shadows,* 147.

223. Ibid.

224. Source: Vass and Rossa B. Cooley, *School Acres: An Adventure in Rural Education,* 100.

225. Alain Locke, "The Legacy of the Ancestral Arts," *The New Negro* (New York, 1968); Dozier, "Black Architects and Craftsman," 5.

226. *Drums and Shadows,* 106.

Bibliography

ARTICLES

Adams, R. F. G., and Ida C. Ward. "The Arochuku Orthography," *Africa* (January 1929).
Armstrong, Robert G. "Glottochronology and African Linguistics," *Journal of African History* 3, no. 2 (1962), 285.
Bascom, William R. "Acculturation among the Gullah Negroes," *American Anthropologist* (N.S., January–March 1941), 43–50.
Bassett, John. "Gullah: A Negro Patois," *South Atlantic Quarterly* (October 1908 and January 1909).
Boilat, Amaat. "Le Tshiluba, langue et intonation," *Africa* 12, no. 3 (July 1939), 267–84.
Bradley, F. W. "A Word-List from South Carolina," *American Dialect Society* 14 (1945).
Chappeke, Naomi C. "Negro Names," *American Speech* 4 (1929), 272–75.
Cohen, C. Hennig. "Slave Names in Colonial South Carolina," *American Speech* (1952).
Curtin, Philip. "Measuring the Atlantic Slave Trade," in Stanley L. Engerman and Eugene D. Genovese, eds., *Race and Slavery in the Western Hemisphere: Quantitative Studies* (Princeton, N.J.: Princeton University Press, 1975), xi.
Curtin, Philip. "Measuring the Atlantic Slave Trade Once Again," *Journal of African History* 7, no. 4 (1976), 597.
Dalby, David. "O.K., A.O.K. and Oke," *New York Times,* January 8, 1971.
Dalby, David. "The African Element in Black English," in Thomas Kochman, ed., *Rappin' and Stylin' Out: Communication in Urban Black America* (Urbana: University of Illinois Press, 1972).
Dillard, J. L. "Non-Standard Negro Dialects: Convergence or Divergence?" in Norman E. Whitten, Jr., and John F. Szwed, eds., *Afro-American Anthropology: Contemporary Perspectives* (New York: Free Press, 1970).
Dillard, J. L. "The Writings of Herskovits and the Study of the Language of the Negro in the New World," Institute of Caribbean Studies, University of Puerto Rico, n.d.
Edwards, Charles L. "Bahama Songs and Stories," quoted in Henry Krehbiel, *Afro-American Folksongs* (New York: Frederick Ungar, 1962).
Garrett, Romeo B. "African Survivals in American Culture," *Journal of Negro History* 51, no. 4 (October 1966), 239–46.
Garvin, Russell. "The Free Negroes in Florida before the Civil War," MS. in Yonge Library, University of Florida (September 1965).
Guthrie, Malcolm. "Some Developments in the Prehistory of the Bantu Languages," *Journal of African History* 3, no. 2 (1962), 277–78.
Hair, P. E. H. "The Enslavement of Koelle's Informants," *Journal of African History* 6, no. 2 (1965a).
Hair, P. E. H. "Sierra Leone Items in the Gullah Dialect of American English," *American Language Review* 4 (1965b), 79–84.
Hancock, Ian. "Gullah and Barbadian: Origins and Relationship," *American Speech* 55, no. 1 (1980), 17–35.
Harvey, Emily N. "A Brer Rabbit Story," *Journal of American Folklore* 32 (1919).
Herskovits, Melville J. "The Social History of the Negro," in *A Handbook of Social Psychology,* Carl Murchinson, ed. (Worcester, Mass., 1935).

Herskovits, Melville J. "The Significance of West Africa for Negro Research," *Journal of Negro History* (January 1936) 15–30.

Herskovits, Melville J. "The Ancestry of the American Negro," *American Scholar* (Winter 1938–39), 84–94.

Johnson, Guy B. "Saint Helena Songs and Stories," in T. J. Woofter, Jr., *Black Yeomanry* (New York: Holt, 1930), 48–81.

Kochman, Thomas. "Towards an Ethnography of Black American Speech Behavior," in Norman E. Whitten, Jr., and John F. Szwed, eds., *Afro-American Anthropology: Contemporary Perspectives* (New York: Free Press, 1970).

Krapp, George P. "The English of the Negro," *American Mercury* (June 1924); also in *The English Language in America,* vol. 1 (New York, 1925).

Labouret, Henri, and Ida C. Ward. "Quelques observations sur la langue Mandingue," *Africa* 6, no. 1 (1933), 38–50.

Migeod, Frederick W. W. "Personal Names amongst Some West African Tribes," *Journal of African Society* 17 (October 1917), 38–45.

Montgomery, Charles J. "Survivors from the Cargo of the Negro Yacht *Wanderer,*" *American Anthropologist* (N.S. 10, 1908), 611–23.

Muffet, D. J. "Uncle Remus Was a Hausaman?" *Southern Folklore Quarterly* 39 (1975), 151–66.

Munday, J. T. "Spirit Names among the Central Bantu," *African Studies* 7 no. 1 (March 1948).

Musgrave, W. A. B. "Ananci Stories," *Folk-Lore Record* 3, no. 1 (1880).

"Negro Names." Editorial, *Opportunity* 5 (February 1927), 35–37.

Neuffer, Claude Henry. "Some Edisto Island Names," *Names in South Carolina* 2, no. 2 (Winter 1955).

Penny, Charles. "A West-Indian Tale," *Journal of American Folk-Lore* 32 (1919).

Personal communication, Countess Martinengo-Cesareso to Miss Elizabeth Carrington, "Negro Songs from Barbados," *Folk-Lore Journal* 5 (January–December 1887).

Phelps, Dawson A., and Edward Hunter Ross. "Names Please: Place-Names along the Natchez Trace," *Journal of Mississippi History* 14 (January–October 1952).

Phillips, Ulrich Bonnel. "The Slave Labor Problem in the Charleston District," *Political Science Quarterly* 22, no. 3 (1907).

Puckett, Newbell N. "Names of American Negro Slaves," in *Studies in the Science of Society,* ed. G. P. Murdock (New Haven, Conn.: Yale University Press, 1977).

Smiley, P. "Folk-Lore from Virginia, South Carolina, Georgia, Alabama and Florida," *Journal of American Folk-Lore* 32 (1919).

"The Speech of Negroes in Colonial America," *Journal of Negro History* 24, no. 3 (July 1939).

Stewart, William A. "Sociolinguistic Factors in the History of American Negro Dialects," *Florida Reporter* 5, no. 2 (1967).

Stewart, William A. "Understanding Black Language," in *Black America,* ed. John F. Szwed (New York: Basic Books, 1970).

Stewart, William A. "Acculturative Processes and the Language of the American Negro," in William Gage, ed., *Language in Its Social Setting* (Washington, D.C.: Anthropological Society of Washington, 1975).

Szwed, John F. "Africa Lies Just off the Coast of Georgia," *Africa Report* (October 1970), 29–31.

Thomas, Gates. "South Texas Negro Folk Songs," in *Rainbow in the Morning,* publication of the Texas Folklore Society (Hatboro, Pa., Folklore Associates, 1965).

Thomas, Gates. "South Texas Negro Work Songs," in *Rainbow in the Morning,* publication of the Texas Folklore Society (Hatboro: Folklore Associates, 1965).

Thompson, Robert Farris. "Black Ideographic Writing: Calaba to Cuba," *Yale Alumni Magazine* (November 1978), 29.

Turner, Lorenzo Dow. "Problems Confronting the Investigator of Gullah," *American Dialect Society* 9 (1948), 74–78.

USA Today. "A Mutombo by Any Other Name," March 1989.

Vansina, Jan. "Long Distance Trade Routes in Central Africa," *Journal of African History* 3, no. 3 (1962), 387.

Vansina, Jan. "More on the Invasions of Kongo and Angola by the Jaga and the Lunda," *Journal of African History* 7, no. 3 (1966), 422.

Ward, Ida C. "A Short Phonetic Study of Wolof (Jolof) as Spoken in the Gambia and in Senegal," *Africa* 21, no. 3 (July 1939).

Westcott, Roger W. "Bini Names in Nigeria and Georgia," *Linguistics* 124 (1974), 21.

White, C. M. N. "The Supreme Being in the Beliefs of the Balovale Tribes," *African Studies* 7, no. 1 (March 1948).

Wieschhoff, H. A. "The Social Significance of Names among the Ibo of Nigeria," *American Anthropologist* (April–June 1941).

Wight, Willard E. "Georgia Post Offices, 1859," in *Williams Atlanta Directory, City Guide, and Business Mirror* (Atlanta: M. Lynch, 1959).

Wood, Peter H. "More Like a Negro Country: Demographic Patterns in Colonial South Carolina, 1700–1740," in Stanley L. Engerman and Eugene D. Genovese, eds., *Race and Slavery in the Western Hemisphere: Quantitative Studies* (Princeton, N.J.: Princeton University Press, 1975).

Woodward, C. M. "A Word List from Virginia and North Carolina," *American Dialect Society* 6 (November 1946).

Wrigley, Christopher. "Linguistic Clues to African History," *Journal of African History* 3, no. 2 (1970).

BOOKS

Abraham, Roy Clune. *Dictionary of the Hausa Language* (London: University of London Press, 1962).

Abrahams, Roger D. *Rapping and Capping: Black Talk as an Art* (New York: Basic Books, 1970).

Abshire, David, and Michael Samuels. *Portuguese Africa* (New York: Praeger, 1969).

Adams, R. F. G. *A Modern Ibo Grammar* (London, 1932).

Aginsky, Ethel G. *A Grammar of the Mande Language* (Philadelphia: University of Pennsylvania Press, 1935).

Alabama: A Guide to the Deep South. Writers' Program of the Work Projects Administration of the State of Alabama (New York: Robert R. Smith, 1941).

Alford, Terry. *Prince among Slaves: The True Story of an African Prince Sold into Slavery in the American South* (New York: Harcourt Brace Jovanovich, 1977).

Arcola, Dongola. *American Language* (New York, 1937).

Atkins, John. *A Voyage to Guinea, Brazil and the West Indies* (1737).

Ballanta-(Taylor) and Nicholas George Julius. *Saint Helena Island Spirituals* (New York, 1925).

Balmer, W. T., and F. C. F. Grant. *A Grammar of the Fante-Akan Language* (London, 1929).

Bancroft, Frederic. *Slave Trading in the Old South* (Baltimore, 1931).

Baratz, Joan C., and Roger W. Shuy. *Teaching Black Children to Read* (Washington, D.C.: Center for Applied Linguistics, 1969).

Bargery, G. P. *A Hausa-English Dictionary and English-Hausa Vocabulary* (London, 1934).

Barnhart, Clarence L. *New Century Cyclopedia of Names* (New York: Appleton-Century-Crofts, 1954).

Basden, George Thomas. *Among the Ibos of Nigeria: An Account of the Curious and Interesting Habits, Customs and Beliefs of a Little Known African People* (London: Cass, 1966).

Bassett, N. S. *Slavery and Servitude in the Colony of North Carolina*.

Bastide, Roger. *African Civilizations in the New World*, trans. Peter Green (London: C. Hurst, 1971).

Bazin, H. *Dictionnaire Bambara-Français* (Paris, 1906).

Bennett, John. *Doctor to the Dead: Grotesque Legends and Folk Tales of Old Charleston* (Westport, Conn.: Negro Universities Press, 1973; reprint of 1946 edition).

Bentley, William Holman. *Dictionary and Grammar of the Kongo Language as Spoken at San Salvador, the Ancient Capital of the Old Kongo Empire, West Africa* (London: Baptist Missionary Society).

Bloodworth, Bertha Ernestine. "Florida Place Names," Ph.D. dissertation, University of Florida, 1959.

Burtt, Joseph, and W. Claude Horton. *Report on the Conditions of Coloured Labour on the Cocoa Plantations of S. Thome and Principe and the Methods of Procuring It.* Publications of the British and Foreign Anti-Slavery Society (New York, 1907).

Campbell, Robert. *A Pilgrimage to My Motherland* (Boston and Philadelphia, 1861); reprinted as *Search for a Place: Black Separatism and Africa* (Ann Arbor: University of Michigan Press, 1969).

Cannecattim, Fr. Bernardi Maria de. *Collectao de observaoes, grammaticaes sobre a lingua Bunda ou Angolense e diccionario abreviado da lingua Congueza,* 2d ed. (Lisbon, 1859).

Carmer, Carl Lamson. *Stars Fell on Alabama* (New York: Farmer and Rinehart, 1934).

Cassidy, F. G., and R. B. LePage. *Dictionary of Jamaican English* (London: Cambridge University Press, 1980).

Chatelain, Hèli. *Grammatica elementar do Kimbundu ou lingua de Angola* (Geneva, 1888–89).

Chatelain, Hèli. *Folk Tales from Angola* (Boston and New York, 1894).

Christaller, J. G. *Dictionary of the Asante and Fante Language Called Tshi (Twi)* (Basel, 1933).

Christensen, A. M. H. *Afro-American Folk-Lore* (New York: Negro Universities Press, 1969).

Collymore, Frank A. *Baradian Dialect* (Bridgetown, Barbados: Advocate, 1957).

Conevin, Robert. *Histoire du Congo,* trans. W. K. Vass (Paris: Editions Berger-Lavrault, 1966).

Cooley, Rossa B. *School Acres: An Adventure in Rural Education* (New Haven, Conn., 1930; reprinted Westport, Conn.: Negro Universities Press, 1970).

Courlander, Harold. *Negro Folk Music, U.S.A.* (New York: Columbia University Press, 1963).

Creel, Margaret Washington. *"A Peculiar People": Slave Religion and Community-Culture among the Gullahs* (New York: New York University Press, 1988).

Crowther, Samuel. *A Grammar of the Yoruba Language* (London, 1852).

Crum, Mason. *Gullah: Negro Life in the Carolina Sea Islands* (Durham, N.C.: Duke University Press, 1940; reprinted by Negro Universities Press, 1968).

Curtin, Philip D. *African History* (New York: Macmillan, 1964).

Curtin, Philip D. *The Atlantic Slave Trade: A Census* (Madison: University of Wisconsin Press, 1969).

Cushman, H. B. *History of Choctow, Chickasaw and Natchez Indians* (Greenville, Tex.: Headlight Printing House, 1899).

Dalby, David. *Black through White: Patterns of Communication in Africa and the New World* (Hans Wolff Memorial Lecture, 1969).

Dalgish, Gerald M. *A Dictionary of Africanisms: Contributions of Sub-Saharan Africa to the English Language* (Westport, Conn.: Greenwood, 1972).

Dard, M. J. *Dictionnaire Français-Wolof et Français-Bambara, suivi du dictionnaire Wolof-Français* (Paris, 1825).

DeClerq, Mgr. Aug. *Dictionnaire Tshiluba-Français.* Nouvelle édition revuée et angmentée par P. Em. Willems. (Leopoldville: Imprimerie de la Société Missionaire de St. Paul, 1960).

Delafosse, Maurice. *Manuel Dahomeen* (Paris, 1894).

Delafosse, Maurice. *Vocabulaires de plus de 60 langues ou dialectes parles a la Côte d'Ivoire* (Paris, 1904).

Delafosse, Maurice. *La langue Mandingue* (Paris, 1929).

Delafosse, Maurice. *The Negroes of Africa,* trans. F. Fligelman (Washington, D.C., 1931).

Dictionary of the Yoruba Language, 2 vols. (Part I: English-Yoruba; Part II: Yoruba-English) (Lagos, Nigeria: C.M.S. Bookshop, 1931).

Dillard, J. L. *Black English: Its History and Usage in the United States* (New York: Random House, 1972).

Dillard, J. L. *All-American English* (New York: Random House, 1975).

Dillard, J. L. *Black Names* (The Hague: Mouton, 1976).

Dillard, J. L. *Lexicon of Black English* (Seabury Press: New York, 1977).

Donnan, Elizabeth. *Documents Illustrative of the History of the Slave Trade to America*, vols. 2 and 4 (Washington, D.C.: Carnegie Institution, 1932, 1935).

Doob, Leonard W. *Becoming More Civilized* (New Haven, Conn.: Yale University Press, 1961).

Douglass, Frederick. *Narrative of the Life of Frederick Douglass* (Cambridge, Mass.: Harvard University Press, 1960; originally published in 1845).

Drums and Shadows: Survival Studies among the Georgia Coastal Negroes. Savannah Unit, Georgia Writers' Project, Work Projects Administration (Athens: University of Georgia Press, 1940).

Du Bois, W. E. Burghardt. *The Suppression of African Slave Trade in the United States of America 1638–1870* (New York, 1896).

Duport, J. H. *Outlines of the Grammar of the SuSu Language* (London, n.d.).

Durham, Frank. *The Collected Short Stories of Julia Peterkin* (Columbia: University of South Carolina Press, 1970).

Eaton, M. A. *A Dictionary of the Mande Language* (Freetown, Sierra Leone: Albert Academy Press, n.d.).

Ellis, Alfred Burdon. *The Tshi-Speaking Peoples of the Gold Coast of West Africa* (London, 1887).

Ellis, Alfred Burdon. *The Ewe-Speaking Peoples of the Slave Coast of West Africa* (London, 1894).

Ellis, Alfred Burdon. *The Yoruba-Speaking Peoples of the Slave Coast of West Africa* (London, 1946).

Ellison, Ralph. *Shadows and Acts* (New York: Random House, 1964).

Fancher, Betsy. *Lost Legacy of Georgia's Golden Isles* (New York: Doubleday, 1971).

Fisher, Henry. *Negro Slave Songs in the United States* (Ithaca, N.Y.: Cornell University Press, 1953).

Fishman, Joshua A., and Dillard, J. L. *Perspectives on Black English* (The Hague: Mouton, 1975).

Flanders, Ralph Batts. *Plantation Slavery in Georgia* (Cos Cob, Conn.: E. J. Edwards, 1967).

Fligelman, Freida. *The Riches of the African Negro Languages* (Paris, 1931).

Fogel, Robert William. Preface, Stanley L. Engerman and Eugene D. Genovese, eds., *Race and Slavery in the Western Hemisphere: Quantitative Studies* (Princeton, N.J.: Princeton University Press, 1975).

Gaye, J. A. de, and W. S. Beecrorf. *Yoruba Grammar* (Lagos, Nigeria, 1923).

Gold, Robert S. *A Jazz Lexicon* (New York: Knopf, 1960).

Goldie, Hugh. *Dictionary of Efik Language* (Edinburgh: United Presbyterian College, 1886).

Gonzales, Ambrose E. *The Black Border* (Columbia, S.C.: State Printing Co., 1922, 1964).

Greenberg, Joseph. *The Influence of Islam on Sudanese Religion* (New York, 1946).

Gregersen, Edgar A. *Language in Africa: An Introductory Survey* (New York: Gordon and Breach, 1977).

Grose, Francis. *A Classical Dictionary of Vulgar Tongue* (Menton Scholar, Yorkshire, 1768).

Guthrie, Malcolm. *Comparative Bantu* (Hampshire, England: Gregg Press, 1967).

Guy-Grand, R. P. V. J. *Dictionnaire Français-Volof, précédé d'un abrégé de la grammaire Volofe* (Dakar, 1923).

Hair, Paul Edward. *The Early History of Nigerian Languages: Essays and Bibliographies* (London: Cambridge University Press, 1967).

Haley, Alex. *The Autobiography of Malcolm X* (New York: Grove, 1965).

Hambly, Wilfrid Dyson. *Ovimbundu of Angola* (Chicago, 1934).

Hamlin, W. T. *A Short Study of the Western Mandinka Language* (London, 1935).

Hammond's New World Atlas (Garden City, N.Y.: Doubleday, 1947).

Hanson, Raus McDill. *Virginia Place Names* (Verona: McClure Press, 1969).

Hava, J. G. *Arabic-English Dictionary* (Beirut, 1915).

Herskovits, Melville J. *Dahomey,* 2 vols. (New York, 1938).

Herskovits, Melville J. *The Myth of the Negro Past* (Boston: Beacon Press, 1941).

Heyward, DuBose. *Porgy* (New York, 1925).

Holloway, Joseph E., ed. *Africanisms in American Culture* (Bloomington: Indiana University Press, 1990).

Holm, John A., and Alison Watt Shilling. *The Dictionary of Bahamian English* (Cold Spring, N.Y.: Lexik House, 1982).

Hurston, Zora Neale. *Mules and Men* (New York: Harper and Row, 1970).

Innes, Gordon. *A Mande-English Dictionary* (London: Cambridge University Press, 1969).

Inventories 1732–1736 of Charleston, S.C., Probate Court.

Jackson, John G. *Introduction to African Civilizations* (New York: Citadel Press, 1970).

Jeffreys, M. D. W. *Old Calabar and Notes on the Ibibio Language* (Calabar, Nigeria, 1935).

Johnson, Amandus. *Mbundu (Kimbundu)-English Portuguese Dictionary with Grammar and Syntax* (Philadelphia, 1930).

Johnson, Guion Griffs. *A Social History of the Sea Islands, with Special Reference to St. Helena* (Chapel Hill: University of North Carolina Press, 1930).

Johnson, Guy B. *Folk Culture on St. Helena Island, South Carolina* (Chapel Hill, N.C., 1930).

Johnson, Henry, and J. V. Christaker. *Vocabularies of the Niger and Gold Coast, West Africa* (London, 1886).

Johnson, Samuel. *The History of the Yorubas,* ed. Dr. Obadiah Johnson (London, 1921).

Johnson, Whittington Bernard. "Negro Laboring Class in Early America, 1750–1820," Ph.D. dissertation, University of Georgia, 1970.

Jones, Charles C. *Negro Myths from the Georgia Coast* (Boston: Houghton Mifflin, 1888; reprinted Columbia, S.C., 1925).

Keller, Bruce, ed. *The Harlem Renaissance: A Historical Dictionary from the Era* (Westport, Conn.: Greenwood, 1989).

Kennedy, Stetson. *Palmetto Country* (New York: Duell, Sloan, 1942).

Kobes, Mgr. *Dictionnaire Volof-Français* (Dakar, Senegal, 1923).

Koelle, S. W. *Outlines of a Grammer of the Vei (Vai) Language, Together with a Vei-English Vocabulary* (London, 1851).

Krehbiel, Henry Edward. *Afro-American Folksongs* (New York: Frederick Ungar, 1962).

Labouret, H. *Les Manding et leur langue* (Paris, 1934).

Labor, William. *The Study of Nonstandard English* (Champaign, Ill.: National Council of Teachers of English, 1970).

Lambert, Pei. *Our Names* (New York: Lothrop, 1969).

Lamen, K. E. *Dictionnaire Ki-Kongo Français* (Brussels, 1936).

Land Patent Book No. 4, Virginia State Library Archive Division, Richmond, Va.

Leith-Ross, Sylvia. *Fulani Grammar* (London, 1851).

Levine, Lawrence W. *Black Culture and Black Consciousness: Afro-American Folk Thought from Slavery to Freedom* (New York: Oxford University Press, 1977).

Long, Edward. *The History of Jamaica* (New York, 1972).

Major, Clarence. *Dictionary of Afro-American Slang* (New York, 1978).

Mannix, Daniel P. *Black Cargoes* (New York: Viking, 1969).

Marie, E. *Vocabulaire Français-Djerma et Djerma-Français* (Paris, 1914).

Mathews, M. M. *Some Sources of Southernisms* (University of Alabama Press, 1948).

Meek, C. K. *The Northern Tribes of Nigeria,* 2 vols. (London, 1935).

Meifhoff, Carl. *Die Sprache der Duala in Kamerun* (Berlin, 1912).

Melzaih, Hans Joachim. *A Concise Dictionary of Biai Language of Southern Nigeria* (London: Trench, Trubner, 1937).

Mencken, H. L. *The American Language: An Inquiry into the Development of English in the United States* (New York: Knopf, 1936).

Mende-English Vocabulary (Good Hope, 1874).

Michiels, A., and N. Laude. *Notre colonie.* (Brussels: L'Edition Universelle, 1938).

Migeod, F. W. H. *The Mende Language* (London, 1908).

Migeod, F. W. H. *The Languages of West Africa,* 2 vols. (London, 1911, 1913).

Miller, Randall M., and John David Smith, eds. *Dictionary of Afro-American Slavery* (Westport, Conn.: Greenwood, 1988).

Mintz, Sidney W. *Caribbean Transformations* (Chicago: Aldine, 1974).

Mintz, Sidney W., and Richard Price. *An Anthropological Approach to the Afro-American Past: A Caribbean Perspective* (Philadelphia: ISHI, 1976).

Mississippi: A Guide to the Magnolia State. Federal Writers' Project of the Works Progress Administration (New York: Hastings House, 1938).

Moreno Fraginals, Manuel. *Africa in Latin America: Essay on History, Culture and Socialization* (New York: Holmes and Meier, 1984).

Morris Dictionary of Word and Phrase Origins (New York, 1971).

Morrison, W. M. *Grammar of the Buluba-Lulua Language as Spoken in the Upper Kasai and Congo Basin* (Luebo, 1930).

Morrison, W. M. *Dictionary of the Tshiluba Language* (Luebo: J. Leighton Wilson Press, 1939).

The New Golden Songbook, arr. Norman Lloyd (New York: Golden Press, 1961).

Nunes, Benjamin. *Dictionary of Afro–Latin American Civilization* (Westport, Conn.: Greenwood, 1980).

Nzongola, Pierre R. K. *Dictionnaire des synonymes Tshiluba* (Luebo: J. Leighton Wilson Press, 1967).

Parrish, Lydia. *Slave Songs of the Georgia Sea Islands* (Hatboro, Pa.: Folklore Associates, 1965).

Peterkin, Julia Mood. *Scarlet Sister Mary* (Indianapolis: Bobbs-Merrill, 1928).

Picq, Ardant du. *La langue Songhay (dialecte Djerma).* (Paris, 1933).

Powell, William S. *The North Carolina Gazetteer* (Chapel Hill: University of North Carolina Press, 1965).

Practical Orthography of African Languages (London: International Institute of African Languages and Cultures, 1930).

Pruitt, Virginia Grey, and Winifred Kellersberger Vass. *A Textbook of the Tshiluba Language* (Luebo: J. Leighton Wilson Press, American Presbyterian Congo Mission, 1965).

Puckett, Newbell Niles. *Folk Beliefs of the Southern Negro* (Chapel Hill: University of North Carolina Press, 1926).

Puckett, Newbell Niles. *Black Names in America: Origins and Usage* (Boston: G. K. Hall, 1975).

Raffalovich, George. *Dead Towns of Georgia* (Division of State Parks, Georgia Department of Natural Resources, 1938).

Rambaud, J. B. *La langue Wolof* (Paris, 1903).

Random House Dictionary of the English Language, unabridged ed. (1970).

Rapp, E. L. *An Introduction to Twi* (Basel, 1936).

Rattray, R. S. *Tribes of the Ashante Hinterland,* 2 vols. (Oxford, 1932).

Rawley, James A. *The Transatlantic Slave Trade* (Norton Publishers, 1981).

Read, William A. *Indian Place Names in Alabama* (Baton Rouge: Louisiana State University Press, 1934a).

Read, William A. *Florida Place Names of Indian Origin* (Baton Rouge: Louisiana State University Press, 1934b).

Robinson, Charles Henry. *Dictionary of the Hausa Language,* vol. 2 (Cambridge, 1913).

Robinson, Charles Henry. *Hausa Grammar* (London, 1930).

Sanders, W. H., W. E. Fay, et al. *Vocabulary of the Umbundu Language,* vol 1 (Cambridge, 1913).

Sayers, E. F. *Notes on the Clan Family Names Common to the Area Inhabited by Temne-Speaking People* (Freetown, Sierra Leone, 1927).

Scarborough, Dorothy. *On the Trail of Negro Folk Songs* (Cambridge, Mass.: Harvard University Press, 1925).

Schon, James Frederick. *Dictionary of Hausa Language* (London: Church Missionary House, 1876).

Sclenker, C. F. A. *Collection of Temne Traditions, Fables and Proverbs to Which Is Appended a Temne-English Vocabulary* (London, 1861).

Sclenker, C. F. A. *An English-Temne Dictionary* (London, 1880).

Seidel, A. *Die Duala-Spreche in Kamerun* (Heidelberg, 1904).

Sell, Edward S. *Geography of Georgia* (Harlow, 1950).

Serjeantson, Mary S. *A History of Foreign Words in English* (New York, 1962).

Sibley, James L., and D. Westerman. *Liberia Old and New* (New York, 1928).

Smith, Reed. *Gullah.* Bulletin No. 190, University of South Carolina. Originally printed Nov. 1, 1926; reprinted Apr. 14, 1967.

Smitherman, Geneva. *Talkin and Testifyin: The Language of Black America* (Detroit: Wayne State University Press, 1977).

Spencer, J. *An Elementary Grammar of the Ibo Language,* revised by T. J. Dennis (London, 1924).

Spieth, Jakob. *Die Ewe-Stamme* (Berlin, 1906).

Stapleton, Walter Henry. *Comparative Handbook of Congo Languages* (Stanley Falls, Congo: Yakusa, 1903).

Steingass, Francis Joseph. *The Students' Arabic-English Dictionary* (London: W. H. Allen, 1884).

Stewart, George R. *Names on the Land* (Boston: Houghton Mifflin, 1958).

Stoney, Samuel G., and Gertrude M. Shelby. *Black Genesis* (New York: Macmillan, 1930).

Stover, Wesley M. *Observations upon the Grammatical Structure and Use of the Umbundu of the Language of the Inhabitants of Bailundu and Bihe, and Other Countries of West Central Africa* (Boston, 1884).

Stuckey, Sterling. *Slave Culture: Nationalist Theory and Foundations of Black America* (New York: Oxford University Press, 1987).

Sumner, A. T. *A Handbook of the Mande Language* (Freetown, Sierra Leone, 1917).

Talley, Thomas W. *Negro Folk Rhymes* (New York: Macmillan, 1922).

Taylor, F. W. *Vocabulary of the Umbundu Language, Comprising Umbundu-English and English-Umbundu* (West Central African Mission, A.B.C.F.M., n.p., 1911).

Taylor, F. W. *A Fulani-Hausa Phrasebook* (Oxford, 1922).

This is Music, Book 5 (Boston: Allyn and Bacon, 1962).

Turner, Lorenzo Dow. *Africanisms in the Gullah Dialect* (Chicago: University of Chicago Press, 1949).

Valdman, Albert, ed. *Pidgin and Creole Linguistic* (Bloomington: Indiana University Press, 1977).

Vass, Winifred Kellersberger. *The Bantu Speaking Heritage of the United States* (Los Angeles: Center for Afro-American Studies, UCLA, 1979).

Waddell, H. M. *A Vocabulary of the Efik or Old Calabar Language* (Edinburgh, 1849).

Ward, Ida C. *The Phonetic and Tonal Structure of Efik* (Cambridge, 1933).

Ward, Ida C. *An Introduction to the Ibo Language* (Cambridge, 1936a).

Ward, Ida C. *Tones and Grammar in West African Languages.* Reprinted from the *Philological Society's Transactions* (1936b).

Ward, Ida C. *Practical Suggestions for Learning an African Language in the Field.* Supplement to *Africa* 10, no. 2 (1937).

Webster's New World Dictionary (Springfield, Mass.: Merrian-Webster, 1988).

Webster's Ninth New Collegiate Dictionary (Springfield, Mass.: Merriam-Webster, 1986).

Wentworth, Harold, and Stuart Berg Flexner. *The Dictionary of American Slang* (New York: Crowell, 1967).

Werner, A. *The Language Families of Africa* (London, 1925).

Westerman, Deidrich. *Die Gola-Sprache in Liberia* (Hamburg, 1921).

Westerman, Deidrich. *Ewe-English Dictionary* (Berlin, 1928).

Westerman, Deidrich. *A Study of the Ewe Language* (London, 1930).

Westerman, Diedrich. *Die Glidyi-Ewe in Togo* (Berlin, 1935).

Wharton, Vernon Lane. *The Negro in Mississippi, 1865–1890* (Chapel Hill: University of North Carolina Press, 1947).

Whitehead, John. *Grammar and Dictionary of the Bobangi Language as Spoken over a Part of the Upper Congo, West Central Africa* (London: Baptist Missionary Society, 1899).

Whitten, Norman E., Jr., and John F. Szwed, eds. *Afro-American Anthropology: Contemporary Perspectives* (New York: Free Press, 1970).

Wightman, Orin Sage, and Marguerite Davis Cate. *Early Days of Coastal Georgia* (St. Simons, Ga.: Fort Frederica Association, 1955).

Wilkie, M. B. *Ga Grammar Notes and Exercises* (London, 1930).

Wilson, Ralph L. *Dictionario pratico: Portuguese-Umbundu* (Dondi, Bela Vista, 1935).

Wolfram, Walt. *A Sociolinguistic Description of Detroit Negro Speech* (Washington, D.C.: Center for Applied Linguistics, 1969).

Wood, Peter H. *Black Majority: Negroes in Colonial South Carolina from 1670 through the Stono Rebellion* (New York: Knopf, 1974).

Woodson, Carter G. *The African Background Outlined* (Washington, D.C., 1936).

Yetman, Norman R., ed. *Life under the "Peculiar Institution": Selections from the Slave Narrative* (New York: Holt, Rinehart and Winston, 1970).

Zaire: A Country Study. Area Handbook Series, Foreign Area Studies (Washington, D.C.: American University, 1979).

Index

Abd Al Rahman Ibrahima ("Prince"), xxiii

African-American: culture, xiii; vocabulary, xv; assessing Africanisms used by, xvi; slang vocabulary of, xvii; basis of African linguistic structure, xviii; dialect of coastal communities, xix

African-American names: naming practices, xvii, 78; African naming practices continued, 80; day names, 80–81; listed in newspapers, 82–84; slave ship listings, 84–85; name shifting, 85; nicknames, 85–87; dual naming system, 86; Bantu spirit names, 87

African folklore: folktales, xi, xviii; proverbs, xi

Africanisms, contemporary, 137–49; foods, 149–52; crops, 152–53; animals and insects, 153; cowboy culture, 153–54; musical instruments, 154–56; dance, 156–58; celebrations, 158; gestures, 158–59; social culture, 159–60

Africanisms, linguistic: sources of Gullah material, xiii; Bantu content of, xiii–xv; survival of, xv; dictionaries of, xvi–xix. *See also* African-American names

African names: in colonial America, 78–79; day names, 80–82; custom of name shifting, 82–85; dual system, 86; spirit names, 86

Akam (West African culture group), xxviii; geographic location of, map 3, xxviii; naming practices in Sea Islands, 80; Africanisms originating in, 138, 140, 143

Alabama place names, 110, map 6, 111

Ambriz (Angolan slave exportation port), xxiv

American English, standard and non-standard, xiii, xv, xvi, xviii, 148

American South: Africanisms on plantations, xvii; Bantu folktales and songs heard in, xxvi; African tourists in, 79; African place names in, 107; style of cooking rice in, 151

Angola: Bantu ethnic groups of, xiii; folktales of, xx; role in slave market xxiv, xxv; percentage of slaves coming from, xxvii, xxix

Animals and insects, 153

Arabic: studied by Turner, ix; words in Gullah, x; source of "jam," "jamboree," 142; term used by Malcolm X, 148; Africanism originating from, 150

Bambara (Mandinka language): Senegambian area, xix; prominent in trade, xx; distribution of Gullah words in, table 2, 4; geographical location of, table 4, 8; naming practices, 80; slave practices, 80; slave with day name "Monday," 82; negative for positive among, 137

Bangala (Central African ethnic group in Lunda Confederation), xxiv

Bantu: Africanisms retained in Gullah, xiii; link for understanding Gullah, xiv; linguistic Africanisms originating in, xvi; content in American culture, xviii; heritage of Americans of African descent, xix; influence predominantly on black culture, xxiv; metallurgical skills, xxv; homogeneity of culture, xxv; survivals in folktales, songs and place names, xxv–xxvi; division by culture clusters, xxvii; percentage from Angola and Congo River area, xxix; vocabulary content of Gullah, 1–2; distribution of Bantu words in Gullah, table 2, 4–5; words in Puckett's *Black Names in America,* 78; "spirit names" among, 87; place names in Southern states, 107–136; vocabulary in contemporary American English, 137–60

Bantu place names in nine Southern states, map 5, 109; listed, 107–136

Bantu Speaking Heritage of the United States, The: list of Bantu words used by African-Americans, xv; Africanisms of Bantu origin in Black English listed in, 93–106; Bantu place names listed in, 107–136

Barbados, Africanisms found in, xix

Bemba (Bantu language): Central African core language of Bantu nucleus, xxv; highest percentage of general terms in, xxv

"Big House," xxiv, 78, 151, 154

Bight of Guinea, source of slaves, 82

Black English: impact on Southern speech, 80; "big eye," term same in Gullah and West African and Caribbean English, 138; occurrence of intonational variations in, 148

Bornu (powerful Chad Basin state), xx

Brazil: period of greatest slave migration, xxv; African heritage of, xxvi

Brer Rabbit. *See* Folklore stories

British Foreign Office, source of information on slave ships, xxv

Cabinda (slave exportation port north of Congo River), xxiv

Cameroon: term for "carry" in, 148; second person form used in, 149

Cao, Diego (Portuguese discoverer of Congo River), xxiv

Caribbean English: relation to Bahamian English, xix; terms incorporated from Africa, 138, 139, 140, 141, 147, 148, 149

Celebrations, of African Americans, 158

Central Africa: diversity of Africanisms from, xiii; baseline for assessing Africanisms in, xvi; search for origins focused on, xviii; percentage of ancestors coming from, xix; ethnic groupings in, xxiv; homogeneous culture of, xxv; percentage in South Carolina from, xxvii; origin of African-American words, 1; importance of personal names in, 82; vehicle of language transmission, 107; terms in contemporary English, 139, 146, 152, 155, 158–60

Chad (Afro-Asiatic state), xx

Charleston, S.C.: examples of iron working in, xxv, 160; Angolans imported into, xxix; progress of slaves learning English recorded in newspapers of, 79; African terms used in, 140, 144; African grass introduced into, 153; African dance introduced into, 157

Congo (Zaire River): source of slaves, xviii, xxiv; percentage from Congo River area, xxix; Tshiluba speakers in, 1; Africanisms originating in, 150, 151, 152, 154, 157, 159

Contemporary Africanisms, 137–49; foods, 149–52; crops, 152–53; animals and insects, 153; cowboy culture, 153–54; musical instruments, 154–56; dance, 156–58; celebrations, 158; gestures, 158–59; social culture, 159–60

Cosmograms, Bantu in origin, xxvi

Cowboy culture Africanisms, 153–54

Crebo, command term originating in, 148

Creole: Louisiana French, x; New Jersey American trade pidgin, xvii; Sea Islands, x, xviii; West African, x; English-based of Sierra Leone, xvii; in South Carolina, 78, 79; Creolized pet names, 86

Crops of African origin, 152–53

Culture groups of Africa, map 1, xxviii

Dahomey: source of voodoo cult in Louisiana, xxvi; term for fetish, 148; witchcraft from, 148

Dances originating in Africa, 156–58

Douglass, Frederick, name changes of, 85

Draine clan (important Ghanian culture group), xx

Dyssli, Samuel (Swiss commentator on South Carolina culture), xxvii

Dyula (Mande linguistic group), xx

East Africa, folktales coming from, xx

Ebo (Iglo, Sudanese language): slave speech, 79; male temporal names in, 80

Ebunde (Mande linguistic group), xx

Edisto Island, S.C., propensity of black Sea Islanders to name everything, 108

Edo-Bini (Sudanese language), tortoise stories among Nigerian peoples, xx

Efik (Benue-Congo language), terms originating in, xviii, 138

English (American): deposits of Africanisms in Black, xviii, xix; spoken by slaves, 79; term for fried cornmeal cake in, 158

Eritrea, okra originating in, 151

Ethiopia, coffee originating in, 150

Europeans: outnumbered by Africans, xxvii; tambourine borrowed by, 155

Florida: dialect, xix; Angolans in, xxix; place names, 113, 116; map 8, 115; vocabulary in, 141

Folklore stories: Brer Fox, xx; Hare or Brer Rabbit, xx, xxiii; Hyena, xxiii; Brer Wolf, xx; Sis' Nanny Goat, xx; Trickster and Hare, xxiii; Uncle Remus, xxiii, xxiv, 138

Fon (Language of Dahomey), term originating in, 148

Foods, Africanisms in, 149–52

Fula (West Atlantic language [Foulah or Fulani]): Folktales brought to America by, xx, xxiii; Soninke language group, xix; terms originating in, 145, 148; contributions to cattle culture, 154

Ga (Sudanese language), terms originating from, xvii, 144

Gambia: Fenda Lawrence from, xxiii, 79; percentage brought into South Carolina from, xxix; personal names from, 80; origin of "good" from, 137

Gbandi (Mande linguistic group), xx

Geechee (South Carolina Creole language), xvii

Georgia: Africanisms heard in, 139, 147, 149, 151; coastal communities' dances, 156; place names, map 7, 112, 113; Savannah grave decorations, 160

Georgia Sea Islands: African folktales retold in, xxiii; Akan naming practices in, 80

Georgia Writers' Project, day name tradition recorded by, 81

Gestures of African origin, 158–59

Ghana, linguistic groupings of, xx

Goree Island, major center of slave exportation, xx

Guinea, Wolof as dominant culture of, xxiii

Gullah, vii, ix, x, xi, xiii, xiv, xvii, xviii, xix, xxiv, xxv; Central African origin of, 1; distribution of African words in, 4; geographical locations of African sources, map 4, 8; vocabulary lists, 9–77; dual naming system, 86–87; vocabulary references, 137, 138, 139, 140, 144, 149, 150, 152

Guthrie, Malcolm: linguistic homogeneity of Bantu identified by, xiii; Luba core language identified by, xxv; starred forms in *Comparative Bantu,* 87

Guyana English, 149

Haiti: Black Haitian French, 149; Congo-Angolan dance in, 157

Hausa (Afro-Asiatic language): Nigerian kingdom of, xx; folktales told in, xxiii; Africanisms originating in, 137, 138, 141, 145, 146, 150

Ibibio (Benue-Congo language): term for "master" originating in, 138; terminology of cattle culture, 153

Igbo (Sudanese language): terms originating in, xviii, 138, 144; tortoise stories in, xx
Indians. *See* Native Americans
Iron working by slaves, xxv, 160
Ivory Coast, West African folktales from, xxiii

Jamaican English: vocabulary listing of, xviii; grammatical forms preserved in, xix; Africanisms found in, 138, 139, 145, 146, 149, 150, 152
Jamestown, Va., first arrival of blacks in United States, xix
Jelly Roll Morton (Ferdinand La Menthe), 85, 143
John Canoe (North Carolina celebration), 158
John Henry, 143
Jula, migration of Mandinka Jula traders, xxiii

Kanem (state in Chad Basin), xx
Kante clan (Mande linguistic group), xx
Kasai River, Bantu dispersal into Central Africa along, xxiv
Khasonke (Mande linguistic group), xx
Kikongo (language of the Bakongo), xiii; Africanisms originating in, 148
Kimbundu (Bantu language): Angolan ethnic group, xiii; Africanisms originating in, 138, 148, 149, 150, 154, 155
Kissi (Liberian county), 141
Kiswahili (Bantu language), Arabized vernacular of East Africa, xiii
Kitungo (Angolan slave exportation port), xxiv
Kongo: Bantu ethnic group named for river, xxiv–xxv; kingdom of the Bakongo, xxiv–xxv; term for Central African in, 139
Koranko (Mande linguistic group), xx
Krio: English-based Creole of Sierra Leone, xvii; Americanisms evolved from, 144
Kuba (Bantu ethnic group, Bakuba), 160

Lady (Billie Holiday), 85
Latin America, 158
Lawrence, Fenda (Gambian slave trader tourist), xxiii; English spoken by, 79
Leveau, Marie, 141
Liberia: trade between Sierra Leone and, xxiii; county of Kissi in, 141; Vai dialect term from, 147
Lingala (vernacular language of Western Zaire), xiii
Loango (slave exportation port north of Congo River), fig. 5, xxiv
Louisiana, xxvi; place names, map 13, 123; Louisiana French, 138; vocabulary in, 139, 141, 149, 157
Luanda (Angola port of slave exportation), xxiv
Luba (Bantu): Baluba of Central Africa, xxiv; core language of Bantu nucleus, xxv; preponderance of Luba speakers, xxvi; Gullah names of Luba origin, 86; courtesy gift of Luba origin, 160
Luba-Kasai (Bantu). *See* Tshiluba

Luba-Katanga (Bantu), linguistic extension south, xxv
Luba-Lulua (Bantu), courtesy gift tradition among, 160
Luba-Lunda (Bantu ethnic group), xxvii, map 3, xxviii
Lunda Empire, vital center of slave trade, xxiv
Lunda of Bushimayi (river), extension of Lunda domination westward, xxiv

Madagascar, 151
Malemba (slave exportation port north of Congo River), xxiv
Mali (powerful West African state), xx
Malinke (Mandinka language), xx
Mande (Mende, Mandinka): vocabulary in Black and Standard English, xv, xvii; percentage of West African ancestry, xix; history of civilization, xx; cultural heritage of, xviii, xxiv; identifying culture in South Carolina, xxvii; geographical location of, map 3, xxviii
Mandinke (Mandingo, West African language group): origin in Senegambia, xix, xx; folktales from, xxiii; Africanisms originating from, 137–43, 145–49
Manikongo, Christian kings of Kongo, xxiv, xxv
Mano River, culture cluster from area, xxvii, map 3, xxviii
Manyika (Bantu language of Shona group), map 4, 8
Mauretanian Marabouts, xx
Mbamba (Bantu ethnic group), xxiv
Mbanza (Bantu ethnic group), xxiv
Mbata (Bantu ethnic group), xxiv
Mbundu (Bantu ethnic group), xxiv
Mende. *See* Mande
Mississippi, place names, 116, 118, map 9, 117
Mpangu (Bantu ethnic group), xxiv
Mpemba (Bantu ethnic group), xxiv
Musical instruments, from Africa, 154–56
Mwata Yamvo (Lunda ruler who extended confederation westward), xxiv

N'Angola (Portuguese term for Angola), xxiv
Native Americans, x, xxiii; Chickasaw, 79; naming practices, 108–109; linguistic amalgamation with Bantu slaves, 110
Ndongo (Bantu ethnic group), xxiv
New Orleans, La.: Congo Square, xvi, 157, 158; Calemba in, xix, 139; slaves sold in, xxiii; iron working in, xxv, 160; one of three main centers of Bantu culture, xxvi; Africanisms used in, 148, 149, 151; African dances in, 157, 158
New World Africanisms: baseline for examining, xv; West African and Central African baselines for assessing, xvi; transplanting of African cultures to, xxvi; common food of Africa and, 150
N'gola, xxxiv. *See also* Gullah
N'gola of Ndongo, xxiv
Niami and Niani (West African states), xx

Niger River and Delta: original location of Ghanian Mande civilization, xx; slave importation, table 1, xxvii; map 3, xxviii; term identifying slaves, 145

Nigeria: languages of, xi; tortoise folktales from, xx; hare and hyena folktales from, xxiii; slave importation from, table 1, xxvii

Non-standard English, xvii

North Carolina: dialect, xix; place names, 118, 121, map 10, 119

Nsundi, Bantu ethnic division, xxiv

Ogeechee River, 141

Oglethorpe, James, xxiii

Ovimbundu (Angolan Bantu culture group), xiii; primary slave exporting group, xxiv; slave importation from, table 1, xxvii, map 3, xxviii; grave decoration customs of, 159

Pidgin, New Jersey American trade, xvii

Pinda (Mpinda), Kongo slave exporting port, xxiv

Place names in the South: important identification of African population areas, xv, xviii; listed, 107–136

"Pombieros" (slave trade middlemen), xxvi

Portuguese: content in Afro-Latin vocabulary, xviii; term for Ovimbundu kingdom, xxiv; spoken by slaves, 79; terms in Africanisms, 137, 138, 152

Prester, John, xxiv

Reconstruction era, xix

Sahel (West African Sudanic zone), xxiii

St. Helena Island, S.C.: location of Penn Center for presentation of Gullah, vii; place of Turner's original research, ix; ritual preparation of fish on, 159

St. Paul-de-Luanda (Angolan slave exportation port), xxiv

Salnia (West African state), xx

Satchmo (Louis Armstrong), 85

Sea Islands: Turner's research in, ix, x; folktales told in, xxiii; survival of Bantu culture in, xxvi; place-naming by residents, 108; origin of term "Gullah" in, 141; growing of tania root in, 152; burial traditions of, 160

Senegal River: Mande civilization beginning by, xx; slaves imported from area, table 1, xxvii

Senegambia: West African culture groups from, xix; Soninke groups living in, xx; languages of, xxiii; craftsmen and artisans from, xxv; cattle culture in, 154

Serer (West African culture group), xix; from Senegambian area, xx; Africanisms originating from, 148

Sierra Leone: source of English-based Krio, xvii; West African trade with Liberia, xxiii; terms originating in, 137, 138, 144, 146, 147, 148, 149

Sisse clan, Mande-speaking Soninke ruling class, xx

Slavery: Herskovits-Frazier controversy over, xv; Africanisms introduced by, xvii; language and linguistic survivals in, xviii; Sudanic empires disintegration at beginning of, xx; folktales brought by, xxiii; Central African role in, xxiv; African skills brought by, xxv; role of South Carolina in, xxvi; statistical table of, xxvi; map of areas of origin, xxix; role of advertising by name in, 78, 79; problem of dual naming in, 86

Social culture, Africanisms of, 159–60

Solomon, Job Ben (Gambian), xxiii

Songhay (powerful Mande kingdom), xx

Soninke (Mandingo-speaking Senegambian group), xx

South Carolina: Africanisms in, xix; Wolof in, xx; Central Africans in, xxiv; migration to, xxv; Bantu survivals in, xxvi; slavery population of, xxvii, xxix; acculturation in, 78; African names in, 80; place names in, 107, 121, map 11, 120; vocabulary in, 139, 141, 143, 150, 151, 152, 154, 156, 157, 159; Georgetown, 146

South Carolina Gazette: Spanish-speaking runaway slaves mentioned in, 79; Akan day names mentioned in, 80; names of African origin mentioned in, 82, 83; dual names of runaway slaves in, 86

South Carolina Sea Islands: Uncle Remus stories retold in, xxviii; Akan naming practices in, 80; basket and community names of children in, 86; Africanisms still current in, 138

Southern cooking: African cooking in the "Big House" creolized into, xxiv; "soul food" of field-slave community developed into, xxv

Spanish: source of Afro-Latin American speech, xviii; runaway slaves who spoke, 79; Wolof term for "banana" adopted by, 137; African-American dance influenced by, 158

Stono Rebellion: effect on slave importation, xxvii–xxix; "talking drums" used in, 155

Sub-Saharan Africa: Bantu language group confined to, xiii; words common to all Bantu languages in, 87

Sudanic empires: Mande civilization most advanced, xix; Mauretanian Marabouts instigators of breakup of, xx; folktales of West African, xxiii; culture groups in Africa and North America, map 3, xxviii; origin of kola nut in, 152; origin of watermelon, 153

Susu (Soninke [Mandingo] state in Senegambia), xx; term for "bug" originated in, 139

Sylla (important Ghanian clan), xx

Tambo (West African kingdom whose prince was kidnapped), xxiii

Tekrur (powerful Mande-speaking state), xx

Temne (Mande-speaking West Atlantic state), xx; Africanisms originating in, 147, 148, 149

Texas place names, map 14, 124
Tonemes, system of marking (Tshiluba), 1
Tortoise stories, xx
Treasury report data, 60% Africans entering South Carolina from Angola, xxvii
Trickster tales, xx
Truth, Sojourner, 85
Tshiluba, xiii, xiv, xv, xviii; orthography of, 1; duplication of words spelled alike, 1; tonemes, system of marking, 1; syntax forms, 2; use of prepositions, 2; use of locatives, 2; tenses, 2; pronominal infixes and suffixes, 2; no gender differentiation, 2; idioms, 2; distribution in Gullah, 4, 5, 6, 8, 9–77; vocabulary, 149, 151, 154, 159
Turner, Lorenzo Dow: biographical data, ix–xi; *Africanisms in the Gullah Dialect,* xiii; multiple African etymologies listed by, xiv; 5,000 West and Central African words listed by, xvi; methodological approach used by, xviii; analyzation of Gullah content, 1; vocabulary list compiled by, 9–77; exception to scholars searching for linguistic Africanisms, 78
Twi (Sudanese language): multiple African etymology of Tshiluba words with, xiv; nicknames originating in, xviii

Umbundu (Bantu language of Angolan Ovimbundu group), xiii
UNESCO, slavery statistics compiled by, xxvi
Uncle Remus. *See* Folklore stories

Virginia, xxvi; place names, 121, 125, map 12, 122
Voodoo cult: Louisiana with double level of Dahomean religion of, xxvi; religious practices of, 142; magic spells and incantations of, 145

West Africa: mistaken assumption of sole linguistic influence of, xiii–xiv; culture baseline for assessing Africanisms from, xv–xvi; Central African source accepted as well, xviii; percentage of African-American ancestors from, xix, xxiv; westernmost part of, map 1, xxi; easternmost part of, map 2, xxii; folktales from, xxiii; tourists from, 79; importance of names in, 82; Africanisms originating in, 79, 82, 137, 138, 139, 140, 141, 142, 143, 144, 146, 147, 148, 149; foods from, 151–52; tree from, 153; musical instruments from, 155; burial ritual of, 160
Western Europe, xvi
West Indies: slaves imported from, 79; Africanisms recorded in, 143; African food prepared in, 150; coco yam eaten in, 152
Wittepaert (Dutch slave ship): slave names listed by, 82; list of slave names on, 84–85
Wolof: Africanisms found in, xvi–xvii; Africans from West African Senegambian area included, xix; kingdoms of Mande civilization included, xx; folktales of, xxiii; Africanisms originating in, 137, 138, 139, 140, 141, 142, 144, 145, 147, 148, 149

Yaka, Bantu pushed westward by, xxiv
Yao (Bantu culture cluster of Mozambique), xxvii
Yardbird (Charles Parker), 85
Yoruba: Black American English nickname from, xviii; tortoise stories told by, xx; Africanisms from, 138, 140; musical instrument from, 155

Zaire: Bantu words presently used in, xiii; link to understanding Gullah from, xiv; Tshiluba, a Bantu language of, xviii; Africans imported from, table 1, xxvii; Luba-Kasai speakers in, 1; Bantu languages of, table 4, 6; vocabulary list of Luba-Kasai words in, 9–77; place names originating from, 107; place names of, 108; Bantu term for "to die" from, 141; musical instrument used in, 155
Zambia, Tshiluba in, table 3, 6

JOSEPH E. HOLLOWAY is Associate Professor of Pan African Studies at California State University, Northridge. He is author of *Liberian Diplomacy in Africa* and editor of *Africanisms in American Culture.*

WINIFRED K. VASS, who grew up in Zaire, is a retired missionary of the Presbyterian Church. She is the author of five books in Tshiluba and numerous works on African subjects, including *The Bantu Speaking Heritage of the United States.*